# APPROPRIATE PAPER-BASED TECHNOLOGY

# Appropriate Paper-based Technology (APT)

## *A Manual*

BEVILL PACKER

INTERMEDIATE TECHNOLOGY PUBLICATIONS 1995

Intermediate Technology Publications Ltd,
103–105 Southampton Row, London WC1B 4HH, UK

This is a revised and updated edition of
*A Manual of APT*, published in Harare, 1989

ISBN 1 85339 268 5

Typeset by J&L Composition Ltd, Filey, North Yorkshire
Printed in the UK by SRP Exeter

# Contents

# Foreword to the second edition

Developments in Appropriate Paper-based Technology (APT) since the publication of the manual in 1989 require a new edition to cater for a wider public and new needs.

Development up to 1988 was outlined in the foreword to the first edition. The manual was published to set the technology on a firm base and to enable the wide variety of people practising APT in Zimbabwe to consolidate and widen their skill. This is happening. The manual has become the text book for students studying APT as part of their courses under the Ministry of Health, the University Medical School, The Harare Polytechnic College for Teachers and other APT enthusiasts in the country.

It has also led to a spectacular expansion of APT beyond the borders of Zimbabwe. The very numerous visitors and ex-patriates who, having heard of APT and visited the Packers' home to find out more, could now go away with a manual to try out and hopefully to teach others the new technology. Jean Westmacott, a physiotherapist working with her husband Kennet at their HEARU Centre (presently part of Greenwich University in London), flew out to learn APT in Zimbabwe. Thereafter HEARU became a centre where, every year, community health workers from all over the world studying at the Centre for Child Health were introduced to APT and went away with a manual. Radio and TV programmes or 'spots' on APT introduced it to listeners and viewers in Australia, New Zealand and South Africa and, via Sky Television, to Europe. Courses have been run by the Westmacotts, myself and others in several countries. There are individuals or groups in every continent and in at least fifty countries familiar with the technology and spreading it. APT features in community health, physio- and occupational therapy courses at several universities. Rehabilitation workers, 'physios' and 'OTs' are, it seems, the fastest growing category of 'Apters', followed closely by those using APT to generate income or create jobs by making 'Aptware' for the market.

The above facts were taken into consideration when preparing this new edition. Material from all the diverse chapters of the original manual has been used by some of its readers. Little has therefore been excised in this edition. The special needs of rehabilitation workers have been better catered for. In the original edition one small section on 'Aids for the Handicapped' was appended to Chapter 4 after the manual had been prepared for the printer. The use of APT in the field of rehabilitation was still in its infancy. The contents of that section were inadequate to say the least. In this edition most chapters have a supplement headed 'In the context of rehabilitation'. These sections draw attention to some of the technology or actual models described in the main chapter which are specially relevant to rehabilitation needs. They also contain diagrams and instructions for making prototypes of rehabilitation apparatus using the technology described in the chapter. These supplements are mere starting points. Rehabilitation workers are compulsive innovators. Once one of them has mastered the technology, seeing the needs of a particular child, or thumbing through a disability apparatus catalogue, will conjure up a picture of the APT model that is needed and they will make it. Hopefully they will publish some of their success stories in an international rehabilitation journal and submit the model for inclusion in a future edition of the manual.

The rehabilitation supplements contain material that will interest many non-rehabilitation Apters. To describe the present situation of the technology one might say that APT is now in orbit, fuelled by its own appropriateness and the enthusiasm of Apters worldwide, but the situation at base is derisory: two elderly pensioners, voluntary workers, ably assisted when needed by part-timer Timothy Gono; premises – a spare bedroom in a home which serves also as a showroom of APT pieces; ground control and communication with Apt-in-Orbit, practically nil.

We express again the hope, first voiced in 1985, that some ministry or non-government organization will adopt the technology and take responsibility for its development. This would seem to involve creating a centre with full-time staff and facilities for running it, as described in the previous edition of the manual. It could, eventually, help in the matter of communication described below.

Apters scattered around the world need to be able to know of each other, to get in touch and share problems and successes. The idea was launched in a letter to some forty individuals and institutions interested in APT in June 1992 but little seems to have resulted from it. How such a network or organization might be initiated is a matter for those concerned to work out. This is a project that we ourselves have neither the means nor the desire to organize but to which we should be glad to contribute if or when it materializes.

## Request

Meanwhile, we should be glad to receive comments of any kind on the manual, especially if they would lead to improvements in a future edition. We should also be very glad to hear of any developments or projects in the APT field. We would endeavour, but cannot promise, to answer any questions, if you should have difficulties in making any of the articles described in this book.

## Thanks

My thanks go to innumerable people – fellow Apters, friends and acquaintances, including those actively involved in the production of the manual. Space only allows me to mention a few by name:
– first, my wife Joan, chief and ever-present helper and advocate, hostess to the increasing numbers of visitors we welcome to our home, which might be called 'the' World APT Resource Centre and Museum!
– and my faithful support team for nearly a decade: Professor Emeritus Robert Steel, Robert Harley Esquire and nephew Professor Brian Bocking. More than all else it has been their encouragement, their advocacy and their initiatives that resulted in the publication of both first and second editions of this manual.
Thanks also to:
– a team of students and staff at Bath College of Higher Education who kindly helped by producing the original version of the second edition, Professor Anne Muir – international ambassador for Apt, Professor Brian Bocking for initiating and co-ordinating the work, Angela Amanatullah for design and layout, and a team of volunteers for typing up the text, including Ann Booth, Pat Caudle, Liz Crabtree, Eileen Dawson, Denise Hart, Sue Hawkins, Anna Jenkins, Marilyn Jones, Alice Kirby, Kay Strawbridge and Helen Waterhouse.
– our daughter Judy Hess, Jean Westmacott, Christa Dill and others for colour photographs,
– Catherine Baron for greatly enhancing my line drawings
– fellow Apters far and near, Timothy Gono in particular, not only for their ideas and models that are included in the manual but for the joy and excitement we have shared in discovering the ever-widening possibilities of this versatile and friendly technology.

A separate and very special word of thanks to the Beatrice Laing Family Trust whose generous financial help has made this second edition possible.

At the launching of the first edition in Harare in 1989 a group of students presented me with a suitably illustrated card bearing the caption, 'You've launched the bird, we'll keep it flying'. They have done just that in the same spirit, and on behalf of the first generation of Apters, I pass on the message to the much wider public that will be reached by this second edition.

*Bevill Packer*
*1 Mulberry Close, Highlands, Harare*
*April 1995*

# Preface to the first edition

Appropriate Paper-based Technology (APT) was first introduced to the IRED partners who attended the workshop on Technology in the Service of Rural Women in 1986. The participants to this workshop requested that IRED organize for them a three-week course solely devoted to making useful articles out of paper. In 1987 a 'Training of Trainers' course was organized. There were twenty participants from Mauritius, Zambia, Botswana, Lesotho and Zimbabwe. They made a variety of useful articles for the home, toys and small items of furniture for the pre-school as well as pushchairs for two severely handicapped children.

As a result of this course, APT has spread like wildfire in Lesotho and Zambia and is slowly taking root in the other countries. In order to maintain this momentum and to transfer this technology more widely to the hundreds of IRED partners who have been making enquiries, IRED now publishes this manual. It is our hope that the millions of grassroot level will have fun in producing durable utensils out of nothing but waste paper, a little porridge, imagination and hard work.

I am grateful to the partners who are supporting the IRED programme in East and Southern Africa without whose financial support this initiative would have remained on the shelf.

*Rudo M Chitiga-Machingauta*

# Foreword

## Origins and history

Appropriate Paper-based Technology originated in Zimbabwe in the late seventies. A sociology lecturer in a College of Education found himself having to teach art. The students would later be sent to schools that could not afford to buy paints or brushes, or even suitable paper and pencils for art and where, for those reasons, art periods were often given over to other subjects.

Students and tutor embarked on a programme they called 'Art that costs nothing' in which they used no-cost materials – clay, grasses, leaves, reeds and waste paper and card – for creative purposes.

Paper and card soon became the most popular medium. From it, using imagination and much ingenuity, they produced a wide range of articles that were remarkably strong and attractive. Many of these were made in order to serve a special purpose in the student's room or at his school. Each succeeding module of students tried to emulate the preceding one - articles became larger and more sophisticated. Eventually in 1981 the first 'Do it yourself' desk and stool was produced. Ten of these were than made and loaned to a school for testing. They passed with honours. It is hoped that some of those who, as students, pioneered paper technology will recognize in this book devices and methods that they invented.

Regrettably, owing to the large sixe of classes and the small amount of time (often only 30 minutes) given to art periods, APT, as it was later to be called, never took off in the primary school system.

In 1982 I retired from college lecturing and my wife, an infant school head, also retired. Together we began exploring the possibilities of technology as a productive adult activity.

More experimentation was done and the technology was systemised and called APT (pronounced 'apt'). The four rules within which it was to operate and preserve its essential character were set down, namely that every APT article was (1) strong; (2) useful; (3) attractive; (4) made from materials that cost nothing.

Friends who saw our work persuaded us to expose it to the public. In August 1983, thanks to generosity of the Standard Bank of Zimbabwe, an exhibition was held in its gallery. The very many enthusiastic comments that were received from viewers confirmed in us the belief that APT could meet many needs and that it should be taken to the people.

Following the exhibition more short courses were given, including a two-week course of three-hour sessions at St Peter's Primary School, Mbare. In that short time eleven pairs of Grade 6 and 7 pupils each made a desk and a stool. They proceeded to make enough to furnish a whole classroom. Some of these are still in use today. In October that year the first 'Full Training' course opened in the Presbyterian Church Training Centre, Mbare. Of the twelve students most were women. Scorning the set hours for work they started at 5 o'clock in the morning and worked until late at night. At the end of the six-week course, with cartons packed with stools, tables, a desk, trays, bowls, toys and other articles they returned to their homes. There they began spreading APT through Zimbabwe by teaching other women in their clubs.

They were reinforced in 1984 by another 28 equally dedicated and fully trained 'Apters' and, with support from women's clubs, various aid organizations and the Ministry of Community Development and Women's Affairs, the spread of APT through the rural areas gathered momentum.

The story of APT in the ensuing years can only be briefly summarized. There was:

- An unfolding of the ever-widening areas in which it was seen that APT could help,
- Continuous exploration and development of new models and techniques to meet new needs,
- Propagation through exhibitions, lectures, demonstrations and short courses of the good news of APT, what it is, what it can do and what are some of its basic skills, and
- Through activities a further widening of the circle of Apters and APT enthusiasts. These included club leaders and skills trainers from Zimbabwe and some from outside; pre-school workers; high school students and teachers; physiotherapists and others rehabilitating the handicapped; conservationists and solar energy protagonists; home economics teachers, nutrition and food security personnel; adult education students ranging from diplomats' wives to gardeners; and most recently a group of unemployed and destitute men who saw in APT a way back to earning a living. In addition, through the visits of scores of interested people from countries all over the world, and through inputs at several international conferences, there are cells of keenly interested people and some APT projects have been started in other countries in Africa and the Western world.

## The present situation

There is another side to the apparent success story that gives reasons for concern. Real progress is being threatened, even blocked. On the Zimbabwean grass-roots scene, where, through people teaching each other, APT continues to spread, there is no organization for monitoring activities and the quality of work can easily fall and thus bring the technology into disrepute; at another level the enthusiastic responses of delegates to conferences and exhibitions can rarely lead to any practical action as we are quite unable to supply the necessary handouts in the form of practical instructions. The causes lie in the history of APT.

What began as the modest retirement activity of two retired people has developed into an enterprise far too great for any two voluntary workers to manage. Since 1984 appeals have been made for some Zimbabwean Ministry or voluntary agency to become involved and to assume responsibility for the development and propagation of the technology by providing salaried staff and equipping them with the necessary facilities for their task. The only responses seem to be requests for more courses! Meanwhile our ability to cope with demands grows less rather than more. The plea for action on this matter is here repeated, urgently.

The second obstacle to progress will largely be removed by the publication of this manual. We and very many people who have glimpsed the potential of APT are deeply grateful to IRED (Innovations et Résaux pour le Dévéloppement) for their initiative.

It is our hope that besides enabling practising Apters to improve and develop their skills and new enthusiasts to launch themselves it will make the technology more widely known. It might even inspire some Ministry or voluntary organization to adopt APT before it is too late, and so to open a new era in its development. It could happen – though for patriotic reasons we should have some regrets – that an APT centre is established in some other country before we manage it in Zimbabwe!

## About the manual: its structure and use

It should be made clear that it was not written to provide interesting reading for those merely seeking information. It is a manual for highly motivated and predominantly practical people to study, and at times to struggle with, in order to make the articles they want.

**Its content:** It is an attempt to set down for future use and reference all the useful knowledge we have gathered about paper technology during the past 10 years.

**Its structure:** It is an attempt to set it down as briefly as possible and in such a way that the Apter who is interested in making a specific article or class of articles can find the information he needs without having to read or hunt through all the book. To avoid needless repetition a reference system has been built into the book.

**Part One:** (Chapter 1) is an overview of APT. It deals with the materials and equipment used in the technology and all the basic processes and techniques. Reading it through once at the outset is a necessity. After that the reader will frequently be referred back to it.

**Part Two:** (Chapters 2 to 10) provides the practical instructions necessary for making (i.e. building and making strong and tidy – not decorating) articles in different categories. Articles are categorized (see chapter headings) according to the forms of paper used in making them and/or the area of use of the article. Each category of article requires some special technology and this is usually explained in the instructions for making one article of that category or type. Thereafter these instructions, like those of Chapter One, are not repeated but are referred to.

**Part Three:** (Chapter 11) on Decorating and Finishing articles is, like Part One, a resource chapter with sections numbered for easy reference. There is however a difference which accounts for the chapter being placed at the end of the book. It describes a wide variety of decoration techniques applicable for the whole range of APT products but no-one needs to know them all before decorating the article. In fact some Apters may opt to do their own thing (as the chapter itself does recommend at one point) without references to Chapter 11. However, reading it through fairly soon is recommended as it contains very many suggestions, some of which will certainly be new to the reader.

**The Glossary:** this follows Part Three. Every technology has its own indispensable jargon. APT is no exception, except that instead of going to Latin or Greek to coin new words it takes well-known and down-to-earth terms and uses them in a special or limited sense. It is hoped that the glossary may come to the rescue when other references have proved inadequate.

It is regretted that this book for some is unnecessarily large and the solar energy specialist has to buy, with the information about his solar cooker, detailed instructions on making a puppet! It is hoped that the manual will be followed by smaller books on special areas of APT as soon as the needs have been identified.

## Thanks

Our thanks go to innumerable individuals and organizations who have given encouragement and help. Space only allows us to mention a few:

- Two great ladies dedicated to the advancement of women and the care of children who have encouraged this project from the start, late Comrade Sally Mugabe, wife of our President, and Comrade Janet Banana, wife of our retired President.

- The pioneers – students who with me laid the foundation at the United College of Education, Bulawayo, from 1977 to 1982; to those first trainers and many other dedicated women who spread the technology around the country; and fellow Apter (since 1982) Timothy Gono. Together we discuss and try out new models and he has helped in several courses.

- Some who gave valued help which enabled the programme to move forward at critical stages – an anonymous donor who sponsored the Launching Exhibition (1983), the Quaker One-per-cent Fund that sponsored the second full-training course (1984); the Royal Netherlands Embassy who sponsored the Up-dating Course (1985) and follow-up tour of Zimbabwe; the Harare Polytechnic College Adult Education Unit who recognised the potential of APT as early as 1984 and has hosted evening courses since then whenever enrolment has justified them.

- For photographs in the Manual – Dick Pitman who donated the black and white photographs taken by him at the launching in 1983; our daughter Judy Hess, who took many photographs and has been responsible for our developing and printing; Kingston Kajese, a former Director of IRED, for the cover photograph and for initiating steps to this publication.

- And my wife, Joan, for total support from the start and all along the way. She helps in all the courses, tirelessly uses her gifts to raise the decorative standards of the technology, and accommodates the innumerable APT articles and bits and pieces that spill out of my spare bedroom workshop into other rooms and the garden sheds outside.

*Bevill Packer*
*1 Mulberry Close, Highlands, Harare*

# PART ONE
# Overview of APT

# Chapter One: Introduction to Appropriate Paper-based Technology (APT)

## 1. Introduction

This chapter is a basis for all that follows. It gives a general view of APT, followed by a detailed account of the materials and techniques needed to make any of the items referred to in subsequent chapters. This information is not repeated in such detail elsewhere in the manual. Therefore, read this chapter carefully and return to it when necessary.

## 2. Overview of APT

APT is a way of making a wide range of strong and useful articles from paper waste. Such waste can be small scraps, strips, sheets or pages of paper of any kind, thin card from shoe or shirt boxes and thick or corrugated card from old cartons. APT is virtually cost-free. Flour to make paste and varnish, if it is used, to finish articles are the only bought materials needed for APT.

## 3. What is Appropriate Paper-based Technology (APT)?

Each word in the name summarizes the key factors of the technology.

**(a) Appropriate** because:

● All APT articles are designed to serve a useful purpose
● It costs virtually nothing

● Nearly everyone can create an APT article that will give him or her pleasure
● By making wood-like articles from paper waste APT helps to conserve one of the world's most precious resources, namely trees, and
● Old, unwanted APT articles can be reused by APT or recycled as paper waste.

**(b) Paper-based** because APT articles are almost one hundred per cent paper or card.

**(c) Technology** because APT is not a craft for making a certain range of articles. It is a body of knowledge, techniques and devices which can be used to construct products as diverse as dolls and solar cookers, armchairs, early-learning apparatus, baskets, and wheel-chairs for the disabled.

## 4. The four rules of APT

APT works strictly within four rules which ensure its quality and preserve its unique character.
**(i) Articles must be strong.** Strength is essential for usefulness. Weak articles, especially furniture, are dangerous. APT items are hard-wearing, bowls can be dropped, even sat upon without noticeable effect. If protected from rain and damp APT work is extremely durable. Some original APT stools show no appreciable deterioration despite 15 years of use.

The high strength of APT articles often

Figure 1.1 *A wide range of strong and useful articles from paper waste*

amazes people. However, it can be easily explained. Paper comes from wood, which is strong. A sheet of paper, considering its thinness, is strong. By pressing pasted sheets of paper together and drying them we are, in a way, reconstituting wood. APT 'wood' cannot crack and is resilient.

APT articles are carefully engineered with systems that can support more than normal weight and strain. APT joins, if correctly made, cannot come apart.

**(ii) Every APT article must be useful.** Every article is designed to serve a useful purpose. In a society where much time and effort is spent securing life's necessities few people have the time or interest to make beautiful things that are not useful.

**(iii) Every APT article must be attractive.** Ancient and traditional art consisted largely of creating useful things that were also beautiful. APT follows in that tradition. The attractiveness of an APT article gives pride to its owner, adds value and helps ensure the item is treated with respect.

**(iv) APT articles must be made from materials that cost nothing.** APT was born in a situation where there was no money or conventional materials available for art. It has been adopted and spread mainly by people from low-income groups, thus the no-cost rule is one reason for the technology's popularity.

The no-cost rule also gives APT its special charm. Decorating an article with materials that have been found necessitates creativity. Every APT product is a unique creation. Those who have attempted to abandon the no-cost rule and bought commercial paints have discovered that their creations lose the charm of variety and uniqueness. Commercial paint looks shabby when applied to the slightly uneven paper surfaces of an APT article, while found materials and home-made paints cover them beautifully.

## 5. Summary of APT method

(a) In basic terms, APT consists of applying paste to paper and, with the help of some kind of pressure, fashioning it to make an article that dries to a wood-like quality.

(b) APT can use any kind of paper. It uses paper in four different forms:

- Odd pieces of paper and card soaked in water, then ground to a pulp, this is called mash or papier mâché
- Paper in sheet form torn into strips
- Pieces of thin card from cereal or shirt boxes used in sheets or strips, and
- Pieces of thick corrugated card from old cartons.

(c) APT articles are made in four stages, which are:

**Stage one, building the article** — for example, layering pasted strips of paper to make a bowl, or joining two vertical boards to make a carcass or base and joining this to a top board, moulding mash around a paper armature to make a ball, and finally allowing the built article to dry

**Stage two, strengthening and tidying** — this includes cutting or rubbing smooth any uneven edges and binding them neatly, strapping and bandaging all joins with strong paper strips, carefully covering the whole structure to give it a smooth, tidy appearance, and allowing the article to dry

**Stage three, decorating** — this is done in a variety of ways, but always involves making the surface of the article wet with paste and, after decorating, letting it dry completely, and

**Stage four, finishing** — this consists mainly of applying varnish to strengthen and protect all surfaces of the article and allowing it to dry.

**Note:** when building some articles, especially furniture, there is a preliminary stage of making and drying components. Actual drying time varies from one hour to a week depending of the size of the articles, material used, the amount of paste used and the weather.

(d) The cycle of making and drying is unavoidable, therefore:

- No APT article can be completed in a day
- Five days is too short for an APT training course, few items are finished in this time, and

- Avoid arranging training courses in wet weather because slow drying leads to poor production levels.

## 6. APT's materials

A thorough understanding of material used is essential for success in any constructive work. In APT much of this understanding can be gained only from experience. However, this chapter is a base from which to start learning.

## 7. Paper and card

There are innumerable kinds of waste paper and card and, although all share common characteristics, each type has its own features which make it suitable for a particular job, or not.

The common types of paper found in Zimbabwe and used in APT are newsprint, newsprint magazines, glossy magazines, duplicating paper, computer paper, cement bag paper (sometimes called strong paper), thin card (for example, from shirt boxes), and thick card (such as corrugated card from cartons). Also, very useful paper arrives in Zimbabwe in the form of magazines, newspapers, envelopes, wrapping paper and very strong thick card.

## 8. Paper characteristics relevant to APT

**(a) Grain** — this the most important characteristic to understand (the word grain is used in this manual in preference to the technical term). It is the direction in which fibres lie. It can be detected by tearing into a sheet of paper or card. The tear will naturally go straight along or down the grain. Grain usually runs horizontally or vertically across a sheet, but in some magazines and duplicating papers it runs diagonally. In Zimbabwean cement bags the fibres are crossed which makes exceptionally strong paper that is difficult to tear straight.

People practising APT must note the grain of every piece of paper they use. With experience it is possible to determine grain without tearing. Work with the grain, never fight it. Tear along the grain. If possible, fold or crease along the grain. In practice, this means doing it the way it feels easiest. If it goes crooked, or the card creases instead of rolling tight you are trying to fight the grain.

Grain also affects the way a piece of paper or a whole article will stretch and curl when it is wetted by pasting, and shrink, with a very strong pull, when it dries. In corrugated carton card the direction of the pipes is equivalent to grain, and for simplicity is sometimes referred to as grain.

**(b) Thickness and thinness** — this makes a piece of paper or card suitable for a job, or not. Very thin paper is unsuitable for most layering jobs. When laminating, the thicker the sheet of card, the quicker and easier the job. Thickness also helps to decide how many layers are necessary to make an article strong enough. Thickness is not always the same as strength.

**(c) Strength** — this characteristic results partly from the type and direction of the fibres. Manila card is thicker than cement bag paper but is not nearly as strong. Airmail newsprint is the thinnest paper used, but also one of the strongest. In most layering work thickness is more important than strength. However, when strapping and bandaging joins and tidy-

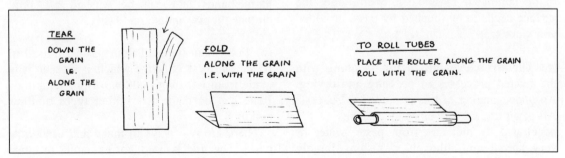

Figure 1.2 *Grain in paper and card*

ing generally strong paper should be used and cement bag paper is ideal.

**(d) Absorbency** — this becomes obvious as soon as the paste is applied. Newsprint and unpapered card absorb water and paste very rapidly. Other materials, such as glossy magazine paper, card with a paper surface, and carton card absorb paste slowly. Some coloured box lids, calendar pictures and thin glossy magazine paper are coated with an almost waterproof material and need testing before they are used for any job involving paste.

For paste to do its work it must penetrate the surface layer at least a little. For good layering work paper and card should be damp right through so it is thoroughly stretched. To help ascertain the absorbency of different papers the following facts should be noted:

● Very absorbent paper that drinks a lot of paste and takes longer to dry adds to the cost, although some claim that the finished article is stronger. To save paste, very absorbent paper may be wetted with water and drained before pasting

● Averagely absorbent paper, for example, from magazines, needs to have paste rubbed over the surface more thoroughly and must be left longer to absorb it and stretch ready for use. Beware of glossy magazine paper which can stick fast to other surfaces when wetted

● Most very absorbent paper is ideal for mash. Exceptions are cement bags and airmail newsprint which, although absorbent, are too stable

● If the card is to be layered in strips it must, like paper, be dampened right through. If it is to be laminated to make a board, only the surface needs to be touched by paste provided you work fast.

**(e) The stretch/shrink factor** — along with the related processes of pressing and drying. An understanding of this is crucial to success. All paper and card swells and stretches as it is penetrated by moisture from paste, water or very humid air, although varnishing largely prevents air penetration. As the material dries it contracts and exerts a very strong pull. The

pull is strongest when the article is finally drying right through.

Shrinkage, unless allowed for and controlled, causes twisting and warping which can be very hard to correct and may render an article useless. If paper or card dries with crinkles or if layers separate, it is usually because the stretch/shrink factor has not be allowed for.

Try to understand the stretch/shrink factor and use it. For example, when layering, paste the paper or card and leave it until the moisture has been fully absorbed and the material fully stretched, then layer it. Finish your layering as quickly as possible so the layering contracts simultaneously and dries like a piece of wood without soft spots or crinkles.

When laminating card use the race-the-stretch method, that is, cover the card very thinly with paste to minimize stretching and work and press very fast, before the card has time to stretch or crinkle.

## 9. Paste

(a) In APT the only adhesive used is paste made from some kind of flour.

The reasons for using flour paste are as follows:

● When it is well-made it is a very strong paste for sticking paper and card because it penetrates both surfaces and bonds them tightly

● Wet flour paste softens the pieces to be joined so they can be crushed, rolled, bent and moulded to lie flat to get a good fit with joins and improve the article's contours

● Flour paste is very cheap. If old *sadza* (Zimbabwe's traditional maize flour pudding) is used it is free, and

● Flour paste is a clean adhesive that does not harm hands and can be washed off skin, clothes, floors, and so on, easily.

(b) Four main types of flour paste are used in APT. The first is *sadza* which is free as it is made from left-over pudding or pot scrapings. Paste can be made from other types of flour pudding.

There are two ways to make and use *sadza* paste. The first is used, for example, to laminate card. Smear water over the card. Take a lump of *sadza* and rub it over the card as if it

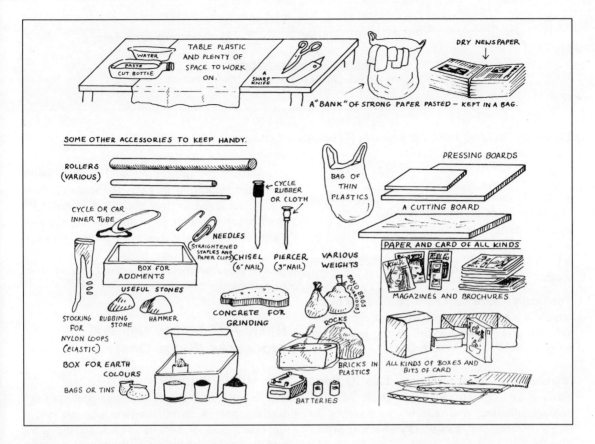

Figure 1.3 *APT tools and accessories – basic kit for most jobs, and some other accessories*

were a piece of soap. Then, with wet hands smear the card all over to spread the paste evenly and fairly thinly. Press the next card on to it. Work rapidly, then press.

In the second method, break the *sadza* into little crumbs and mix thoroughly in hot water. The mixture should not be too thick. Work it thoroughly with hands. Stir and add water as necessary.

The advantages of *sadza* are:

● It costs nothing
● Well-used it makes hard strong articles
● It is the best paste for mash-making.

The disadvantages of *sadza* are:

● It is not quite so easy to use as normal flour paste
● Its large grains make it unsuitable for fine work, and
● Little bits of *sadza* seem messier than other types of flour paste.

The second type of flour paste is paste made from left-over porridge (*bota*). To make this excellent paste, porridge is simply diluted with water. Or thin porridge can be made in the usual way.

Paste made from household or plain flour is the third and most widely used APT adhesive. To make approximately 500cc of thin paste *thoroughly* mix a heaped dessert spoon of flour with a *little cold water* until it is about the consistency of cream and there are no lumps. *Rapidly* pour into the mixture about 500cc of *boiling water, stirring hard*. Continue stirring for a while.

Making paste from household flour is a simple task, *but failure to follow the procedure described above will result in poor, even useless, paste*. The theory behind the method is that stirring in cold water floats and separates the flour's grains so that when boiling water is poured into the mixture each grain is touched and releases gluten, which is a sticky substance.

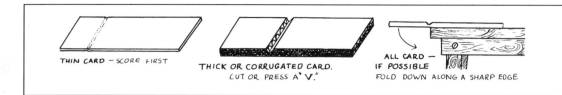

Figure 1.4 *Folding card, particularly if corrugated and across the grain*

Note that:

• It is possible to vary the amounts of flour and water to make thicker or thinner paste
• Thin paste is best for most jobs
• If self-raising flour is used, allow the cold mix to stand for 20 minutes before adding hot water.

The fourth type of flour paste is cornflour paste, which is a good, clean paste but more expensive. To make this paste follow the plain flour paste method.

(c) Use hands to apply paste. **Two Ps Spell Stick** is an APT slogan. Flour paste is not a contact adhesive, and requires pressure to do its job. Remember, **Paste + Pressure = Stick**.

## 10. Tools and accessories

APT does not need expensive tools. However, the technology does require a lot of no-cost equipment. Individuals practising APT should collect gadgets, home-made tools and oddments to facilitate the work.

The *basic APT kit* needed for almost every job consists of:

• A plastic sheet to work on
• Paste in a wide container
• Water in a container
• Pieces of pasted cement bag paper kept moist between plastic, and
• A sharp knife and, if possible, scissors.

Other standard items include: plastic bags; thin plastic; cutting boards; pressing boards; bricks; sandbags and smaller weights; old stockings for string; a piercing tool; a chisel-like tool to cut holes; a grinding or smoothing stone; needles made from box staples; at least three round sticks or tubes of different thicknesses to use as rollers; and paraphernalia to make and use earth paints.

**Measures** — dimensions and measurements are often important in APT, but most of these can be achieved without the use of rulers. APT uses measures, that is, templates or strips of card cut to the right size to measure, for example, seat width or leg length. When a more precise measurement is required, use a ruler to make a measure to use on the job.

## Basic APT techniques and processes (Stage One)

### 11. The time factor

Much work and, therefore, time goes into the construction of an APT article. An extremely important part of APT is organizing the work and finding time-saving methods and devices. However, never take short cuts that reduce strength or quality. One way to save time is to build a supply of long rails and large boards to cut to size when they are needed.

### 12. Tearing and cutting

Tear paper and card rather than cutting it. Tearing is quicker and leaves a bevelled edge which sticks down firmly. Cut edges make a ridge that easily comes unstuck. Tearing is best done when paper and card is dry but that is not always possible, for example when tearing layered strips. Tear along the grain if possible, but tearing across it is sometimes necessary. If you must tear across the grain, crease sharply where you have to tear, place the crease along the edge of a table and tear downwards. Thin card can be torn across the grain in the same way, but should be scored first. Cutting is sometimes necessary, for example if a straight edge is required, perhaps when decorating. Scissors are usually used to cut paper and a knife to cut card. Cut card on a cutting board.

## 13. Folding

Note the grain and, as for tearing, fold along it. Card may be scored and bent over a sharp-edged table. If thick card (carton) has to be folded, a deep V shape should be cut or pressed into the card along the line where it is to be folded.

## 14. Mash (papier mâché)

There are many ways of making mash. Some people use resins or commercial glues to get a very strong, water-resistant mash. APT mash is not waterproof. It is made by the simplest of methods and takes only a few minutes. To make mash, soak pieces of paper or card, for example, newspaper, in water, preferably over-night or longer. Take handfuls of the soaked paper and with a tool, such as a rough stone, rub, grind or pound it to a pulp. The finer you grind it the easier it is to work. Squeeze very hard to expel water. Put the mash in a strong plastic bag. Take a little thick paste or break some old *sadza* into little crumbs and work it into the mash until it has the consistency of moulding clay. Only use a little paste or *sadza* or the finished article may attract weevils.

### Using mash

Very small articles, such as jewellery or chess men, can be made just by building them of mash. Normally, an armature is made over which mash is moulded.

To make small mash items using an arma-ture, first construct the armature. It must be hard and tight. Smear paste over it. Press and mould the mash on to the armature and mould into the shape desired. The mash should be 1cm thick, not less. Finish by working the surface all over with pasty fingers.

Dry the mash article with air circulating around it. Check often as it dries. Press any cracks together and squeeze the mash closer on to the armature if necessary, improving the shape as you do so.

In stage two, strengthening and tidying, cover the mash article with at least three layers of cement bag paper, applying them in strips and small pieces.

## 15. Layering

Layering is used in the production of every APT article. It consists of placing and pressing pasted strips of paper or card on to the surface of an article or a mould. Layering is used to strengthen, tidy and decorate the article. Each complete covering of the object by layering is called a 'course'.

Layering can be used to actually make an item by applying courses of three- or four-layered strips instead of single pieces. This is called thick layering. Important facts to remember about layering follow (refer to grain and stretch/shrink discussed earlier in this chapter):

● Moisten and stretch, that is paste, all paper and card before using it. Except when you are layering decorations, tear and paste large pieces or sheets, single or layered, and tear the layering strips or pieces from these when they have stretched

● On curved surfaces use narrower strips and smaller pieces. Larger pieces can be used on flat surfaces, but extra care is needed during the drying stage to prevent warping

● Work with pasty hands. Press and massage your work quite heavily all the time. If layering coloured paper, handle and mould it through a thin sheet of plastic

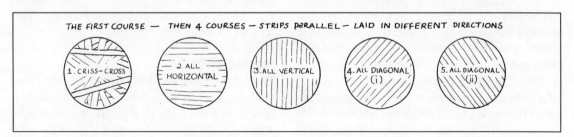

Figure 1.5 *The five courses of thick layering*

Figure 1.6 *Rolling card or paper to make tubes*

● Every piece must lie flat. Lift any piece that is not flat and tear into it if necessary to relay it
● Achieve an even surface. Find how to tear into a piece of paper to layer it over a corner and mould it tidily through thin plastic. When tidying tear suitably shaped pieces to get a neat finish, and
● Always be conscious of the grain. Remember that the stretch and pull is in one direction – between the fibres, that is, across the grain. Alternate the grain in successive courses of layering.

The following points are relevant to thick layering. They have been written with the layering of a bowl in mind (see Figure 1.5), but apply generally:

● To build an average-size bowl or similar article by layering you will need 15 to 20 layers of paper. To save time, these are applied as three- or four-layered strips. Five courses are applied to complete the job
● To neutralize the pull of drying, each course is applied in a different direction, that is, one course in which all the strips cross and four parallel courses layered in different directions
● Continually press the work making it tight and squeezing out excess paste
● The number of layers depends on the size of the article, the thickness of the paper and the purpose for which the article is intended. It is better to make the article too thick than too thin, and
● Thick layering can be applied on the inside of a mould, for example a bowl. The process is not difficult and small children can do it. Extra paste usually has to be squeezed out afterwards. A bowl made inside another bowl may not have a good flat base on which to rest.

## 16. Moulding (and pressing)

Different materials are moulded by the hands. These are:

● Mash is moulded over an armature or mould that is removed
● Soft paper mixed with paste makes a kind of instant mash which can be moulded in the same way. This material dries faster, but moulding it is more difficult than moulding mash
● All layering work involves pressing with the hands to improve the shape and strength of the article or a join. This process is described as moulding, and
● A piece of card can be cut and strapped into the shape desired. then layered over and moulded to complete the item.

## 17. Tubes

Tubes are made in different sizes and strengths according to their function. Strong hard tubes are used for lampstands, pillars, legs, rails for furniture, for pegs, hinges, axles and bearings and so on. Hard tubes are usually made of card. However, paper and especially the strong outside paper of a corrugated card box can make excellent tubes, although they take longer to dry. Soft tubes of paper or card are used in construction work, particularly to bond and strengthen long angle joins. They are crushed flat while still soft and folded along their lengths to make an angle piece.

### Making tubes

This can be simply done using the following method. First, find or make a smooth roller. A broomstick is a good size for a roller with which to make a table leg or rail. Polyvinyl chloride (PVC) tubing is also excellent for the job. If reeds or sticks are used they must be of

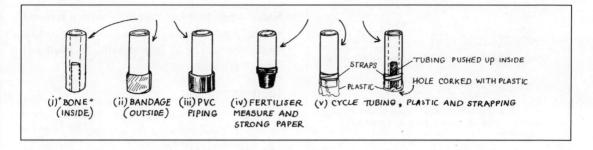

Figure 1.7 *Ways of reinforcing and waterproofing tube ends (feet)*

even thickness and free from ridges or lumps on the surface.

Next, prepare for rolling. Place the card on a flat, clean plastic surface with the grain lengthways. Preferably, see that the front and back edges of the card are torn and not cut. Smear paste lightly over the card but check that it covers the card to its edges. Paste the roller well.

Then, place the roller along the grain. Roll the card tightly on to the roller and continue rolling it in your hands until the edge of the rolled card sticks down, at which point pull the tube off without delay. If necessary, stick the edge down with a pasted paper strip. Finally, dry the tube off the ground and turn occasionally to avoid the risk of bending. Soft tubes are made of soft card or thick paper and can be rolled without a roller.

*Tube-rolling hints*
To get a tight roll, especially in the case of narrow tubes, two devices are used. The card is given a practice roll first (either wet or dry). A narrow strip of strong paper is pasted along and underneath the front edge of the card with approximately 1cm projecting. The projecting paper will grip the roller and start the card off correctly.

If the tube does not come off the roller, it has either stayed on too long or the roller was not well-pasted. Try twisting the tube in reverse and pull. If that fails, unroll the tube, find out the problem and roll again.

*Paper tubes*
Making tubes from paper is feasible. All the original APT furniture has legs made from cement bag paper. Thick business brochure paper is easier to use. Well-made paper tubes

are harder and, for their thickness, stronger than card tubes. However, the process of making paper tubes is slightly slower and trickier than for card tubes.

To make tubes from paper use the following method:

● Use a smooth roller. Wrap a well-pasted thin plastic around it
● Paste and layer five two-layer sheets together, if you are using thick magazine paper. Iron each double sheet flat with your hands. Work quickly
● Roll the sheets around the well-pasted plastic-covered roller, overlapping each new sheet with the previous one. Carefully pull the tube off as soon as it is finished
● Check and turn the tubes during drying to prevent bending, and
● Improve your technique with experience.

*Strengthening tubes*
To reinforce the ends of tubes, for example stool feet, several options are available:

● To strengthen a tube on the inside, find or roll a hard tube about 10cm long that will just fit inside the wider tube. This new inner tube is called a bone. Paste the two parts well. Screw or force the bone right in the original tube
● To strengthen a tube on the outside find a long strip of card with the grain running across it. Give it a practice roll around the tube. Then paste the card, roll it tightly around the original tube and layer over it
● To make a super-strength leg end, for example, for a push-chair, force a segment of PVC piping over the tube end. Layer over it and bind it to the leg.

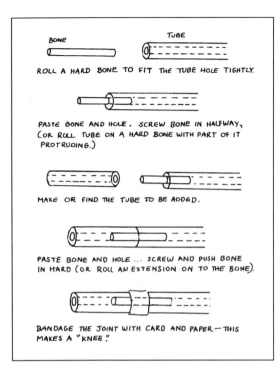

ROLL A HARD BONE TO FIT THE TUBE HOLE TIGHTLY.

PASTE BONE AND HOLE. SCREW BONE IN HALFWAY, (OR ROLL TUBE ON A HARD BONE WITH PART OF IT PROTRUDING.)

MAKE OR FIND THE TUBE TO BE ADDED.

PASTE BONE AND HOLE ... SCREW AND PUSH BONE IN HARD (OR ROLL AN EXTENSION ON TO THE BONE).

BANDAGE THE JOINT WITH CARD AND PAPER — THIS MAKES A "KNEE".

Figure 1.8 *Joining tubes (lengthening)*

*Waterproofing chair and table feet*
Find a length of cycle tube, approximately 10cm long. Stretch it and fit on to the tube. Pull 5cm of it up the leg, like a sock. Push the remaining piece up inside the leg and force in thin plastic to cork it.

*Lengthening tubes*
Lengthening tubes may mean either extending a tube such as a leg end or joining two pieces of tube to make one long tube. The method is basically the same as for reinforcing tube ends, but the bone has to fit into both tubes and the join must be reinforced outside as well as inside. There are two ways of fitting the bone and extension:

● To join a long piece on a tube use ready-made tubes. Force half the bone into one tube end. Screw and push the other tube right on. Bandage the join with the thin card and layering, to make a knee

● To add on a short extension, force the bone into the tube end with a piece projecting just the length of the extension. Roll card on until it is the same thickness as the leg. Bandage and layer over the join.

**Note:** when building an article with a join and a knee, plan it so the join does not have to bear much strain. Try to incorporate the knee into the design of the article.

## 18. Laminating

(a) This term is used for layering card pieces on top of each other to make a board (see 8e, The stretch/shrink factor).

(b) The thickness and composition of boards depends on:

● The intended purpose, and
● The material available to you.

(c) Different boards have various qualities:

● Boards of thin card may have as many as 12 layers. They are easy to make and very thin, strong and stable. These are the best boards for tables and chairs
● Carton boards of two or more layers are easy to make but slow to dry right through. They are not as hard as thin card boards. Sitting on them can make depressions. Humid weather makes them slightly soft, especially if they are not varnished. Carton boards are very useful as the bases of utility-type furniture and in all solarware. They are also heat and cold-resistant
● Sandwich boards of one or more carton cards in between thin cards (at least two on each side as one tends to come unstuck). have harder surfaces than carton boards. They are easy to make, but need care when drying. These are also called hard-top carton boards. Sandwich boards are recommended for the seats of utility furniture, and
● Paper boards, if well-made, are extremely hard and strong (see (g) below).

(d) To make boards from thin card, first get all your cards ready. Layers need not consist of whole cards. Pieces of card fitted together can also be used. Arrange cards so when you layer, the grain of the cards alternates. Then:

● Smear paste all over one surface of the first card. Place the second card on it, paste its surface. Continue in that way
● Work quickly to race the stretch (see 8e, The stretch/shrink factor)

Figure 1.9 *Laminating – work quickly, race-the-stretch*

• Bind the edges roughly, especially at corners, wrap in a sheet of newspaper
• Tread all over, and
• Press on a flat surface under a heavily weighted board (see 21a, Pressing and drying).

(e) To make boards from thick (corrugated) card use the same procedure as for thin cards. However, when pressing with feet tread cautiously to avoid footprints. Tube direction in corrugated card is treated as grain, but thick corrugated boards do not warp as much as thin card boards. Therefore, you can laminate thick carton boards with the grain of nearly all cards in the same direction. This will result in a board which is stronger in a certain direction to bear extra strain. For example vertical boards for chair sides have grain running vertically as pressure is downwards (see Chapter Four: Utility approach two). Seat boards are made with grain running across supporting rails.

(f) Some people practising APT use bars for rails, especially where thin card for tubes is hard to obtain. First, laminate a thick board of carton card, wide enough to make all the bars you need, with grain lengthwise. Cut fairly wide bars from the card. Bind the bars strongly with double layering. Control when drying as they tend to warp. Most models and instructions are for tube rails. Bars require no design modifications and fitting instructions are basically the same.

(g) Boards made from paper are hard and strong, but tricky to construct (see 15, Layering). To make paper boards:

• Layer and press flat a number of five-layer sheets with the grain in one direction as for bowl-making. Count each five-layer sheet as equivalent to one card
• Laminate in the usual way but iron well with the hands to get all surplus paste out, and
• Press and dry. This is the tricky part (see 21, Pressing and drying).

## 19. Joining

The term means fixing together components of an article. The noun 'join' is used here rather than joint which often means fitting one piece into another. In APT pieces are sometimes fitted together, but most joins are made by

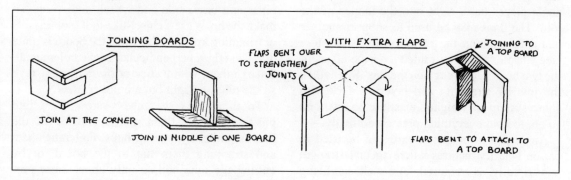

Figure 1.10 *Angle pieces*

13

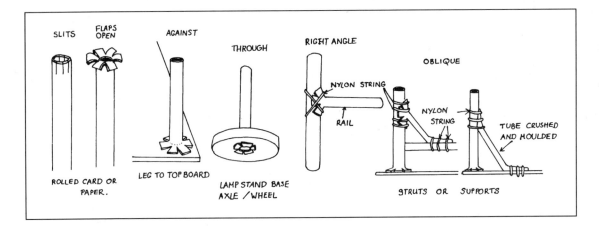

SLITS  FLAPS OPEN  AGAINST  THROUGH  RIGHT ANGLE  OBLIQUE

NYLON STRING

RAIL

NYLON STRING

TUBE CRUSHED AND MOULDED

ROLLED CARD OR PAPER.  LEG TO TOP BOARD  LAMP STAND BASE AXLE / WHEEL  STRUTS OR SUPPORTS

Figure 1.11 *Joining of tubes*

the components being pressed or crushed together (and usually secured with string), and then strapped and layered to make the join strong. Angle pieces, which are pieces of thin card folded to make an angle, and crushed tubes are also used, pressed along the join.

The following standard methods have proved satisfactory and are commonly used, sometimes with modifications. There are others, each APT user inventing his or her own.

**(a) Board joined to board**, for example, in box-making — the join may be at the end of both boards or in the middle of one of them. Angle pieces and strong paper are used. They may need to be cut into, to make flaps, if three boards are to be joined. It helps to use nylon string or wooden nails to hold the parts in place while you work.

First, paste the angle pieces. Let them stretch. Paste the joining areas. Press the two boards together where they are to be joined. Press the angle pieces hard, right into the angles of the join. The flaps may be used to support another board, for example the top of a utility-style stool (see Chapter Four), or folded over the edges of the two boards to strengthen the join. Strengthen the join by strapping and layering. Dry with some system of weights, elastics, boards, and so on, to hold everything pressed correctly.

Angle pieces of carton card can be used in carton board structures where special strength and rigidity is required. As well as being pressed hard along the angles and to the boards, they may be tied or nailed in place.

**Note:** arrange the card with its tubes across the angle. (see Chapter Two: Rehabilitation and Chapter Four: Armchair).

**(b) Tube joined to board** — there are three systems for doing this (see Figure 1.11 above): *(i) Tube against board*, for example, to fit a leg to a table top) — cut slits up into the end of the tube to make, say, four flaps about 15mm long. Dip the tube end in paste, open the flaps and flatten them. Press the tube hard against the board, checking that it does not try to jump away from the board (in which case the flaps are not bent enough). Hold the tube pressed in that position (you may use your chin). With your hands strap over the flaps with strips of double strong paper. Press little triangles of card on to the strapping between the flaps and strap over it all again. Tubes joined to boards need strut supports (see Figure 1.11 above). *(ii) Tube through board*, for example, chairs (see Chapter Four: Utility approach two), lamp pillar and base, axle and wheel, and so on. To make the holes use a chisel-like tool (not scissors or trimming knives). Cut when the board is quite dry. Cut edges perpendicular. Make holes small. Enlarge them with a stick or piece of rusty pipe so the tubes fit tight but are not crushed.

To fit and fix the tubes, screw them into position. Secure them on the outside of the boards, either by cutting flaps, flattening them and strapping them flat to the board, or by cutting the tube end so only about 3mm projects, opening the end and burring it over with a rounded stone or some other tool.

LAMINATED BOARD →    ← ROUGH BINDING    EDGE OF BOWL    TIDY BINDING

Figure 1.12 *Binding*

On the inside, secure the tubes by collars of card (see Chapter Four: Chair, Figure 4.13). Wrap the collars tightly around the tube. Press and strap the flaps to the board.

*(iii) Tubes supporting boards*, for example, going through the side boards of a chair (see Chapter Four: Utility approach two), and supporting a seat board. Obviously the size and strength of the tubes will be related to the strain they will have to bear.

Press soft tubes of card or paper along the angle where the tube meets the seat board (17, Tubes). Strengthen the join further by paper or card layering over the tube and on to the board.

**(c) Tube joined to tube** — two types of join are used:

*(i) Right-angle join* (for example a rail to leg) — slit and open flaps as in previous examples. Place the joining tube in position against the other tube with two flaps embracing the tube and the other two flaps against it. Tie over the flaps in all directions with thin nylon string. Then, strap and layer over the join.

*(ii) Oblique join*, that is, a strut or support, for example, for a lamp pillar or table leg. The method is basically the same as for a right-angle join, but the tube ends may be crushed, moulded and tied to the leg without flaps being cut. Struts are crushed and joined to boards in the same way with or without being tied.

Other joining techniques are in the sections dealing with articles that require them.

## 20. Strengthening and tidying, including binding (Stage Two)

(a) The *strengthening* stage in APT has its own techniques. The strengthening of joins includes forcing card pieces or lightly pasted paper into sharp angles and cavities, then moulding strapping and layering over them. Tubes and flat surfaces are also strengthened with strong

layering. It also includes binding all open edges as is described below.

(b) *Tidying* consists of more careful layering all over, often with larger pieces carefully torn to shape so that when applied they give the whole article a neat, smooth surface with absolutely no soft spots or loose bits. APT often favours rounded rather than sharp edges and corners, particularly for utility furniture and articles for children. Edges are often rubbed with a stone rather than being precisely trimmed with a knife, and then bound and worked with the hand to get a final smooth finish.

(c) *Binding* refers to pasting and pinching together the open edges of an article (a layered bowl or a laminated board), and binding them tightly with pieces of paper. It can be done when making components or at the strengthening or decorating stages. As the final appearance of some articles depends largely on the neatness of its edges a few technical hints are offered. They apply particularly to bowls. Note therefore:

● In binding, each piece of paper or card just overlaps the other

● Paste along all edges to be bound. If layers are separating open them and spread paste between them. If there are thin or uneven spots, add small pieces until the surface is uniform. Pinch edges together and make them smooth between fingers, before and after binding

● Do not use very long strips even for binding straight edges

For curved edges, the pieces should be about 1cm wide, and

● Remember grain as you bind. It is best to use the grain direction to help the paper bind tightly. Experience will tell you what that direction is in each case.

(d) *Saving time* is an issue because the stages that have already be discussed are time-consuming. People practising APT need to think

Figure 1.13 *Pressing and drying – a few examples*

and plan as they work to find devices and methods by which they can work more speedily, and still achieve best results.

## 21. Pressing and drying

(a) APT articles must be dried. Most, but not all, need some pressing so they keep their shape and dry hard. The two processes take place over the same period but not always at the same time, and are different. Pressing can slow down or prevent drying. A grasp of the stretch/shrink factor will help you understand the reasoning behind this advice:

● Drying is an essential part of making an APT article and must never be left to chance, which could cause irreversible damage. (A note to APT teachers: there may be a time gap between lessons, but drying articles must still be watched by you and hopefully by students who must also learn the drying process)
● Devise a way to enable all parts of the article to dry evenly. Dry articles off the ground, on racks or egg boxes or in nests of paper. Turn them
● Boards need to be taken out from their presses from time to time to facilitate drying. They must be observed and returned at the first sign of warping
● Never dry in radiant heat (sun or fire). It will rapidly dry and lift the top layer and cause warping (mash is an exception to this rule), and
● Articles are not safe until they are dry right through. It is easy to be caught out. Judge dryness by feel and weight, not appearance.

The strongest warping occurs in the last stages of drying.

(b) Suggestions for successful pressing of articles follow:

● Card and carton boards are pressed, initially wrapped in a sheet of newspaper, on a flat surface under a heavily weighted board. Do not press with stones or bricks and no board. Bricks used as weights are best wrapped in plastic, for example, in plastic bags
● If you have to press a decorated surface, cover it with a clean thin plastic sheet, but you cannot be sure some colour may not come off
● Bags of sand (which do not leak) of various sizes are essential for a number of pressing jobs where surfaces are not flat and boards cannot be used, such as inside bowls or round stools, along edges, and so on, and
● Individuals practising APT must devise all sorts of ways to press articles inwards as well as downwards. They use boards of various sizes, belts of cycle tubing or nylon string and much ingenuity!

Figure 1.13 gives examples of APT drying and pressing.

## 22. Decoration (Stage Three)

The field of decoration is so wide that Chapter Eleven is devoted to it. Dip into Chapter Eleven as and when you need information on a particular form of decoration. A quick glance at its contents at this point is useful:

- The no-cost rule is strictly followed
- Decoration often involves applying a fairly plain decoration on to which various kinds of finer decoration can be added
- An endless variety of materials and techniques are used, especially in finer decoration, such as coloured papers torn from boxes, magazines, envelopes and wallpaper or pictures from calendars and old books. In addition, the APT user creates original designs by using home-made earth paints and brushes for stencilling and printing and by cutting out shapes and patterns. Pressed flowers and leaves are sometimes used.

### 23. Finishing (Stage Four)

Finishing an article is dealt with in Part Three of this manual. The process uses size and varnish to give a permanent finish.

### 24. Care of APT articles

It has already been stated that APT articles are stronger than many comparable wooden articles and should last indefinitely, if they are properly cared for. The material does not crack like wood. APT joints, if properly made, cannot work loose. Surfaces are not affected by a little water or spills if they are wiped soon afterwards. If little fingers do manage to tear off some of the decorative surface it can be replaced by the owner with a minimum of APT decorative knowledge.

However, prolonged exposure of APT articles to sun is not recommended. Using legged articles for a long time on uneven floors is not good for them. Leaving APT products out in rain or in damp night air, and, especially, standing them on damp ground or wet surfaces will definitely harm them if it happens with any frequency.

If an APT article comes to the end of its useful life it can be taken to pieces, parts may even be soaked in water, and the materials reused, probably in a different way. As the articles are almost ninety-nine per cent waste paper, they should be recyclable as paper.

### 25. Making a start

Now is the time for action. You have read enough to fill three full days of workshop. In fact, you have read too much to absorb. Make a start before you forget what you have retained. We suggest you read the introductory sections to Chapter Two and Chapter Four. Select the article you want to make first. The bowl in Chapter Two or the square-based stool in Chapter Four are good for beginners. You could make both the bowl and the stool by making the boards for the stool and pressing them, and then starting on the bowl.

Read the instructions. Make your paste. Spread a plastic sheet on a table. Place all the items you need on it and plunge in. You will find the material easy to work with and will learn as you go along. Follow instructions carefully.

## In the context of rehabilitation

This manual is about technology. Rehabilitation workers, using little technology, find or make very useful apparatus, some permanent, some throw-away. Also, there is need in rehabilitation work for really strong durable items of equipment that meet patients' needs. This manual aims to help produce them.

Factors to remember when you make rehabilitation items follow.

(i) All APT material is friendly. The main material used in rehabilitation models is corrugated carton card, which is particularly friendly in texture and flexibility to the user and maker. Parts can be lengthened, shortened, thickened, strengthened, rounded, moulded bent, and so on, by the technician. Errors can often be corrected. Have confidence as you handle and manipulate your material, but also learn from it.

(ii) It pays dividends and saves time to plan, design and work carefully and accurately.

(iii) These days, much rehabilitation work is done with children less than five years' old who have cerebral palsy. Aids are intended to assist and correct development. Apparatus made solely to give support could do harm. Wherever possible, a physiotherapist should play a part in designing equipment, prescribing measurements and checking the apparatus with the child during and after its construction (see Measures, p. 8).

(iv) Desirable features to be aimed at in APT rehabilitation items include; strength with lightness; rounded edges, no sharp corners, nothing sticking out; made to suit a particular child, but if possible, adjustable, capable of being enlarged as the child grows or being used by other children, or serving more than one purpose; and no larger than necessary, easy to house, and, for multiple items, stackable.

(v) Rehabilitation workers often need long boards. APT long boards on their own are not strong and may tend to warp. Some workers overcome the problem by using them flat on the floor. This is not a very hygienic solution as the boards are sometimes used the wrong way up, get dirty and go soft.

Long boards should be made reasonably thick. Corrugations should run lengthwise. The boards should be strengthened by strapping at least two long tubes or thick bars along their length underneath in suitable positions. This raises the boards from the floor, keeps them strong and flat and provides thickening for holding any pegs firmly (see Chapter Two: *In the context of rehabilitation*).

(vi) Time spent on decoration is well-spent.

Children love decorated apparatus, which brighten a room. Decoration enhances the value of the article in everyone's eyes, and earns more care than drab apparatus will receive. However, children enjoy pulling things apart. Therefore, if possible, paint decorations on an article. If you use pictures, tear, rather than cut, their edges, give them rounded corners and two coats of varnish.

(vii) In many countries genuinely nontoxic varnish is unobtainable. Toxic varnish does no harm when it is dry unless it is sucked or eaten. Rehabilitation workers will take local advice from a paint firm and know what precautions if any, they should take.

(viii) APT in the context of rehabilitation, as presented in this manual, is still in its infancy. Individuals in various corners of the world are experimenting and developing new techniques and models. It is hoped that they will get in touch with one another, share ideas, and ensure that valuable new findings are published and communicated to the author for inclusion in future editions of this manual.

# PART TWO
# Making Specific Articles

The general plan of chapters in this section is:

- A general introduction to the APT area to be covered
- Construction of one APT article in detail, and
- Further examples of articles of the same type with diagrams and a brief description of the technology.

Several types of APT article are described in some chapters. It is assumed that readers have a grasp of basic APT principles and techniques described in Chapter One.

# Chapter Two: Articles made from paper and card

## Three basic approaches to paper layering

Almost any article, any size, can be made by layering paper. However, for large items the process is difficult, and drying long and tedious. If card is available it should be used for larger articles. Before proceeding, refer to Chapter One:8e, The stretch/shrink factor.

## 1. First approach to paper layering

In this approach a weak or unwanted article is layered over in order to strengthen it and make a new, and often different, article.

### Example: A box

A shoe box turned into a strong and attractive container with a fitted lid (optional) and handles to convert it into a basket (optional). As this is the first article described in this manual, detailed instructions for Stage One, Building, are given.

(i) First, look at your shoe box and plan how you want it to be. Do you want to reduce its height, change the shape of its top edge, and so on?

(ii) Prepare your basic kit (see Chapter One,10). Have sheets of newspaper or magazine paper ready for layering.

(iii) Get ready to layer the box. Take a pile of eight to ten sheets of the paper with grain running in the same direction. Measure the box's length along the grain. Tear the sheets across the grain to the length measured (see Figure 2.1a and b). Then, tear the sheets down the grain to make conveniently sized pages (about 30cm wide). Stack them tidily.

(iv) From these sheets make a number of three-layer pages as follows. Smear paste on a space on your table plastic. Place a page on it. Smear the page with paste. Lay another page on the first one, with grain in the same direction, and paste it. If desired, paste a third page. Repeat the process, but lay the pages across the first three-layered page.

Continue making more three-layered pages, each one lying across the previous page. Keep pressing and ironing the pages, with your hands, pressing out surplus paste. Lift the pile. Turn it over and place it down. One by one lift up each three-layered page. Place them loosely together and make sure they do not stick to each other. Next, take two or three of these layered pages. Tear them down the grain to make strips for layering approximately 5 to 6cm wide. Place the strips tidily one by one, for example, on the table plastic, for ease of handling.

(v) Refer to Chapter One:15, Layering. Understand the following additional information about layering over rectangular boxes of thin card before you start layering:

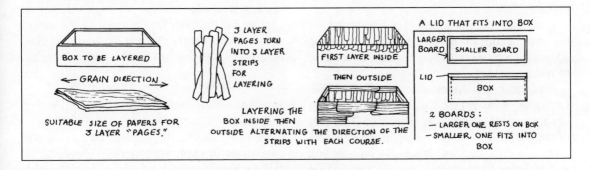

Figure 2.1 a and b *Layering over a shoe box to strengthen it*

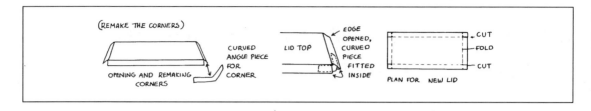

Figure 2.2 *Adjusting the original lid or making a new lid*

● You can use fairly wide strips, but do not let a strip go over more than one angle of the box. Start on the inside of the box, layer one course horizontally to cover it, and then one course vertically with strip ends going neatly over the box edges to bind them. Develop a technique for layering close into angles and corners, and over them (when layering the outside)

● Press and iron the sides and bottom against the table plastic

● Layer all over the outside in the same way (at least two courses). Sides bulge out because they swell. Pinch corners and angles to make them sharp. Press and hold the sides in as you layer, and during drying

● Finish by ironing the bottom and sides against the table plastic, and

● Dry off the ground, correcting its shape as it dries.

(vi) Now, proceed to Stage Two, Strengthening and tidying. When the box is dry or nearly so, strengthen it if necessary. Then, layer it tidily all over with single pieces of paper (not long strips).

*The lid*
Read Chapter Four: Utility approach three, Lids. Decide what kind of a lid you want to make.

A lid that fits into a box (see Figure 2.1) is the easiest lid to make and can easily be adapted if you want to add handles to the box to make a basket.

First, tear the edges off the original lid. Laminate on to it (see Chapter One:18) three or four more thin cards, the same size. This part of the lid will rest on the box. Cut three or four more thin cards that will fit loosely into the box and laminate them in their correct position on to the large lid part. Test the lid by placing the box opening over it or wrapping it in plastic and trying it in the box. Adjust, layer over it and press to dry. At some point dry it in position on the box.

A lid that fits over the box sides can be made in two ways. In the first method, adjust the original lid by undoing its corner joints and bending the lid's sides outwards. Strengthen the corners in their new position by inserting two or three small angle pieces of thin card along the lid's sides. Bind and layer the sides in their new position. Layer strongly over the whole lid. Dry it pressed. At some point, dry the lid in position on the box, separated from it by thin plastic.

**Note**: if you are still not satisfied with the fit you could improve it by cutting triangular shapes out of the four box corners, moistening and bending the sides in at the top and remaking the corners with strong binding and strapping. Dry with the lid pressed on to the box, but insulated by plastic.

The second way of making a lid that fits over the box sides is to make a new lid. To do this cut the shape as shown in Figure 2.2 to fit on to the box, but make it about 3mm bigger all around. Score and fold the edges sharply (see Chapter One:13). Strengthen the lid by laminating two more thin cards inside it. Strap the corners firmly in their correct angles. Layer all over as for the box. Dry pressed in its correct shape. When nearly dry test its fit on the box. Add more layering inside the edges if necessary.

*Making the box and lid into a covered basket with handle*
First, make and fit the handle. To do this prepare strips of card, grain mainly crosswise, to make a long handle piece of the desired width, five layers thick. Use shorter pieces, end to end

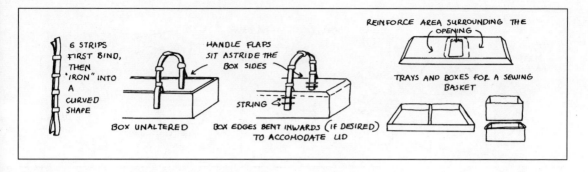

Figure 2.3 *The box made into a basket*

to get the correct length if necessary. Bind around the strips in about five places with strong paper (see Figure 2.3). Bend the handle piece into its correct shape by 'ironing' it with the hands until the strips slide into position. Open flaps at each end. Place the handle with flaps astride the box sides, exactly perpendicular and central. Tie and strap the flaps in position. Layer strongly all over the handle and dry it held in its correct position.

Adjusting the lid to fit the handle depends on what type of lid you have. For a lid that fits into the box adjustment is simple and instructions unnecessary.

To make a lid that fits over the box (and handle), adjust the original lid as follows. Dry the box sides and the handle pressed slightly inwards (you may have to remoisten the parts to do this if the box has dried). Work with the lid upside down on the table.

After measuring carefully, cut an opening across the middle of the lid about 1cm wider than the handle to where the edges bend up. Test that the fit is loose and the lid fits well either way around. Strengthen the edges thoroughly with extra card pieces and strong binding. The top, especially around the opening, may need to be strengthened with extra card.

For a new lid follow the same method. In this case, the process is easier because the lid is already two or three layers thick and fits fairly widely over the box. The handle may not need to be pressed inwards.

**Note**: to make the basket into a sewing basket add divisions and small fitting boxes or a tray.

**Other articles made by the same approach**

Articles are grouped according to the material of the covered-in item in order to show the versatility of layering to strengthen an object (letters in brackets refer to Figure 2.4 and Figure 2.5). The technique hardly varies, but some materials are more difficult to layer on to than others.

**Note**: most objects are rigid and will not warp. Card objects, especially rectangular boxes and flat surfaces, need pressing during drying (see *box* and *lid*) in order to control their shape.

*Layering over flat card:*

• From shaped pieces of sandwich board (see Chapter One:18) make table mats (a), and coasters (b).

*Layering over card objects:*

• From a toilet roll and base of thin cardboard make a pencil holder (c)

Figure 2.4 *Other articles made by the same approach – card armatures*

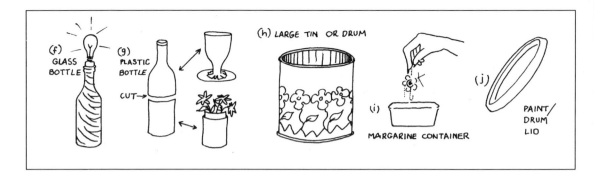

Figure 2.5 *More Approach One articles – a variety of armatures*

• From a cut cereal box or dog biscuit box build an office tray (d), and
• From a cereal box (cut differently) construct a letter rack (e).

*Layering over plastic and glass objects:*

• From a bottle make a lamp stand (f). Weight the bottle with sand
• From a plastic bottle (cut to size) construct a mug or a flower vase (g). The layering must stop well below the mug's rim. Make the rim smooth
• From a margarine container make a small box or casket (i) (see the third approach to paper layering later in this chapter).

*Layering over tin objects:*

• From a paint drum lid make a heatproof tray (j). Rust can be a problem. Get rid of all the rust you can from the lid. Insulate the rest with a circle or two of plastic. Straighten the feet, and, with crushed tubes (see Chapter One:17, 19) and layering, enclose them in a ridge so the finished tray stands off the ground on both sides. Avoid using a lot of paste. The tray centres or inside angles may pull away from the armature. Surgery and skilful pressing should solve the problem
• From a paint tin make a waste paper basket (h).

**Note**: other useful articles that have rusted can be renovated by completely enclosing them in paper or card layering, for example coal scuttles, trash bin cans and so on.

*A flat file*
To make a flat file (see Figure 2.6):

• Find, or make by joining, a long piece of thin card (approximately 55cm) with the grain across it and wide enough to accommodate your papers
• Fold and crease it hard down the middle inside out. Then, more gently and without scoring, fold the covers back again so you leave about 25mm of double card for the ridge on which your papers will be filed
• Paste inside this ridge; put three or four nylon stitches through it near the second folds to stop it separating too much
• Strengthen the covers of the file on the

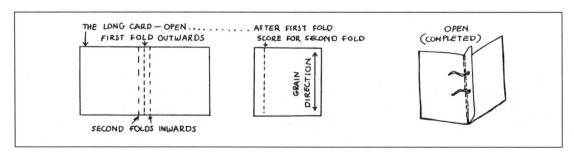

Figure 2.6 *A flat file*

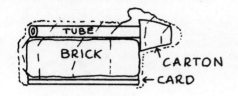

PRESS PAPER HARD AROUND IT,
THEN TIE IT FIRMLY TOGETHER
TO MAKE A GOOD FOUNDATION
SHAPE.

Figure 2.7 *Armature for an animal door stop*

inside with thin card (grain alternated) and paper layering
● Bind and tidy the file, and
● Dry in the first stages with plastic underneath, two cards covered in plastic between the covers and plastic under a weighted board on top.

## 2. Second approach to paper layering

In this approach an armature is made and layered over. The approach resembles the first, but the whole operation is creative and the layering techniques free. Traditionally, this approach is used by moulding mash over an armature. However, if you have a little artistic ability and some layering experience you will find it quicker to layer with paper. The resulting article is not inferior and is lighter and stronger than a mash creation. Only two examples are given. More example are to be found in Chapter Eight.

### Example: dog or cat doorstop over an armature

Make the armature. The armature shown in Figure 2.7 is a brick wrapped in card with a wide tube strapped to the top to make it round, like a back. A small cream carton stuffed with paper is pressed and tied to the tube end for the head. More paper is tied tightly around it to improve the shape. The armature is tightly bound with nylon string to make it a firm and good shape.

Layering will probably be done in three steps. First, prepare some loose sheets or pieces of paper to use with a little paste, and crush to make padding. You also need a large quantity of three- or four-layer strips, which can be up to 2cm wide.

The first stage is to apply a foundation course of layering that you can build on. Especially layer the base. Then, stand the article on plastic and do the rest of the layering without moving it. Work to improve the creature's shape, adding lumps or rolls of crushed pasted paper and strapping and layering them in place to make an ear or the nose. If necessary, press, even cut, into the foundation layering to get the shape you want. When you are fairly satisfied and the shapes are well-held with tight strapping and layering, let the thing dry. Check it as it dries.

The next step is to further improve and tidy the door stop. During drying it will have lost some of its shape. Dents and sharp corners will have appeared. Work on these in any way you think fit. Get a good shape. Leave to dry fairly thoroughly. This step may need repeating.

The last step is the final tidy layering.

### Layering paper over clay articles

Although this process is not well-known it is a very useful. Clay is abundant in Zimbabwe and almost any clay can be used. Almost anyone can obtain clay and can mould it with some skill. Sometimes, beautiful articles made by children crumble or fall to pieces as they dry. Following the method described here, clay articles can be preserved by paper-layering and beautified by decoration.

To make an ornamental bird:

● First, make a hard paper armature on which to mould the clay bird
● Mould the clay bird on the paper armature. Put it to dry. Observe it. Let it dry as far as it can without cracking. Check it as it is drying
● When the clay is no longer soft, very delicately apply your first course of layering. If possible, use cement bag paper in small pieces, with, if necessary, airmail newsprint.

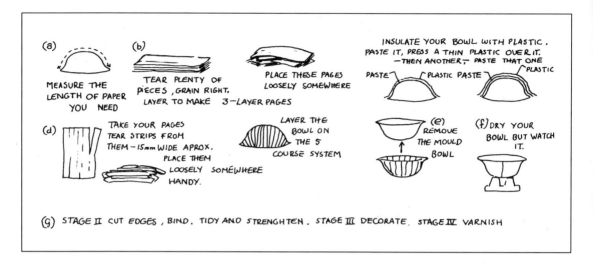

Figure 2.8 *Layering paper to make a bowl*

When you think it is strong enough let it dry, and

• As it dries the paper will shrink and the clay armature inside may break up a little. Do not worry. You now have a strong shape to work on. Do more layering, probably with single pieces of paper, to tidy and finish the article.

## 3. Third approach to paper layering

In this approach, paper or card is layered over a mould. The mould is then removed and the creation finished. It may be a replica or something new.

This kind of layering, which is often linked to papier mâché, has been known and used for a very long time. It is taught in some schools. APT developed from papier mâché and paper layering and it is still a very important part of APT.

APT layering differs from traditional ways of layering in that:

• The APT process is extremely simple and rapid.
• The range and variety of APT articles made by layering is very great
• Card is layered as well as paper and large sturdy articles are made, and
• The four rules, especially the no-cost rule, and the use of earth paints, give APT layered work a unique character.

### Example: layering a replica of a bowl

As this may be the first job you tackle full instructions are given. First, prepare your basic kit (see Chapter One:10). Obtain a well-shaped bowl, two pieces of very thin plastic big enough to cover it, a tidy pile of 20 to 30 sheets of not very thin newspaper or other fairly absorbent paper, with grain running lengthwise, and a drying rack (letters in brackets refer to Figure. 2.8).

Tear or cut the sheets, several at a time, across the grain (see Chapter One:12) to make them the right length for layering, that is about 2cm longer than the distance over the inverted bowl from rim to rim. Tear these wide pieces down the grain and make pages about 20cm wide. Place them in a tidy pile (a) and (b).

Working rapidly, smear paste on your working plastic. Place a page on it, smear paste over the page. Place and paste a second page on the first. Then, paste a third to make a three-layer page. Make a second three-layer page lying across the first. Prepare many three-layer pages. Separate these pages and place them tidily and loosely somewhere (b).

Place the bowl, dome upwards, on the plastic. Paste it. Place a thin plastic over it. Smooth it down tight on the bowl. To ensure your bowl will separate easily you may add a second, dry plastic. Smooth it down with paste (c).

Take a three-layer page. Tear strips from it about 15mm wide. Prepare 20 or more strips, and place them down tidily, for example hang each strip separately over the edge of the table.

Layer the bowl on the five-course system (Chapter One:15) as follows (d). In the first course of layering, criss-cross long strips layered across the bowl in different directions crossing at different points (do not make lumps). Finally, use shorter pieces to close any gaps that remain on the sides of the bowl. Mould tight with the hands.

The second, third, fourth and fifth courses of layering (the parallel courses each in a different direction) are the ones that wrap around the bowl and pull everything together. Start with a strip across the centre. Lay another on the far side just overlapping it. Continue in that way, wrapping the strips tightly around the bowl. When you have finished, turn the bowl around and complete the other half. Complete the other courses in the same way, turning the bowl so it is always in the best position for layering. When the fifth course is complete, tear or cut off any very long ends and mould the bowl once more, heavily, with pasty hands.

Pick up your work. Hold it the right way up in two hands. Ask a friend to lift the mould out and then the plastic (e). If he fails try pulling at the plastics, and attempt to rotate the bowl in either direction, then try to lift it out again. If it is still stuck fast repeat the process less gently. If all else fails invert the bowl. With a sharp instrument pierce right through your bowl until you feel the mould. Lift the base of your bowl slightly to let in the air. Turn the bowls upright again and lift out the mould (using two plastics avoids this problem). Dry your bowl off the ground. Tend it as it dries (f).

When the bowl is dry it is time to strengthen and tidy it. First, cut around its rim with a knife or scissors. Do not cut outside the mark of the original bowl's rim. Study your bowl critically to decide what has to be done to tidy it. Is it really round? Does it sit straight? Are there lumps to be pushed out? Hollows to be filled? Ridges to be smoothed? Does the rim need thickening in places? Having decided, moisten your bowl with paste and work on it till you are satisfied.

Next, bind the edges (see Chapter One: 20c) (g). Finally, dry it again, checking it and correcting any faults.

## Making other articles by layering over moulds — general points and examples

Large articles need to be thicker. Achieve this by using thicker paper or card, or by using four or five layer strips. Use the five-course system.

Deep articles can present two problems. First, it can be difficult to remove the mould. Using two insulating plastics will ease the problem. Second, articles may collapse or crease when stood up to dry. If this threatens, dry them upside down to start with, and fill them with crumpled soft paper so they rest on a cushion of paper with the rim just off the ground (see Chapter One: 21).

When layering over square and rectangular articles, including trays, there are three points to note:

● Because there are no curves to be layered, wider strips may be used

● Corners control and give strength to the sides and thus the whole article. Layer them with care using narrow strips and possibly some extra pieces, and

● Large flat areas of layering, especially if they are thin, tend not to dry flat. Trays tend to warp. Pressing during drying is the main treatment. Thicker layering may warp less. Adding extra sheets of card does not necessa-

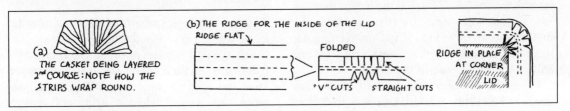

Figure 2.9 *Casket on margarine carton*

rily solve the problem (see Layering a tray, below).

*Casket, layered over a margarine container or other rectangular container, with a lid*
Two ways of making a fitted lid have already been described in the first approach to paper layering, earlier in this chapter. The method suggested here is for making a lid with a tidy fitting ridge from a thin strip of card. Start with the lid as it needs time to dry.

To make the lid laminate four thin cards, grain alternating, to make a lid slightly larger than the box all around. When dry, cut the lid to its correct size and bind the edges.

To make the casket, layer as for the bowl previously described. However, use narrow strips. Follow each strip with your fingers and press it down where it wants to go, but if strip ends are making any part too thick, tear them short.

To make and fit the lid ridge, take a thin card strip, approximately 2cm wide, with grain running lengthwise. Score and fold it down the middle (see Chapter One:13). Score it again along lines about 4mm from the middle fold and bend the edges (flaps) outwards. Mark on the lid where the ridge should be, but actually make the ridge slightly inside the mark.

Work out where the ridge piece must bend and make cuts into the flaps to make it bend easily (straight cuts on the outside and V-shaped cuts on the inside. See Figure 2.9). Strap and bind it in place. Press to dry under plastic.

*Layering a tray over another tray (or mould of clay, polystyrene, wood and so on)*
The process of layering a tray is not basically different from that of layering a bowl. The advice on layering larger articles and rectangular articles applies. To avoid the lumps that can easily occur when strips are criss-crossed in the first course of layering, strips on rectangular trays are crossed so that some cross in one half of the tray, some in the other.

Drying is not easy. The bottom of the tray needs to be evenly pressed. One way to do this is to cut three or four carton cards that fit the bottom exactly. Use these cards on a plastic sheet with a heavy weight spread over them for pressing. The sides also may need controlling during drying.

**Warning**: no other article seems to present drying problems like a layered tray. As well as the base being a thin large board, the sides can cause problems. They are angular and very strong when they contract. Sometimes, cutting into them to release tension is the only way to get the tray to dry straight. But layered trays can be successfully made and they are strong and light. Some APT users claim that extra thick layering solves the problem (see Chapter Four for an alternative method).

*Large ball (netball) for use on soft ground*
The mould for this ball is a balloon. Blow the balloon up to slightly less than the right size. Tie it securely, but so that it can be undone. Try to squeeze it to the right shape and keep the shape by layering some circular belts of strong paper directly on to it. Leave the teat protruding so that you can blow it up again when it is getting soft.

To layer the balloon use the five-course system using three or four layered strips, plus some extra layers of strong paper. A few small problems need to be solved, which are:

• Layered strips resting on the ground or a table tend to come off. Therefore, layer with the ball resting in the top of a pot or tin with no rough edges. Rotate as you layer
• It is difficult to see where a course begins or finishes when the ball is rotated. Using a different paper for successive layers helps. However, layer more by feeling the thickness in different areas than by carefully following rules
• The layering must be thicker than for a bowl and is done in at least two stages with drying periods in between.

At least two layers of strong paper are needed to strengthen and tidy the ball.

Dry the ball in a net or orange bag, turning it from time to time. Keep the teat hole uppermost and open so you can re-inflate the balloon when necessary. Undo the string and remove the balloon when it is no longer needed, and so that the ball can dry thoroughly on the inside.

Figure 2.10 *A netball*

After removing the balloon push out any dents with a stick.

Close and layer over the hole only when the ball is one hundred per cent dry inside and out.

**Note**: these balls are meant for use on soft ground. Experience shows they do not crack rapidly. They get soft on the outside and remain airtight for a long time on the inside.

*Hats*

Hats produced by APT are made in many different ways. They can be very comfortable and endure several years of quite rough wear and some rain. They need resurfacing occasionally. The hats should be as light as possible. A hard wood-like hat can be dangerous.

A well-fitting hat just rests on the hair, or lightly on the sides of the head, not on the ears. It has space for air to circulate near the top and has air vents.

Three models of hats are described:

● A small-brimmed hat — made in one piece like a bowl. Its edges are opened a little and strengthened, fashioned and tidied by any suitable means to make a brim (see Figure 2.11i)
● A brimmed hat with a straight-sided cylindrical crown — school boater or top hat (see Figure 2.11b and g), and
● A brimmed hat with a rounded crown (most of the other hats shown in Figure 2.11).

The last two types of hats are made in two parts, brim and crown, which are then joined. To make a crown for a straight-sided hat, card of suitable height and grain is made into an oval, say two layers thick, the same size as the brim opening. Add 2cm to the height in order to make flaps at the bottom.

For a rounded-crown hat layer over a mould and leave strips projecting at the bottom for flaps. Make the first layering quite thin and fashion the shape you want.

The mould can be a plastic bag filled with plastic or crumpled paper tied to the right size and shape or a cooking pot, fattened and shaped into a mould by tying paper around it and covering it all in plastic, or it could be a real head with a little padding and plastic over it.

Figure 2.11 *Hats that can be made by APT*

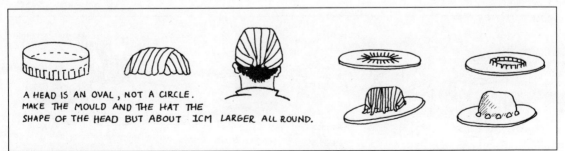

Figure 2.12 *Crowns and brims and joining crown and brim*

29

Figure 2.13 *Liquid containers in holders*

To make the brim, cut thin card into an oval the (outside) size you want. Cut a hole, approximately 10cm, at the centre. From that hole, cut into the brim to make flaps. Bend the flaps upwards. Finally, put the brim on the head and crease the flaps sharply to make the opening about 1cm too big for the head all around. Layer another piece of card of the same size on to it.

To join crown to brim, use the flaps and strap and layer when the crown is not very dry. Precise instructions are not needed. The hat must be tried on and adjusted. The brim, as well as the crown, has to be moulded to a pleasing shape.

The hat will shrink slightly as it dries. Make it too tall and a little too large. You can easily reduce its size where it sits on the head by extra layering, but to enlarge it is difficult.

Have adequate air vents. Cut slits and open them a little, with the knife pointing upwards so the slit has a little lid above it. Make or find a plastic cover to fit over the hat in wet weather.

*Masks*
The technique of layering masks over clay moulds needs no special explanation. Masks can be layered over the future owner's face, by a quick team. Openings must be made in the plastic and layering to allow breathing.

*Boxes, office trays and the like*
These can be made over moulds such as wrapped bricks, books and shaped blocks of Kaylite.

*Layered holders for liquid containers*
The first approach to paper layering described an easy way of layering holders on to plastic or tin containers. However, the holders were permanently attached to them which could be a disadvantage when washing up.

Using the third approach to paper layering, containers fit into holders and can be removed (see Figure 2.13). Large and attractive flower bowls and vases can be made over large containers.

The shrinkage of the holders is quite considerable. Before layering, wrap the container around with at least two layers of thin card covered with plastic. Also, pay special attention to drying the bottoms flat.

## Layering card

The basic techniques are the same as for paper. However:

● Because card is used for larger items, strips may be wider
● The thickness of one card strip equals approximately five paper strips

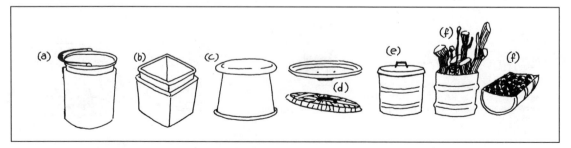

Figure 2.14 *Examples of card-layered objects*

- Card strips are usually layered singly, and
- Card-layered outside surfaces are more uneven than those layered with paper. If a smooth surface is required, a card surface may need patching and rubbing with a smoothing stone followed by a covering or two of layered paper.

### Examples of card-layered articles
See Figure 2.14:

- Waste-paper basket over a bucket (a)
- Waste-paper basket over a square flower pot (b)
- Stool over a bucket — a laminated top was strapped and bound on top to make a flat seat (c)
- Round tray over a (nearly) flat dustbin lid — during layering the handle was left protruding. After layering the tray was removed, placed flat on plastic-covered table and worked to get the bottom quite flat. The tray needed a lot of pressing until it was quite dry (d)
- Kitchen trash-bin holder over oil drum — the lid was made to fit by adding a circular ridge (see how to make a lid for a casket earlier in this chapter) (e), and
- Holders for coal and wood containers made over oil drums cut in two different ways (f).

**Note**: for containers of dirty matter (trash, coal, logs) the original tin moulds (oil drum sections), although removable, should be left inside.

## In the context of rehabilitation

Several models described in the chapter are suitable for use in rehabilitation situations. You will have thought of other models. It is possible to make an artificial limb using APT.

The *first approach to paper layering*, that is, layering over an article to strengthen and transform it, can be employed as *therapy* for rehabilitation patients. As an occupational therapy exercise this approach is very versatile. It is straightforward. Young children and severely disabled people can do it in its simplest form. It can also be done with much skill and artistry to make beautiful and useful articles and, if desired, can earn income.

The first approach to paper layering is also used for *making equipment* for use by disabled people. This could involve:

(i) **Adapting** tools, pencils, eating utensils, and so on, to the grasp of a disabled person. Further instructions are unnecessary, except that either mash or paper may be used to build up and cover in the part needing modification.

(ii) **Larger rehabilitation apparatus and equipment can be made by reinforcing and layering paper over cartons**, either in their original shape or with excisions or modifications, or both. This technique has been pioneered and used extensively by a number of therapists. APT students, once they have mastered the techniques, will constantly be inspired by a child's need or by looking through a catalogue and will confidently set about making the aid that is needed.

In the rehabilitation context the word strong means able to bear much weight and also misuse by children and some adults. The following advice will help to make such strong equipment:

- To strengthen surfaces (tops and sides of boxes) laminate one or two additional sheets of carton card to the inside surfaces. Press well (see Chapter One:18)
- To strengthen angles and so make the structure rigid use wide, long angle pieces of thick carton card cut so that the pipes go across the angle. Bend straight and sharp (see Chapter One:13). Fit the piece tight all along the angle. If desired, hold it in position with nylon string loops. Dry held or pressed in its correct shape
- To hold the sides and/or support the top with rails (see Chapter Four: Utility approach two, railed chair) fit the rails where they are needed. Secure them at each end with flattened flaps layered to the outside of the structure and collars to the inside, and
- To enlarge, reduce or modify cartons use common sense plus any suitable APT techniques and be thorough. If necessary, carefully unmake a carton, study how it was made and remake it to the size and shape you want. Make new folds. Flatten old folds where necessary, laminating an extra piece of card with its grain across the old fold to keep it flat. Bind any newly cut edges strongly.

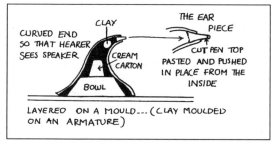

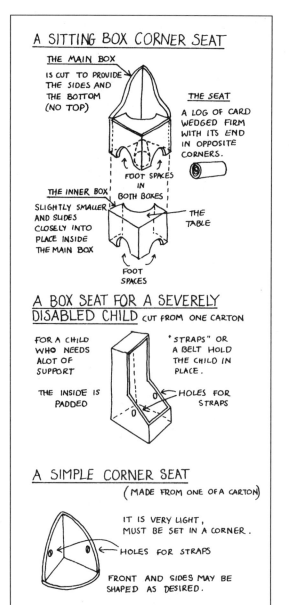

Figure 2.16 *Ear trumpet*

## Ear trumpet

The ear trumpet described here is approved by a UK hearing specialist as useful for helping children with some hearing to hear better. The device is curved so that the deaf child can see the speaker and his or her lip movements while holding the trumpet in his ear.

To make the ear trumpet:

● Make a mould the size and shape of the trumpet you want (see Figure 2.16 for a suggested mould). Cover the mould with plastic while it is still soft. Work the clay through the plastic to get exactly the right shape and a very smooth surface. Cover it with two more thin plastics

● Layer on to the mould using two-layered strips and roughly following the five-course system. Add extra courses as the trumpet gets wider towards its rim

● Remove the trumpet very carefully. Skilfully repair any damage, especially near the narrow end and put it to dry. When it is dry, cut and bind the edges and tidy the trumpet in the usual way. Make the inside surface very smooth, right up to the narrow opening

● Find a suitably shaped ear piece, for example, a tapered pen cap. See that it has a clear smooth hole through it and make it a little bit round and very smooth to fit into the child's ear. Test it with the child. With the narrow end of the trumpet still slightly soft, put paste on the ear piece and gently force it into position from inside the trumpet. Add more layering as necessary to be sure the ear piece is firmly fixed with the plastic end protruding about 1cm beyond the paper, and

● Decorate the inside of the trumpet, for the speaker's benefit, as well as the outside.

Figure 2.15 *Making apparatus by shaping parts cut from thick card boxes/cartons – layering over to strengthen them. Examples of apparatus made by staff and mothers at the Children's Rehabilitation Unit, Harare*

The *third approach to paper layering* described in this chapter, that is, thick layering over a mould of any shape to reproduce that shape in the form of a new strong article, can also be used in rehabilitation, for example to make an ear trumpet (hearing aid).

# Chapter Three: Layering thin card to make stools and tables

Making furniture using APT is a responsibility. Weak articles could cause serious accidents and discredit the technology. The furniture may be sold and thus scrutinized by customers.

Therefore, APT furniture demands first-class workmanship, and a thorough understanding of APT processes and principles, and of basic engineering. This includes, for instance, the strength of different components, shapes and constructions, for example bars and tubes; triangles and squares, cubes, pyramids, cylinders, spheres, stresses and support systems. Design is therefore crucial, but it is largely a matter of common sense.

## Furniture design

Two paramount requirements of design are:

- The article should be strong, and
- The article should be stable, stand firm and not be easily tipped over.

Appearance is also important, but must not conflict with strength and stability. When designing APT furniture remember:

- **Bases** — wide bases stand firm. For smaller articles, especially tall ones, carcasses must be wider at the bottom, for example, legs splayed out. However, bases must be kept within the line of the top edge, or they will catch people's feet as well as look ugly.

- **Tops** — all APT boards need well-spread supports under them. Carcasses or struts must support the top to within 2cm of its edges. Corners particularly need support. Legs or boards of carcasses should be attached so they support corners, otherwise use strong struts. Seats must be designed to bear very heavy weight. They may be stood on

- **Corners** — sharp corners can be dangerous. Also, they are easily spoiled if knocked. Whenever possible make rounded or cut-back corners, and

- **Small is strong** is an APT slogan. Do not make articles larger than necessary.

- **Chairs** (especially chairs for children) — should be designed to reduce the risk of being tipped backwards (and of children falling). This can be achieved by making relatively large seats, with low backs and legs that splay out and especially backwards.

The models described in this chapter evolved in the early days of the technology from layering paper over moulds (see Chapter Two: Third approach to layering). Card pieces are layered around a mould to make the carcass. A top is made by laminating thin card and fitted to the carcass. Moulds are usually either round or square (cut cones or pyramids). Other shapes can also be used.

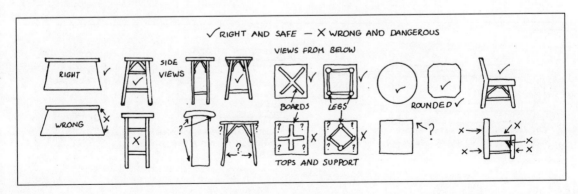

Figure 3.1 *Design in furniture*

33

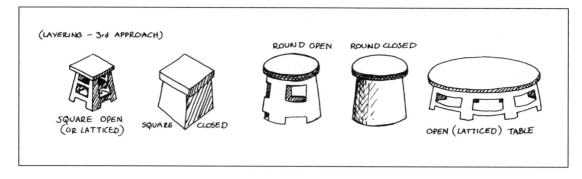

Figure 3.2 *Four designs of furniture made by layering card (or paper)*

The strips or pieces may be layered to leave a pattern of openings (windows) to make so-called open or latticed tables, or cover the mould completely making so-called closed stools or tables. Open models are lighter and more attractive. They are used as tables. Closed models are heavier, stronger and used as stools or tables. This style has been largely superseded by the classic and utility styles that evolved later.

APT layered furniture-making is often omitted from short courses as the method does not serve as a basis for many other models. However, it is a style of construction worth learning because:

● It follows on from paper layering and beginners learn it easily
● It is a relatively quick method. Parts can be made and the article built in a single session.
● The furniture can be made using otherwise useless strips and pieces of card which supports conservation, and
● The closed stools and tables, round and square, are some of the strongest articles produced by APT.

## The approach to making square and round models

The method, as for most APT articles, is simple. However, it includes some unconventional procedures, gadgetry, and so on, necessary if the work is to be done efficiently. Instructions will be detailed.

First, to summarize the approach:

● A suitable mould is found and covered with plastic. Six to eight courses of prepasted thin card, strips or pieces, are tightly layered to the mould, their grain running vertically down the carcass. Cuts about 15cm deep are made in the top of the carcass. The layers are separated and bent to a sharp 90° angle, some inwards, some outwards, to make a flat ridge for the top. The top is a circle or square of six to eight thin cards, laminated and pressed, but not necessarily dried. It should be about the same size as the bottom of the carcass, not

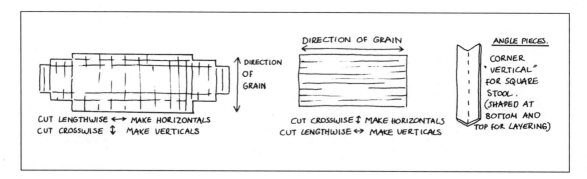

Figure 3.3 *Card box off-cuts make angle pieces*

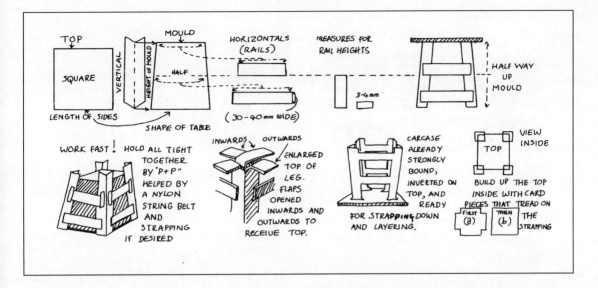

Figure 3.4 *Square stool, open style. The mould gives the measurements*

bigger. The top is placed in position. The article is inverted. The two components are strapped, layered and pressed together

● Moulds may be square and round flower-pots or 5-litre beer containers, or they can be made to any desired shape or size by moulding them in clay (over an armature) and covering the mould with thin plastic. Duplicate moulds of two or three layers of thin card can be made over original moulds. Or make a mould follow-ing instructions supplied at the end of this chapter

● Angle pieces (see Chapter One:19) are essential for making the open models. Ideal angle pieces are the sides and ends cut from shirt boxes because they are already creased. Other angle pieces can be made from cereal or shoe boxes and from any thin card.

Each angle piece must be applied either as an upright (vertically) or as a belt (horizontally) according to whether the grain runs along it or across it. Grain must always run down the carcass. Figure 3.3 shows how horizontals and verticals are differently cut according to the grain of the box.

**Note:** advantages of card moulds are that they are light and easy to carry or store. Any num-ber of moulds can be made for courses or by participants for their use.

## Examples

### Square table, open pattern, latticed
To make this table:

● Find or make a suitable mould. Laminate the top board (see Chapter One:18), about eight layers of thin card, square, the same size as the bottom of the mould. Press until you need it, and

● Before building the carcass and joining the top, read the instructions below. Then, work quickly.

Prepare:

● An elastic belt; two card measures, one for the height of the underneath of the bottom rail (approximately 3cm from the base), the other for the underneath of the top rail (about half-way up the mould)

● Twenty-eight vertical angle pieces, the same height as the mould and roughly the same widths. Cut at an angle at the bottom to stand right at the corners

● Twenty-four horizontals (grain is not important) for the top rails, measured to be a little shorter than top of mould, and approxi-mately 35mm wide, and

● Twenty-four horizontals for the bottom rails, slightly smaller than the width across the mould half way-up and approximately 40mm wide.

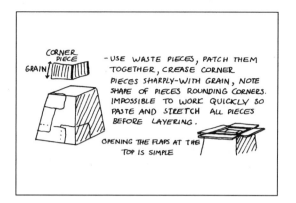

Figure 3.5a *Square closed stool or table*

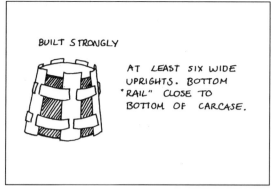

Figure 3.5b *Round open stool or table (latticed)*

To build the table:

● Paste at least half the pieces of each kind. Separate them so that they do not stick together. Keep moist under plastic

● Press two verticals hard to each corner of the mould, hold them in with elastic

● Separate the inside edges of verticals to insert one horizontal (bottom) and one (middle) all around. Press and make them tight against mould

● Build on five or more courses (verticals and horizontals)

● Bind and remove from mould

● Cut down each corner to an equal height. Bend flaps until they stay at an angle of 90°. Weave the inside flaps on top of each other. Pinch and press corner angles to 90° or less

● Invert the carcass and make it stand square and straight, with flaps flat on the table plastic

● Stand the carcass up. Take the top board. Position it carefully. Attach it with a little strong strapping. Check it again. Invert the table and adjust again if necessary. Get it right

● Begin joining with double strapping over flaps on to the top board, outside and inside

● Cut about three strengthening pieces of thin card (see Figure 3.4) that fit flat to the inside part of the top board and which tread on the strapping but not the flaps

● Paste and place one card. Add a layer of strapping, another card, and more strapping, until the centre is level with the flaps. Cut and paste a card piece that will cover the inside. If you wish, have flaps to hold on to

the sides of the carcass, which strengthens the top, and

● Dry and press. First, check everything is straight. Cut two carton cards to fit inside. Place them inside on plastic with a fitting heavy weight on top (sandbag, bricks and the like). Devise a means to keep sides in and corners sharp during drying. Place a lightly weighted board across the bottom, resting on all four feet.

**Square stool, closed-style**

Refer to summary of approach earlier in this chapter and the previous example. The process and techniques are broadly the same as for the open pattern. However, note the following differences:

● Use pieces with vertical grain to bend sharply around corners, for example angle pieces from box sides. Elsewhere grain direction of pieces is less important, but try to alternate grain from course to course when possible

● Pieces of any shape or size (but not too large) can be used. Patch them together overlapping preceding pieces. Small gaps between pieces do not matter

● Five or six courses are sufficient

● One cut for flaps at each corner may be enough for joining. Instead of weaving the inside flap ends at the corners cut a triangle off the flaps to make them lie flat, and

● During drying the board across the top must leave space for air to pass.

## Round table or stool, open-style (latticed)

The main advantage of this stool is it is light and attractive (see Figure 3.5b).

Follow the procedure of square stool, open-style, but incorporate the following modifications:

- Have at least six verticals (legs) at least 7cm wide, slightly curved at the bottom to stand well on the floor
- Normally use fairly short horizontals that fit in between each pair of verticals. If you prefer to use some long horizontal belts, they must be shaped to a slight curve upwards in order to lie correctly on the carcass and not turn downwards
- Make three or four cuts for flaps in the top of the verticals for joining
- Feet need to be reinforced and very strong. Use one or two thin card layers and some strong paper such as the top layer of corrugated (carton) card and triple cement bag to do this
- To join and strengthen the top read the instructions for the next example.

## Round stool, closed-style

This is one of the most popular, and possibly the best, child's seat made by APT. It is light and extremely strong. It has no sharp corners. It can be used as a seat, step, drum, building unit, or a receptacle for toys. It must be well-made.

Reread summary of approach earlier in this chapter and square open table and square open stool examples. To make a round stool, closed-style, note that:

- Pieces or strips can be used, but the grain must be vertical
- Six courses are usually adequate
- Strengthen the bottom. After layering invert the stool to check the bottom. If there are spaces between layers push in pieces of layered card to fill them. Make the bottom strong, strongly bound and level
- Check the evenness of the side angles as well as the level of the top. These must be right before joining. Mistakes can happen
- Dry as for square closed stool. Leave room for air to circulate.

To join and strengthen the top of the round, closed stool:

- Make the cuts about 15cm apart. It is easier to cut if the carcass is dry. As you bend the flaps out, pinch the sides of the stool together. With a measure check the flap ridge is level. Press the top accurately in position. Strap it to hold it in place
- Carefully invert the stool and work first on the inside. Strap the flaps down
- Cut about five circles of card, three that will fit inside the circle of the flaps and two that will lie flat across the top and the flaps inside the stool
- To join the top press one pasted circle inside the flaps, on top of the strapping, with a course of strapping to hold it down. Repeat with a second and third circle to make the surface level. Then add the two circles that cover everything. Finally, layer right across the circles and slightly up the sides
- Stand the stool up and work on the outside.

Figure 3.6 *Round closed stool*

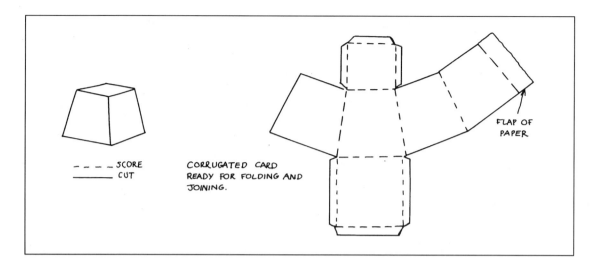

Figure 3.7 *A square-topped mould*

Cut back any projecting flaps. With strong paper pieces, bind the flaps to the stool top
● Take a 5cm strip of strong paper long enough to encircle the top. Paste it. Roll it tightly to make a belt. Wrap it tightly in the angle under the top, over your binding. Press and mould it, squeezing out all the paste. Add a final layer of strong tidy binding and layering over the belt and the edge of the top.

### Round closed stools made from paper
This is not difficult. To make a round closed stool from paper by the simplest method:

● Prepare a lot of long curved pieces the same height as the carcass and made of five layers of paper each. They can be made from double pages of magazines in which the grain runs vertically. Layer these, as if they were card pieces
● Press and rub pasty hands over the work so all the layers lie flat
● Tops can be laminated using five-layer strips in the same way
● Pressing, drying and layering over with strong paper must be done thoroughly.

### Larger layered tables
These can be made on any of the patterns previously mentioned. Because small articles of furniture are stronger, low tables are stronger and also are usually more attractive than tall ones. The principles of design mentioned at

the beginning of this chapter should be observed.

### Making moulds from card
To construct a square mould:

● Cut a template the shape and size of the mould you want
● If possible, find one piece of carton card large enough to cut from it the shape shown in Figure 3.7. (If you cannot obtain card big enough for the mould make a large piece by joining pieces of card.) Use the template to provide the measurements, and
● Score V-shaped lines in the card along the dotted lines and fold the flaps up (see Chapter One:16) to make the mould.

The following hints may help make the mould:

● Flaps help, but are not essential
● Scrape away all but the outside paper of your flaps to make them thin, and
● Fold angles hard so the card pieces stay in position even before you strap them down.

To make a round mould of thin card:

● Make the sides from one piece of card, whole or joined, with grain vertical to make rolling easy
● If possible, find a suitable flowerpot on which to make the mould
● To mark the side piece with the correct curves, slowly roll the flowerpot over the sheet

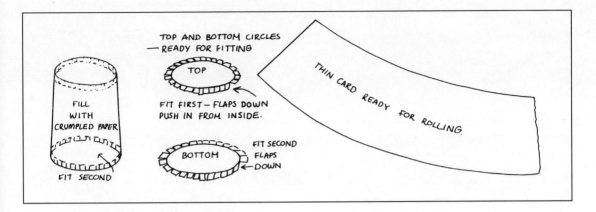

Figure 3.8 *Mould for round stool*

of card marking the lines where its two ends roll

● Roll the side piece tightly on to the flower-pot, overlap and strap down the join. Check that top and bottom edges are correct. Take it off the mould and check that it stands straight

● Measure the top and bottom circles of the mould. Score them for folding, then draw another circle about 15mm bigger outside the scored line. Cut around the bigger circle, cut the flaps and fold them up at 90°

● Paste and fit the top first, with the stool inverted, flaps down, strapped firmly down inside

● Stuff the mould with dry, crumpled paper. Fit and strap down the bottom circle, flaps down outside, and

● Bind all joins and layer all over with strong paper — at least two layers.

If you do not have a suitable mould to start with, take a piece of card wider than the height of the mould you want. Make a template (see Figure 3.7) about 19cm across the bottom and 16cm across the top, from another piece of card. Then, roll the whole piece of card and pin it in what you think is the right shape. Using the template to give you the size and shape across the middle, adjust the pins and cut the top and bottom edges until the shape and size is correct.

Check the size and shape of the mould from all angles. When you are satisfied make and join the top and bottom circles and strengthen the mould.

**Note:** check any mould you make and correct it during and after drying. Cover the mould with thin plastic before layering over.

### In the context of rehabilitation

The square closed stool is particularly suitable for rehabilitation situations. It is a very strong and stable model, and easy to make with waste pieces of thin card.

# Chapter Four: Using laminated corrugated card to make a full range of furniture

Figure 4.1 *Illustrating the three main utility approaches*

## Utility style

Carton-card furniture is called utility-style furniture. Characteristics that distinguish utility-style articles from other APT products are:

- They are cheap because they take comparatively less time to make
- Articles made are often large and in demand and difficult to make using other APT materials and techniques
- The technology is simple. People with a fairly limited grasp of APT can do it, and
- Utility articles are not intrinsically attractive. Their large expanse of flat card surface requires a lot of decorative cover. The most economic and convenient way of decorating them is with earth paints. In fact, earth colours

are becoming a distinctive feature of APT utility ware. Good decoration can render utility-style furniture some of the most interesting and attractive work that APT produces.

## Utility-style boards and flat board models

Making boards is dealt with in Chapter One:18. Instructions will not be given about what type of board to use for a specific article. Use your common sense. Consider how much use the board will get, the weight it will carry, the support it will have underneath, and how big it will be. Carton, rather than thin card, tends to be used for big boards. To familiarize yourself with this material make a thick board tray first.

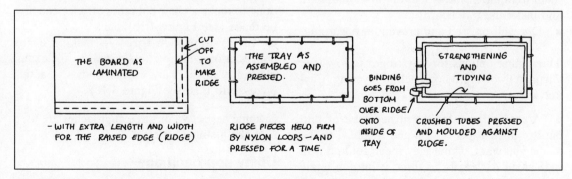

Figure 4.2 *A thick board tray – two-layered corrugated card*

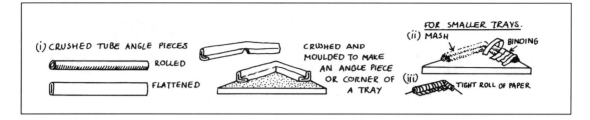

Figure 4.3 *Alternative tray ridges*

## Thick board tray

Advantages of this model compared to the layered tray (see Chapter Two: Third approach to layering) are that it is less liable to warp, can be made any size or shape, and is more heatproof.

To make a thick board tray:

● Make a hard-top board using only two or three layers of carton card (Chapter One:18c). Press and dry it totally flat
● To make the ridge for a rectangular tray add extra length and width to the size of your tray board in order to cut from it also the four ridge pieces (see Figure 4.2)
● When the board is dry, cut the pieces accurately. Bind them with a layer of paper to prevent cards from separating. Cut the cards to the right length — the end pieces must fit between the side pieces. Paste the board lightly where they will fit. Tie them firmly in position and secure them with strapping
● When you are satisfied all is correct, cover the ridges with thin plastic and press them under a lightly weighted board
● When dry tidy the ridge pieces. Strengthen them with crushed tubes pressed along their inside angles and strong tidy strapping over them from the inside of the tray, over the ridge and under the tray board
● Dry well pressed and prevent any warping.

Three other options for tray ridges follow (see Chapter Two: Third approach to layering; Casket with lid):

● A card ridge using a crushed tube of thin card or thick paper. Crush and mould it to the shape you want, which may mean folding it in half along its length, to force it into an angle piece. Cut triangles out of it as shown to bend it round corners (see Figure 4.3i)

● A ridge made of stiff mash, made very tidily and layered over when dry. This is a very straightforward method if you do not make things too wet (see Figure 4.3ii), and
● A tightly rolled tube of paper, applied in the same way as mash (see Figure 4.3iii).

The last two methods are not suitable for very large trays.

## Simple picture frame

Make this in the same way as the thick board tray. Choose the method of making the outside frame that will suit the shape you want. Paste the picture in the frame (see Chapter Eleven: Fine or detailed decoration (a)). You can devise a way of fitting glass, but see Chapter Five: Picture frames before doing so.

## Utility-style furniture

Three approaches to making utility-style furniture are described in this chapter:

● **Utility approach one** — using a carton board base to support a top, for example of a stool or table and so on (refer to Figure 4.1a)
● **Utility approach two** — joining two carton board sides using tubes of rolled card that support another board or boards. This is often done to make a chair but other articles can also be made (see Figure 4.1b), and
● **Utility approach three** — making a box construction with five or six boards, for example solar stove, baby-walker body, or actual boxes with lids (see Figure 4.1c).

In some cases two or three approaches are used to make a single article.

## Utility approach one

In this furniture-making method a carton board base is used to support a top.

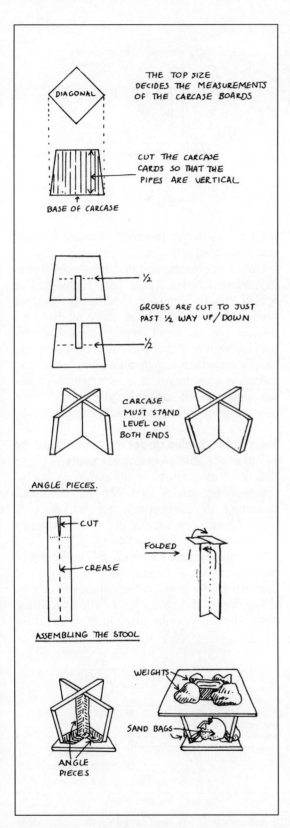

Figure 4.4 *A square-top cross-based stool*

## Example: square-topped stool with a crossed board carcass

This article is recommended as an introduction to furniture-making (Chapter One: 25).

Before you build this stool you must make its components and allow them to dry. Do this by deciding the size of top you want. Cut a card template for it and laminate a hard-top carton board for the top (see Chapter One: 18). Make a template for the cross boards. Calculate measurements from the top board, for example, width at top, about 2cm less on each side than a diagonal of the stool top, width at bottom, almost as long as the top diagonal, and height not more than the width of the top board. The cross boards' grain should run vertically. Laminate the two cross boards, five cards thick (about 15mm).

Now you are ready to build the stool (Stage One). To do this:

● Tidy and correct the size and shape of the cross-boards. They must be identical. Utility furniture usually has rounded edges. Rub the edges of your boards before they are quite dry, with a rough stone, or on a concrete surface to tidy them. If necessary, hammer the edges with your stone or smoothing tool. When the edges are correct, bind the sides' and bottom's edges with strong paper and dry them, pressing again if necessary

● When the boards are dry measure and cut the grooves of the halving joint (see Figure 4.4). The grooves should be wide enough to fit closely, but not too tightly. Each groove should extend just over half way up (or down) the board. They must be absolutely perpendicular. Do a trial fit, without paste, and make adjustments

● Paste all the parts to be joined. Assemble the carcass. Check it by standing it the right way up and upside down on the table. It must stand flat, without rocking on its top or on its base. Plug any gaps in the join with small pieces of card or pressed paper

● To join the carcass to the top place the top board, best side down, on the table. Paste the surface, that is make all the surfaces of the top and carcass sticky with paste. Place the carcass on the top. Check it is central, and that the two boards stand perpendicular and at right angles

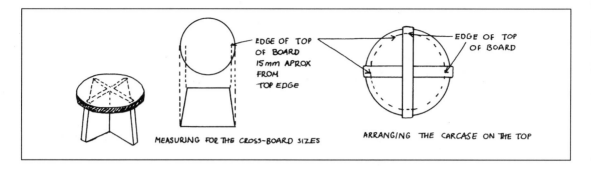

Figure 4.5 *A round cross-based stool*

to each other. Press the carcass down, you might even place a small weighted board across its feet. Prepare and cut to suitable sizes some angle pieces (see Figure 4.4 and Chapter One:19b). Still pressing the carcass down in its correct position, press pasted angle pieces along and right into all joins and corners. Tear into them where necessary to make them lie quite flat. Strap them down with double cement bag paper. See that all surfaces are covered with at least one layer of card pieces. Finally, layer tidily over the whole stool, and
• Dry the stool inverted with a weighted board across the feet and sand bags or other suitable weights pressing the angle pieces and strapping to the top.

Strengthen and tidy the stool (Stage Two) when it is dry (see Chapter One: 20).

Stand the stool up and check that it stands straight, the top is level, and so on. Blunt or cut the corners. Correct mistakes. Layer all over again tidily. Add extra strong binding to give the feet long wear. Check again how the stool stands. Dry upright, under a weighted board

placed centrally. Incorrect weighting will make the stool crooked.

Utility approach one, that is, a board base supporting a board top, is very versatile. The boards can be arranged in different patterns according to the size and shape of the top. Boards can be fitted into grooves horizontally, as well as vertically. Additional supports can be added. In larger models, in which the carcass is quite heavy, it is necessary to secure the carcass to the top with nylon loops before fixing it with angle pieces and strapping.

### Nest of two tables under a mother table, or set of stackable play school seats
This item of furniture is an extremely useful space-saving model that can be decorated according to the purpose for which it is made. Constructionally, it is a combination of utility approaches one and two.

The mother table has three rails at the top of the carcass boards to give added support as it may be sat or stood on sometimes. Refer to utility approach two for information on fitting rails. The rails can be fitted in grooves cut in

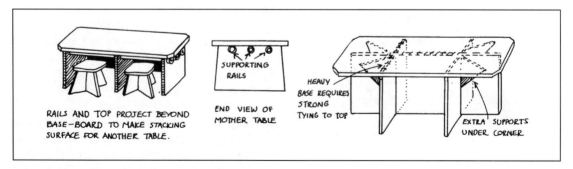

Figure 4.6 *Stackable seats for play centre or nest or tables/stools (a), and large rectangular table (b) for children*

44

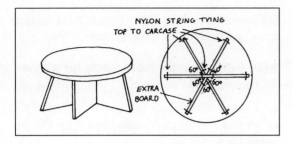

Figure 4.7 *Low coffee table (utility-style)*

the top of the side boards instead of in holes cut through them.

When designing this item of furniture:

● Make the stools so they fit in their nests with plenty of room to spare. Both the stools and the nest walls will be fattened by layering. Blunt corners on the stools are essential
● For stackable tables make the top board project at least 4cm each end. Support the board underneath by making the rails project too
● All stackable tables must be identical in size and small tables interchangeable, and
● Make the front edges of the carcass the same pattern as the boards of the stools, that is wider at the bottom.

### Large rectangular children's table
Adequate leg room is a priority of this item of furniture. Therefore, it is necessary to break the rule for the diagonal direction of carcass boards. To compensate for this transgression:

● Make the top thicker than normal, and
● Devise strong supports for corners, but they must not inconvenience the children's knees.

The table is quite weighty (see Dining table in Utility approach two). The base is heavy and

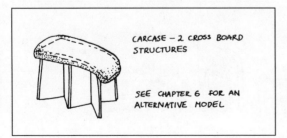

Figure 4.8 *A footrest*

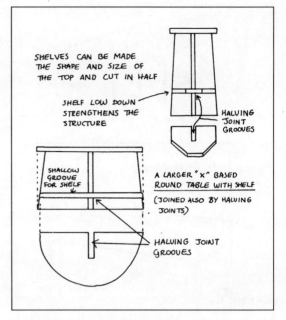

Figure 4.9 *A cross-based stool*

the table will be lifted by its top. Thus, attach the top first by strong, tight nylon loops to all the carcass boards. Do not lift the table by its top until it is dry.

### Round table with a six-board base
The six boards used in the construction of this item which give the table top more support are in fact two full-size boards and one cut in half. To avoid a clumsy appearance do not make the boards very thick. Measure and fit the boards so they are, approximately 35mm in from the top's edges.

The heavy carcass will tend to pull away when the table is lifted. Tie it securely to the top at 12 places (see Figure 4.7). Do not lift the table by its top during drying.

See Figure 4.7 for bending the joins of the first two boards to 60° to make room for two extra boards (x in diagram). Strap the carcass to the top very securely. Dry with pressure on strapping and the table inverted.

### Footrest
If required, cut the carcass boards to shape to get a slight slope. See the classic-style footrest in Chapter Six especially for the top board.

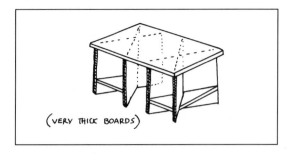

Figure 4.10 *Work bench*

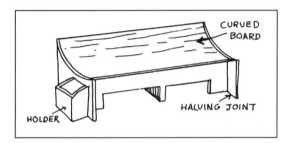

Figure 4.11 *Baby changer (for use on a table)*

## Large, shelved versions of the cross-based stool (models designed and made by Harry Finken-Flagel) (Figure 4.9)

Shelves are necessary to give strength and stability to large models. The lower the shelf, the bigger it is and bigger shelves are more useful than small ones.

The best way to make and fit shelves is to build two boards, each board comprising two shelves.

The shelf boards fit into one cross board by a halving joint, and into shallow grooves on the other cross board.

## Work bench

In this model boards should be at least 2cm thick. The design is basically the same as for the footrest, but the cross boards have square ends and shelves on three of their sides.

## Safe baby changer that stands on a table

To construct this article:

● Find a suitable curved mould, for example an oil drum. Laminate, mould and press the top board on it
● Shape the tops of the upright cross boards to accommodate the curved top
● Make grooves in the top part of the cross boards to hold the long support bars, which may also need grooves to make halving joints
● Cut away part of the centre cross board to give working space on the table, and
● Make and fit shelves and holders to suit your needs.

## Utility board chair with no rails

This is a slightly awkward chair to make because it is big compared to the seat space it provides. However, the model is very strong, easy to make once your plan is right, and does not need rails (see Figure 4.12).

Use two sets of halving joints. Experiment without cutting to make sure the halving joint for the two main boards is correctly placed to support a good-size seat.

Figure 4.12 shows how the chair's components fit together. Once assembled, sections of the boards with no structural or strengthening function can be cut away to lighten the article and make it more interesting.

## Utility approach two

In this approach, two shaped carton-board sides are joined by rails that support another board or boards, for example, to make chairs, cupboards, beds, and so on.

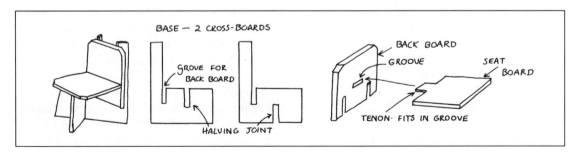

Figure 4.12 *Cross boards based chair (a model by Harry Finken-Flagel)*

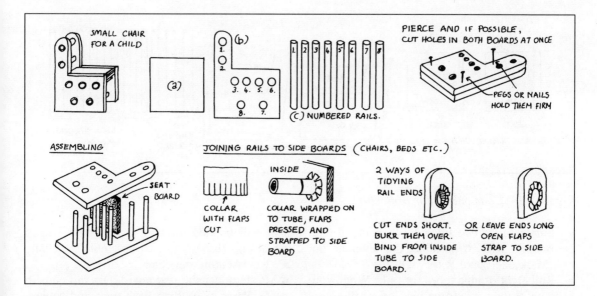

Figure 4.13 *A railed chair – Utility approach two*

This utility style originated when making a small chair. It proved unexpectedly robust. As a result, other models were developed using the same approach.

This utility approach is an extremely versatile basic plan used to make stools, benches, chairs, tables, shelves, and numerous rehabilitation items. The approach is used, in conjunction with approach three to make cupboards and coffins.

In this utility approach the size and shape of the side pieces, as well as where you plan the rails, determines almost all of the article's other features. These two factors decide whether the item will be useful and comfortable and strong, or not. When planning the side pieces take care to remember that:

● **Small is strong**, do not make an article or a part of it bigger than necessary
● The user wants comfort as well as usefulness. Test for comfortable height and shape. Plan rails so they do not obstruct legs and cannot be trodden on
● Strength depends less on the thickness of the boards than on the strength of the rails, where they are sited, how they are attached to the boards. The rails have two functions — to support boards, particularly seat or top boards, and to strengthen side boards and hold them rigid, and

● You must think where weight will be heaviest and prepare for this by bigger rails or extra rails. Remember that people will mistreat the article (children stand on tables, beds and so on). Plan additional rails to hold the side boards firmly in parts that are narrow and a long way from the seat boards.

To decide whether to use tubes or bars as rails, and for information on laminating boards refer to Chapter One:18. For details about cutting holes, fitting and fixing tubes see Chapter One:19.

### Example: small chair for a child
To make this item use the following instructions (letters in brackets refer to Figure 4.13).

● Make a seat board of the right size, or bigger so it can be cut (a)
● Make one side template and plot the holes on it and number them
● Take the size of the child into account. Test for height with the child. Allow plenty of seat room all around. Plot the seat holes very near the top so the seat board will be a bit higher than the side boards
● For a small chair four or even three rails for the seat may provide enough support. The front rail must be very near the front of the seat board. If extra rails are needed at the bottom, make them very strong and out of the way of feet

47

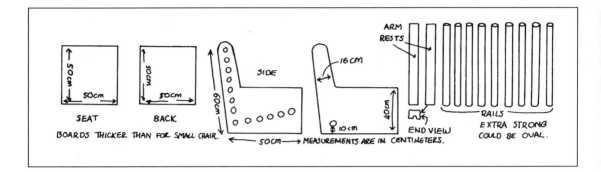

Figure 4.14 *Components for armchair*

● Laminate the two side boards, made of five cards each, with, if possible, the template on top. Mark one board R for right (b)

● Roll eight or nine tubes for rails. When you fit them in they should be just longer than the width of the seat board, plus the thickness of two side boards. Mark them with numbers one to eight in the middle and with an R near one end to show that end will fit into the right board. Dry the rails (c)

● Tidy the boards and make them identical in shape. Cut the holes with a chisel. If necessary, make a chisel by hammering and sharpening the head of a big nail and fixing it into a handle. Cut one card, take out the circle, then cut the next (do not use scissors or trimming knives). To cut efficiently place one board exactly on top of the other. Keep them from moving by pushing three or four sharp pointed nails or pegs through them. Mark the holes by pushing a piercing tool right through to the lower board. Either cut the holes right through or separate the boards to cut them. Cut with perpendicular sides. Test each rail in its numbered hole (d)

● Do a mock assembly — place one board flat on the table. Screw the correct end of each rail into its hole. Place the seat board in position

● Find or make a measure, for example a rail, the same length as the seat width. Place the second board on the rail ends. Guide each rail into its hole, screwing it as you do so, and press the board down hard, bit by bit, until it is hard against the seat board. Use your measure to be sure the side is pushed down to the correct points on the other rails. Stand the chair up. Correct everything to make it stand firmly and with the seat level, and so on. Pierce pairs of holes through the seat where, next time, the

seat will be tied through to the rails. Thread the strings through (e). Disassemble the chair

● Re-assemble the chair

● Paste under the seat board. Dip rail ends in paste. Press everything very tight and square. Tie the seat to the rails, and join it underneath to the sides with angle pieces and to the rails by crushed tubes of thin card and much strong layering

● Stand the chair upright on a flat surface. Check everything is correct. Place a weighted board (not a brick) on its seat

● If the rails are too long, cut them to the same length, projecting about 3mm at each end

● Fix the rails firmly to the side boards (f), (g). Tidy the tube ends with binding so the holes are part of the design or close them with discs of card and tidy layering if desired, and

● Give a hard smooth surface to the seat by laminating two sheets of thin card on to the carton board, with the top sheet wrapping just over the side board.

### Adult chair

This is made in exactly the same way as the child's chair but stronger, for example with oval rails under the seat. Do not make the back high.

### Armchair

The method is basically the same as for the other two chairs. However, an extra board is needed for the back. Seat rails must be very strong. Remember **small is strong** and there is no advantage in making a chair bigger than necessary. The pattern shown in Figure 4.14 has proved satisfactory and comfortable. The

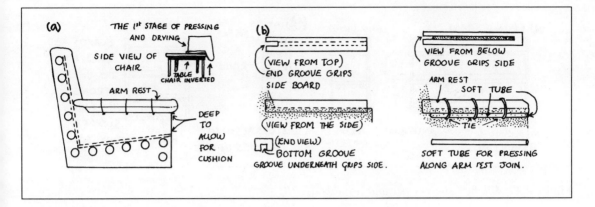

Figure 4.15 *Armchair (utility-style) and making and fitting armrests*

back of the seat is 10cm from the floor. The seat and the backboard are about 50cm square, that is the distance between the two sides is 50cm. Rails are just over 55cm long.

Armrests that fit very securely to the arm part of the side boards are optional. Armrests are a major problem in armchair-making as they must be capable of bearing a lot of strain. The owner rests all his or her weight on the armrests to sit down or get up. Also, an armchair may be lifted by its armrests.

To make the armchair, first construct all the components, including the armrests. Approximate dimensions are shown in Figure 4.14 in centimetres. Note that:

● Rails should be very strong and could be oval-shaped
● The back board and height of the side boards could be slightly larger than shown in the diagram, which is a shoulder-height chair, and
● The narrower the armrests are the less strain there will be on their joins.

Make a vertical groove at one end of the armrests to grip the side board and a groove all along the underneath of the armrest to grip the side board. The groove underneath can be made by laminating narrow strips, or cut out when the armrest is dry. Use strong carton card. Bind strongly over and along the groove.

Assemble the armchair using the same procedure as for the small chair. Join the components very strongly. The parts that need special strengthening are the two sides from the seat upwards, because this is where the greatest

pressure will be on the chair and there are no rails holding the sides together.

To strengthen the sides:

● Fit and tie a strong soft tube across the front edge of the seat board. Bend its ends around the side board, tie and strap them firmly, and
● Find some large pieces of good corrugated card which will, with grain running across the joining angles. Cover the whole of the seat area, starting just below the armrest on one side, going down the side across the seat and up to the armrest on the other side. Plan and score the cards. With the aid of nylon loops, press and hold the cards close to the chair's sides and right into the angles. Dry under pressure (Chapter One: 21).

Next, the grooves made in the armrests should be corrected so they grip. However, the grooves alone do not hold the side very strongly. To secure the armrests to the chair's sides, string is tied through the armrests near the edges and through the side boards. Then,

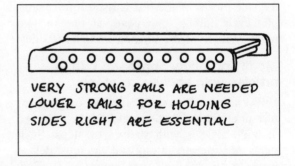

Figure 4.16 *A junior bed*

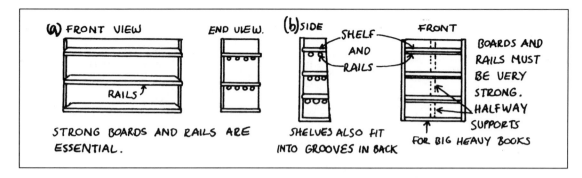

Figure 4.17 *Kitchen shelves (a) and a bookcase (b)*

long tubes of freshly rolled card are forced under the strings, and crushed and pressed into the angles of the join. More than one tube may be used for each join if desired. The joins must be strapped over very strongly.

To fit the armrests place them flat on the table, with the groove upwards. Assemble the armrests with the chair inverted, and side boards firmly pressing into the armrests. The armrests should not project forward beyond the side boards.

## Junior bed

Make this bed before attempting a full-size one. Take care not to make it too narrow. The model has low sides or strength. A raised edge is necessary if a mattress is used, otherwise it is a nuisance (Figure 4.16).

The lower rails are vital in order to keep the sides vertical. Check that the rails hold the sides perpendicular. Dry in that position.

A head-board can be made separately. Think of it as half a bed standing against the wall and attached at the bottom to the bed by holes and pegs. Foam rubber pads at the back of the head-board protect the wall. A nonslip device under the side pieces of the bed is useful, for example, cycle tubing underneath at one or two points, held by string stitches through the sides.

## Modifying utility approach two — articles with shelves or steps

Utility approach two, i.e. making carton card furniture with supporting rails, can be modified to build articles with shelves or steps. Such items must be very strong and you must devise ways to ensure this (see Figure 4.17). Two points to remember are:

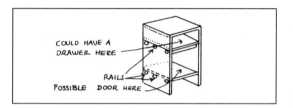

Figure 4.18 *A bedside cabinet*

● Any APT board will sag if weight is continually placed on it, unless it is built with strong supports under it. Tubes can provide some support but under continuous weight may sag. Vertical boards (with tubes vertical) arranged at intervals under the shelf boards provide the best support. Make the spaces between the supporting vertical boards as narrow as your model will permit, and

● For strength and stability shelves should have a back board as well as side boards. Grooves or ridges are made in or on the back board to support the shelves at the back. The bottom board, or the tubes or rails supporting it, should rest on the floor.

Design shelves for the articles they will hold.

## Book shelves

Making the bottom wider than the top allows for big heavy books to be kept on the bottom shelf. It is also necessary for helping the book shelf to stand firm. Long shelves need dividers (or vertical rails) in the middle to provide extra support.

## Bedside cabinet (Figure 4.18)

No new construction features are required to make this article. To fit a hinged door see Chapter Five: hinges.

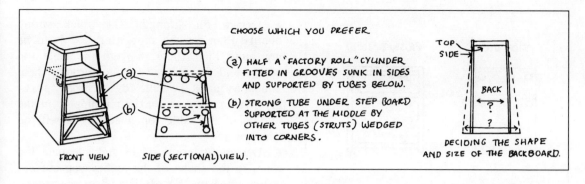

Figure 4.19 *High stool/step – showing alternative systems for making front rails very strong*

## Tall stool or a set of steps

Strength and stability make the design for this article distinctive. All the sides are wide at the bottom. The top is small. All the shelves (steps) have extra-strong support systems at the front. Shelves go right to the back, and so give useful storage space.

This model (Figure 4.19) is not an easy one for a beginner. If you are experienced you may have your own ideas. However, a recommended method follows:

● Cut three strong card templates. Make the top as small as possible to avoid having to make the bottom of the carcass too wide and lower rails too long and therefore weak, but do not make the top too small for it to be a comfortable seat and top step

● The two side boards must be the same as the top step at their top ends. The front edge extends outward a little more than the back one

● Carefully mark on the side templates the lines of the two steps and the supporting rails underneath them. If you can find a hard, wide tube used by paper factories to roll paper on, use it for the front supports instead of rails. Cut it in half, lengthwise. To fit it cut grooves in the side pieces instead of cutting right through

● Plan a supplementary support system for the front of the steps, for example, tubes tied and strapped to the sides. In this support system, the lower tube supports the rail under the bottom step. The tube itself rests on the bottom rail which rests on the floor. The upper tube, strapped to the bottom step, supports the rail under the second step in the same way

● Stand the three templates in position on the floor on their back edges to decide the shape and size of the back board and the boards that will be steps. Also decide the lengths of the rails, and

● Make all the components. When they are

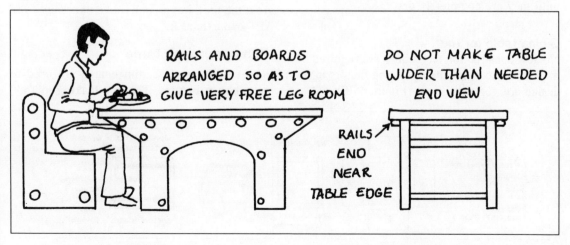

Figure 4.20 *A dining table for four*

51

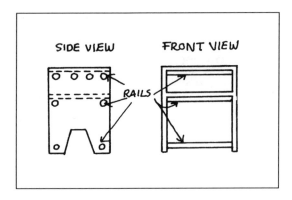

Figure 4.21 *A scholar's desk*

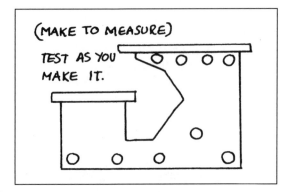

Figure 4.22 *Play desk for pre-school child*

quite dry assemble the stool first as a structure of two side boards joined by rails with a back board held between the side boards. When everything is satisfactory proceed to add the other features, including the top using techniques already described. Do not test the steps until they are completely dry.

## Dining table for four

No new construction techniques are required to make this table, but the following factors in its design are very important (Figure 4.20):

- Design for strength. Use thick strong boards. Plan for the supporting boards to be not more than 10cm in from the table top edges, and for the rails to go through them almost as far as the table edges. Strong, possibly oval, rails give maximum support in the middle of the table top. One day it will be stood on
- Design for comfortable and adequate leg room in the shape of the arches you cut out in the supporting boards, and when positioning the rails to hold the side boards together. Test this with different people sitting up at the table. Legs must be completely free of obstruction. Make the bottom rails extra strong. Fix almost at floor level, out of the way of feet
- **Small is strong**. Remember this when planning the size, and particularly the width, of the table.

### Scholar's desk

This model has one problem (Figure 4.21). The bottom rails, essential for holding the side boards together, are a nuisance as they get in the way of the feet and could get broken. Make them very strong and site them just above the floor. The legged desk (see Chapter Six) is a much better model but needs thin card.

### Small child's seat and desk unit

The model is very simple, but must be made to fit the child (Figure 4.22). Test the unit with the child sitting at it, and getting in and out, as you make it. Before very long the child will out grow the unit, but an individual experienced in APT can extend it.

### Utility approach three

In this utility style carton boards are used to make box structures. The box-making method

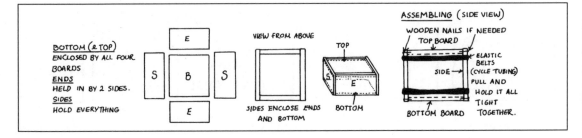

Figure 4.23 a and b *A box – standard APT pattern*

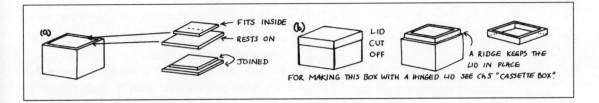

Figure 4.24 *A lid that fits into a box (a) and a lid that fits on to a box (b)*

described here is simple. However, the procedure can be used to make boxes of any size from thin card or carton boards. Usually templates are made, and boards are made slightly larger than the templates. The boards are then cut to the correct size, with sharp straight edges for assembling.

Boxes usually require five or six boards of the same thickness. It saves time if you can laminate boards as large as possible and cut components from them when they are dry.

### Example: simple box pattern
The bottom is the inside size of the box. The ends are the same width as the bottom. The two sides are the length of the bottom, plus the thickness of the two end pieces.

The bottom of the box is enclosed by the two end pieces at its ends and by the side pieces which also enclose the ends (see Figure 4.23a). To assemble the box (see Figure 4.23b):

● Prepare two elastic bands (inner tubing) to encircle the box, and wooden nails if you intend to use them. Wooden nails (sharpened pegs) are not recommended for small boxes, but can be useful for large or awkward structures
● Rub paste into the joining edges and make the inner surfaces of the boards sticky with paste
● Press the parts together with one band around the very bottom and one near the top to help you. Strengthen all the corners with angle pieces with flaps – first inside then outside – strap, then layer over everything with strong paper, and
● Dry with a system of weights, bands, boards, and so on checking they hold the box in its correct shape.

### Lids
Lids can be classified as fitting into a box, on to a box, or over it (Figure 4.24). Lids in each

category can be made in several ways. Four ways of fitting lids have been described in Chapter Two.

Making a lid of thin card to fit over a box was described in Chapter Two: Approach one. Making a lid of thick card to fit over a box can be done in the same way if the card is bent sharply and accurately (see Chapter One:13). Alternatively, this can be constructed from component boards.

### Coffin
Few people enjoy making coffins. However, making good inexpensive coffins out of waste material is a service to others and saves valuable wood from being burned. The coffins made by APT described here comply with the four basic rules of APT. A prototype has been approved by local and national health authorities. Countries have laws on coffins. Make enquiries before embarking on coffin-making.

The plan described here is suitable for coffins of all sizes (Figure 4.25). Its railed structure and boards, laminated to alternate the grain, ensure strength. However, the coffin should not be stood on a wet surface for long, or exposed to a lot of rain. The coffin must be lined with plastic and probably should not be left closed with a body in it for more than a day before it is buried.

To design a coffin use a combination of the second and third utility approaches of furniture design. Rails join the sides and support a bottom board above ground level, but the coffin is built as a six-sided box, strengthened by the rails. The top board that fits level, but inside the side boards, is the part of a two-part lid that fits into and on to the box. The coffin must be made to provide space around and above the body. The part below the bottom board should not be high.

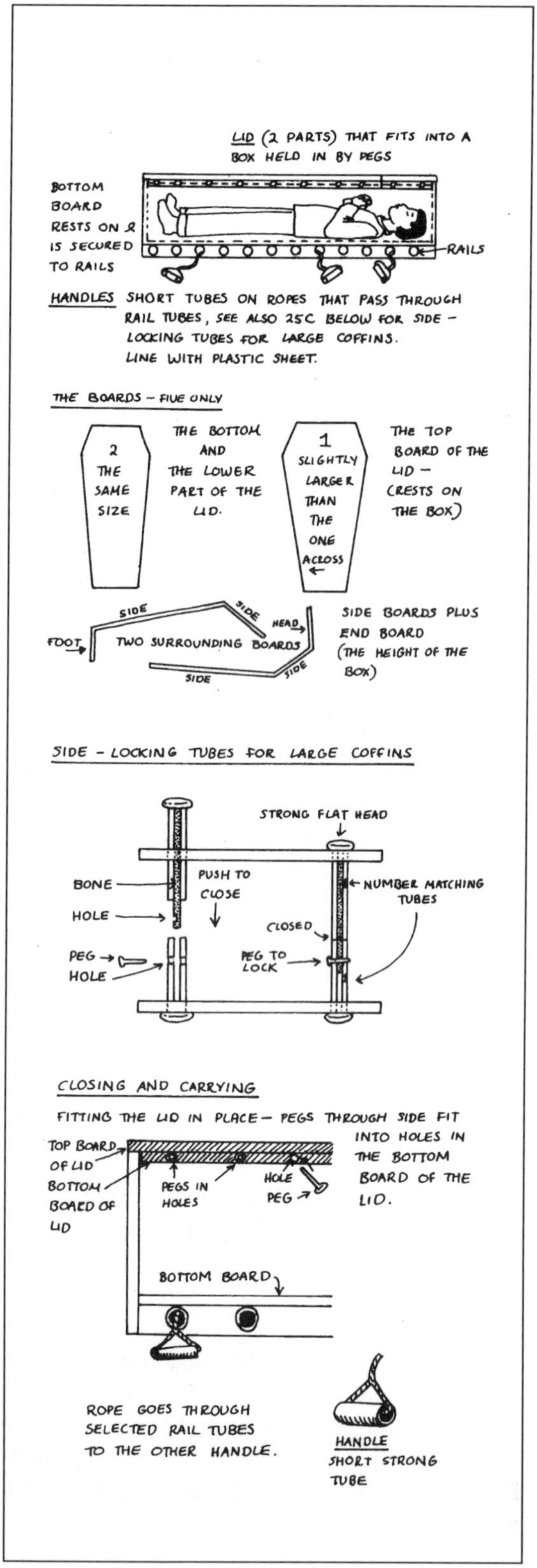

LID (2 PARTS) THAT FITS INTO A BOX HELD IN BY PEGS
BOTTOM BOARD RESTS ON & IS SECURED TO RAILS
RAILS
HANDLES SHORT TUBES ON ROPES THAT PASS THROUGH RAIL TUBES, SEE ALSO 25C BELOW FOR SIDE-LOCKING TUBES FOR LARGE COFFINS.
LINE WITH PLASTIC SHEET.
THE BOARDS – FIVE ONLY
2 THE SAME SIZE
THE BOTTOM AND THE LOWER PART OF THE LID.
1 SLIGHTLY LARGER THAN THE ONE ACROSS
THE TOP BOARD OF THE LID – (RESTS ON THE BOX)
SIDE
SIDE
HEAD
FOOT
TWO SURROUNDING BOARDS
SIDE
SIDE
SIDE BOARDS PLUS END BOARD (THE HEIGHT OF THE BOX)
SIDE – LOCKING TUBES FOR LARGE COFFINS
STRONG FLAT HEAD
BONE
PUSH TO CLOSE
NUMBER MATCHING TUBES
HOLE
CLOSED
PEG
HOLE
PEG TO LOCK
CLOSING AND CARRYING
FITTING THE LID IN PLACE – PEGS THROUGH SIDE FIT INTO HOLES IN THE BOTTOM BOARD OF THE LID.
TOP BOARD OF LID
BOTTOM BOARD OF LID
PEGS IN HOLES
HOLE
PEG
BOTTOM BOARD
ROPE GOES THROUGH SELECTED RAIL TUBES TO THE OTHER HANDLE.
HANDLE SHORT STRONG TUBE


Figure 4.25 a, b, c and d *A coffin*

The coffin incorporates the following:

- Five boards, and between four to eight rails depending on the coffin size
- Side and end boards should be laminated as two long pieces, and deeply and accurately scored to wrap closely around the corners of the bottom and top boards
- Pegs, for example, bamboo twigs with slightly large heads, which fit through neat holes prepared in the sides and ends and into holes in the lower part of the lid
- Four or six handles which are strong short tubes joined, through selected tubes at the bottom of the coffin, by a loop of rope. The knot is worked into the tube, out of sight, and
- Side-locking tubes, which are recommended for large coffins in order to hold their long sides rigid when the body is in place and ensure the lid pegs hold the lid all along. There could be three or four side-locking tubes in the middle area.

The coffin is made by standard box procedures, but the rails must be fitted during the process. To build the coffin:

- Prepare the boards at least three strong stretchy belts, a device for supporting the lid, and some wooden nails
- Do a mock assembly without the rails. The sides must wrap very closely all along and around each corner. Score widely and deeply cutting through layers if necessary to bend the boards sharply (see Chapter One:13). Use a few nails to hold everything together. Plan and mark where the rails must be
- Disassemble and cut the holes. Then, assemble with paste
- Wrap the top board in plastic. Paste all the joining parts and assemble starting with the rails. Assemble the box, pulling everything together with tight elastic belts and securing the joins with nails and angle pieces. The top board can be removed for a while (but should be replaced for the start of the drying stage, held in place by temporary rails. Tie the bottom board to the rails and dry with weighted boards on the bottom. Dry for a time, remove the top board. Laminate the top board of the box to the top board of the lid. Tie the two boards together in a few places. First, dry pressed flat and then in place on the coffin and pressed but not too heavily

- When it is convenient fit a carton card lining. If possible, use one whole piece carefully cut to fit. Otherwise, use two or three pieces (see armchair earlier in this chapter). Its top edges should just reach the bottom of the lid when in place
- Strengthen and make the lid fit perfectly
- If necessary, fit three side-locking tubes just below the lid and sited in the middle section of the box (see Figure 4.25c). Calculate tube lengths. Open flaps carefully at each end and build up to make strong, flat heads. Cut each tube approximately in half. Mark matching halves. Fit a bone into one half with 6 to 8cm projecting to fit into the matching half tube. Make suitable pegs and pierce tidy holes for them to lock the two halves together
- Prepare uniform-sized round pegs. Segments of bamboo or other twigs wider at one end are excellent. Plot the holes for holding the lid in place and pierce them carefully to hold the pegs firmly
- Make and fit the handles (see Figure 4.25d)
- Decorate with attractive grained earth colour (see Chapter Eleven). If possible, varnish the inside and outside, and
- Fit a plastic sheet with no holes in it as a lining. If there is no better method, sew it near the top edge through the sides with long stitches on the inside and almost invisible ones outside.

## In the context of rehabilitation

For rehabilitation workers, Chapter Four is one of the most useful in this manual. Corrugated card from cartons is often available in rehabilitation situations. The material is easy to work and the finished products are solid and friendly in texture to children and disabled people.

Several models previously outlined in this chapter are already popular in rehabilitation situations, either as described or with minor modifications. A number of other models which have proved their use in rehabilitation centres are described in this supplement. They are arranged under the same main headings that have been used in the chapter. In some cases instructions are brief, but where special procedures or devices are recommended detailed information is given. Rehabilitation workers should not attempt to make these models before they have made, or closely studied, the relevant section in the chapter and if possible made one of the model described there.

Mobility is a priority in rehabilitation work. Chapter Seven deals with wheeled models. Where wheels are an integral part of a model it will be dealt with in Chapter Seven, even if the item is made by the utility style of APT.

## Boards in the rehabilitation context: accessories fitted to boards

Boards (see Chapter One:25) in rehabilitation situations (standing, prone, side-lying, and so on) usually have accessories either as permanent fixtures, or as removable fittings.

### Removable fittings

Make removable fittings with large flat bases whenever possible. The simple method is to fix pegs firmly in the accessory which, in turn fit into holes in the main board. However, carton boards are soft and such fittings may work loose. Accessories can be made with tenons that fit into mortises, but the same problem may arise.

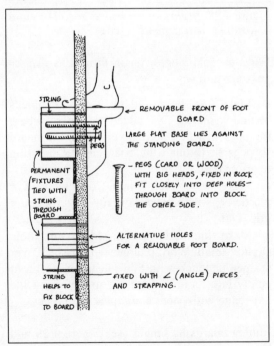

Figure 4.26 *Fixing and fitting accessories (that is, removable or permanent), blocks to boards, for example a foot board or standing frame*

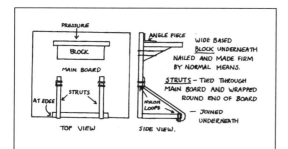

Figure 4.27 *Boards fitted at right angle to main board*

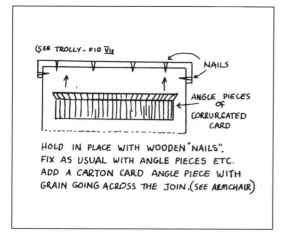

Figure 4.28 *Right-angled board at end of main board and bent around its corners*

Ways to make peg or tenon fittings as firm as possible follow:

● Make the boards thick, or add blocks behind them to give added thickness where the pegs will fit. Alternatively, plan the board so pegs fit through the board into supporting tubes or bars
● Make the pegs full length. Cover wooden or plastic pegs with paper layering to get a better grip, and
● Make the fitting tight. Make the hole slightly small. Work it larger with paste. Cover the peg or tenon with thin plastic and force it gently into its hole. Leave it to dry. Bind the hole edge with paper and repeat the process.

Joining boards by hinges (see Figure 4.29 and Figure 5.5) is quite straightforward. The larger the board and its hinges, the simpler the job. Hinge rods can easily be removed and replaced so the fitting is either removable or permanent.

## Permanent fittings

The following suggestions apply particularly to joining accessories to boards as permanent fittings (see Figure 4.26 and refer to Chapter One: 19):

● All blocks should be held in place with wooden nails or nylon loops, then fix firmly with angle pieces and layering
● Boards fitted at right angles to the main board may need a lot of support according to the strain they will bear, where the pressure will come from, how high they are, where they are sited on the board, and so on
● Boards can be given extra support if they are fitted to the main board, but not at the edge. To make boards firm and strong support them at each end by tube struts. The tubes should be flattened at one end and tied to the main board, and the opposite end wrapped over top edge of the accessory board and tied through the back of it (see Figure 4.27)
● For low boards, crushed tube angle pieces or low blocks should give adequate support. For higher boards, larger higher blocks can give great support underneath. However, angle pieces of carton card, and probably end struts as well, are needed to make the fitting really rigid (see Figure 4.27)
● Boards fitted at right angles to the edge of the main board need a great deal of support. Hold them firmly in place with wooden nails or strong nylon loops.

Where possible, wrap the accessory board around the corners of the main board and secure it there with strong nails (see Figure 4.28)

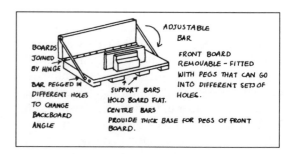

Figure 4.29 *A side-lying board*

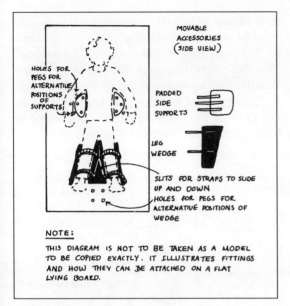

Figure 4.30 *A flat-lying board*

As well as normal angle pieces, cut an angle piece of carton card with grain that runs across the join. Score and bend it sharply. Force it tight into the angle and hold it in position with nylon loops through it and through each board, and

• Alternatively, hinges and struts can be used (see Figure 4.29).

The following models incorporate some of the technology mentioned above.

### Side-lying board

A side-lying board's components, and their requirements are as follows (see Figure 4.29):

• Main board – suitable size for the child's body and legs, lying on his or her side against front board. Support bars underneath sited to provide thickness for pegs of front board. Two to three sets of holes for front board pegs

• Front board – height and length suitable to hold a child's middle. Supported by a high block. Pegs are fixed in block to match holes in main board, and

• Back board – attached by hinge. Held in the correct position for keeping a child's body close to a front board, by adjusting bars that are pegged to board edges.

### Prone-lying board (front or back) for posture control

Make this board large enough to accommodate a child in required prone position. Site support bars to provide thickness for holding pegs. Wedged between legs is a strongly fixed block, with slits for holding two straps on each side. The side supports are moveable with two sets of holes. They are suitably shaped fairly high blocks padded on the sides that hold the child's body.

### Standing boards

Two types are described here. Type A is a straightforward board with accessories that latches onto a table edge. Type B (originated by Mrs Archie Hinchcliffe in Lusaka) is an independent unit that stands alone, complete with play tray (see Figure 4.31).

For type A, make the board the right height to fit at the correct angle on to the table which will support it. Mark where the foot board must be to give the child free arm movement on the table. Also, make the board narrower at the top for free arm movement and broad at the base for stability.

In type A:

• The table-gripping groove is made by fixing two bars with a space between them across the board at the top

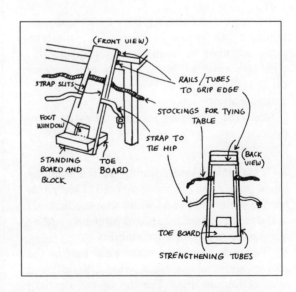

Figure 4.31 *Prone board/standing board*

• The foot-board window is square, at least the width of three little feet. Fix a long toe support board across the back of the board at foot window level. This reinforces the board, weakened by the window hole and slits, and provides extra thickness for pegs

• The top strap ends secure the board to the table. Lower straps hold the child to the board. Slits allow straps to slide into the correct position. Make long narrow cuts with a knife. Widen by pasting and working a thicker tool covered in plastic up and down. Bind the edges. Dry with plastic-covered card in the slits, and

• A removable foot board is shown in Figure 4.31 to allow the standing board to be used as a prone board if desire. Otherwise fit the board as a permanent fixture.

Type B, a posture-control standing board unit, is a pair of steps with a tray fitted across the top. The standing board proper is made to measure to fit the child. It is fitted with a foot and toe board at the bottom of a foot board window. Two side supports, fitted with pegs and belts, control the child's standing posture.

To build type B, take the measurements listed below from the child. Incorporate them in the standing board's templates. Check the board with the child at several points during its construction (letters in brackets refer to Figure 4.32).

To make the standing board's components laminate two very large boards with the templates arranged on them as the top layer. This will save time as many boards of the same thickness are needed. When dry, cut out the components.

Make the templates for the following components and laminate them as previously described:

• Two main boards, which are the standing board proper and the support board. The boards are the same height and width (not too narrow) at the top. The standing board proper should be quite wide at the base for stability

• Two side boards to make each half of the pair of steps, about 10cm wide ( therefore a total of four boards). The top of the standing board's side boards must be widened to 20cm

(see Figure 4.32). The bottom of the boards must be cut so they stand at the angle required

• Six cross boards (steps) of required lengths. The top cross board of the standing board should be as wide as the top of its side boards

• The tray board, which is at least as wide as the base of the standing board proper and a little deeper than the child's reach

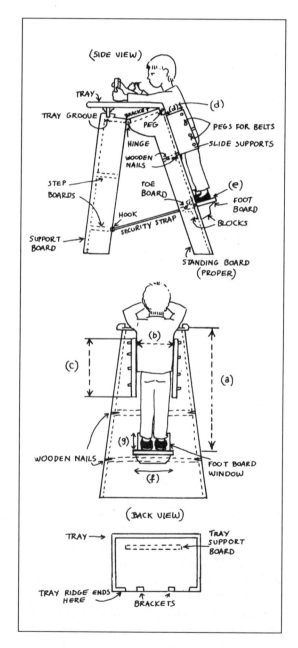

Figure 4.32 *A posture-control standing board*

58

| Child's measurements | Measurements on the standing board |
|---|---|
| From the child's heel to comfortable level for the tray | Distance from the top of the standing board to the foot board (a) |
| Widest part of the thorax | Distance between the side supports (b) |
| Inside the armpit to beyond the hip | The length of the side supports (c) |
| Front to back of thorax, minus approximately 3cm | Height of side supports |
| Length of foot, plus approximately 4cm | Length of foot board (e) |
| Width of two feet, plus approximately 4cm | Width of foot board (f) |
| From heel to below knee | Height of foot board window (g) |

*Type B standing board's measurements (letters in brackets refer to Figure 4.32)*

• Side supports and foot board – use the measures you made to construct the templates
• Foot board and foot board window — mark on the standing board template where these will be fitted, and
• Blocks, brackets, tray support, and so on – cut when exact sizes are known.

Next, assemble the two main components (the steps). To do this, fix the parts together initially by wooden nails. Hold each part of the steps together by belts of cycle-tube elastic or nylon stocking. When all is correct, join firmly and strengthen with angle pieces, and strong layering. Note that the large boards are fitted between the edges of the side boards. The middle step of the standing board should be sited level with the foot board window to serve as the toe board. Fitting a large hinge is straightforward (Chapter Five). The tubes project beyond the board ends.

To complete the standing board carry out the following tasks:

• Fix the accessories – the side supports must be firm. Struts or high blocks can be used on the outside and crushed card tubes on the inside
• Make and fit the tray (see Chapter Four: Board tray) – the raised edge should stop near the corners on the side of the tray in front of the child. Calculate the height of the tray support and fit it
• Brackets (short lengths of narrow tube) are tied and strapped under the tray edge nearest the child. Long pegs are fitted through the tubes into the standing board to attach the tray where it is needed
• The tray groove is made by attaching fairly tall bars to the top of the support board. If extra firmness is required, put a peg through the groove boards and the tray support
• Security strap – a strong string, or some other device could be used to ensure the steps, once set, do not open wider, and
• Belt(s) over the child's back – ideally, a wide sewn belt of cloth permanently tied to one set of pegs, with four strings at the other end to tie as required to hold the child in the right posture. Alternatively, use straps.

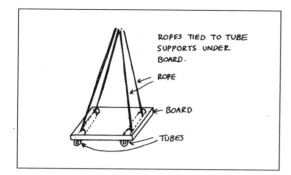

Figure 4.33 *A platform swing*

## Rehabilitation models (built by the three utility approaches)

### Utility approach one

Utility approach one is used to construct crossed board bases for stools, tables, and so on. The flexibility of the approach, and all necessary techniques have been described in the chapter. Rehabilitation workers will be able to develop the technique further to serve special needs. However, remember that large flat board tops must be given adequate support, and the bases of large articles tend to be very heavy. Bases can be lightened by cutting away parts, but often the item can be made also by utility approach two and will then be much lighter.

### Platform swing

The swing board must have supporting tubes across its weaker direction, underneath. Ropes are tied through the board and over the tube supports (Figure 4.33). Rails can be fixed around its upper circumference (see round rocker for method of fixing rails to supporting tubes).

### Utility approach two

In utility approach two, pairs of boards are joined by tubes supporting a top. It is essential that the processes and technology for making the small railed child's chair and the armchair are mastered. Then a rehabilitation worker will be able to create new models to meet special needs. Two prototypes of special rehabilitation chairs are described in this section, which have proved their use and can be modified to cater for specific needs.

### Invertible two-level chair

The invertible two-level chair is an enclosed chair, that is, the sides are rectangular boards and the user sits in the chair (Figure 4.34).

First, make the boards and rails. Plan where to site the seat rails to get the seat boards at the two different levels you require. Cut holes. Fit the seat rails and tie the boards on temporarily each side of the rails. Test, then mark holes for the back rails. Disassemble, cut the back rail holes and reassemble with paste. Tie on the back boards. Keep checking the seat in its two positions. Layer all over with card strips and pieces to enclose all the rail and board structure and give the inside of the chair a comfortable rounded surface, with a moulded seat if required.

### Chair for a severely disabled child

Again, it is essential to have made the small railed chair and the armchair described earlier in this chapter before attempting to construct this prototype.

This chair is an upright armchair made to fit a specific child.

Other features that distinguish it from the standard armchair are: its profile (side boards widen at the bottom for stability); a front board and foot board are added; the back board may

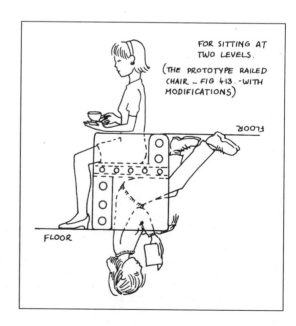

Figure 4.34 *An invertible chair*

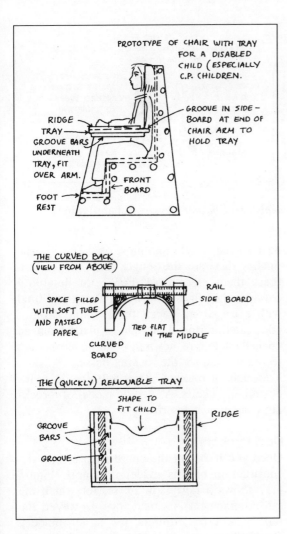

PROTOTYPE OF CHAIR WITH TRAY FOR A DISABLED CHILD (ESPECIALLY C.P. CHILDREN.

RIDGE
TRAY
GROOVE BARS UNDERNEATH TRAY, FIT OVER ARM.

GROOVE IN SIDE-BOARD AT END OF CHAIR ARM TO HOLD TRAY

FOOT REST

FRONT BOARD

THE CURVED BACK
(VIEW FROM ABOVE)

SPACE FILLED WITH SOFT TUBE AND PASTED PAPER

CURVED BOARD

TIED FLAT IN THE MIDDLE

RAIL
SIDE BOARD

THE (QUICKLY) REMOVABLE TRAY

SHAPE TO FIT CHILD

GROOVE BARS

GROOVE

RIDGE

Figure 4.35 *The chair – prototype of chair with tray for disabled child (especially C.P. children)*

be curved; the seat can be moulded to suit the child; an easily removable tray slides into position on the side boards; and there are no armrests.

Constructing this chair (see Figure 4.35) involves no new technology except for the (optional) curved back board. Calculate the size and shape of the back board and laminate it with six or more layers of thin card, grain lengthwise, on a curved surface such as an oil drum. When it is dry, but not stiff, make two lines of holes about 10cm apart down the middle of the board so the middle part of the board can be tied flat to the back rails. Tie it. Mould

the board with pasty hands so it lies against the side boards. When you are satisfied, strap the board in position with card pieces. Build up and fill the spaces behind using wide thin crushed tubes and pasted paper padding. Watch carefully. Press as needed as it dries.

The chair's tray must be easily removable in case of choking. It is a wide board that extends over the side boards (arms) and is shaped on the inside to accommodate the child's body.

The tray has two groove fittings on each side so it slides into position. Grooves made by pairs of high bars under the tray fit closely over the arms and a groove, say 3cm deep, is cut in the side board at the end of the arm so the front edge of the tray fits into it. For additional stability large-headed, and easily removable, pegs can be fitted through the groove bar and the side board on one or both sides of the tray. Alternatively, for quick removability of the tray, pegs can be fitted through the tray into the arm (Figure 4.36).

### Pushchair with insertable wheels

Adapt the prototype of the chair for a severely disabled child to make a pushchair with insertable wheels. Do this by adding the following features:

● Legs – chair legs with reinforced feet are very desirable. They facilitate tipping the chair, especially if the chair is large. Feet also give the chair extra stability and reduce wear on the base. Where possible, the legs are fitted to lodge against projecting tube ends. The front legs are fitted on the inside in the angle between the front board and the side board and through the foot board. Legs take a lot of strain, so tie and nail them in position and attach strongly with crushed tubes, strapping, and so on

● Shoes – these could be segments of strong polystyrene piping, radiator hose, and the like (see Chapter Five: *In the context of rehabilitation* – crutches)

● Handles – these take a lot of strain. If possible fit them so that back rails and the back board help to hold them. Fix a joining rail between handles to help hold them rigid

● Accessories for the tray board – which can be hand grips in the form of strong wide pegs

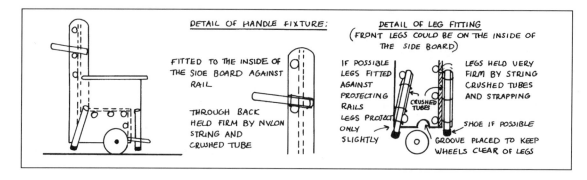

Figure 4.36 *Wheeled push-chair (for insertable wheels see Chapter Seven:* Rehabilitation)

fixed permanently in the tray, or book-holders or mouth-writing boards, that is, hinged boards fitted very firmly when they are needed (see Chapter Five: A music stand), and

• Wheel assembly and groove – this needs to be planned very carefully near the front of the pushchair (for stability), but where there is no obstruction from other rails or fittings. For instructions on how to make and fit independent wheel assemblies see Chapter Seven: *In the context of rehabilitation.*

## Rocking apparatus

The apparatus is designed to minimize risks of accidents to users and people nearby. Rocking boards are the key components.

The curve (see Figure 4.37) is a gentle curve that flattens out to prevent accidental over-rocking. Trial and error is necessary to get a model right.

The rocking boards must be strong as they bear all the weight and most of the wear. The thicker they are the longer they should last. Press them extra hard. For extra durability oversew the edges with nylon string and bind with extra strong paper, for example, from a corrugated carton. Long shoes made from an opened cycle tyre, sewn through the rocker are recommended for the rocking horse.

Models of rocking chairs vary, as do styles of ordinary chairs. A specific model of a rocking chair is not described.

## Rocking horse

Once you have got the board shapes right the construction of this model is simple. Figure 4.37 shows a fairly low horse, for which the rail arrangement is satisfactory. However, the rails would be different for larger models. Correct balance is essential. The seat is in the horse, but additional back support should be arranged. The seat is slightly nearer the back

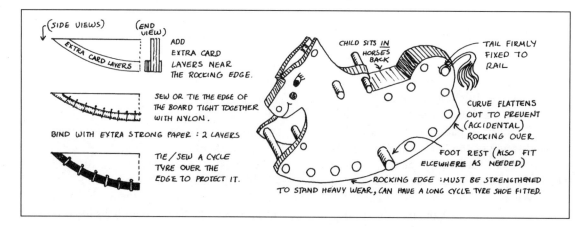

Figure 4.37 *Rocker boards, which take a lot of wear and need strengthening, and a rocking horse*

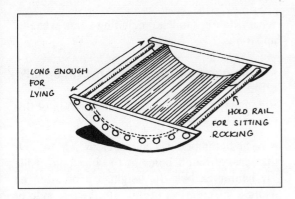

LONG ENOUGH FOR LYING

HOLD RAIL FOR SITTING ROCKING

Figure 4.38 *Cradle and/or sitting rocker (balancer)*

than the front but should allow for the child to move a little to adjust his or her balance. Footrests and hand-grip tube should be very strong and reinforced with collars. Site them after checking with the child.

When assembling the horse the boards should almost meet at the horse's ears, and widen out to the desired distance between the rocking boards at the bottom. The top and top end parts are closed by thin boards resting on the tubes and level with the sides. The head can be attractively moulded in paper.

The horse is mobile and dangerous. Users may need supervision.

## Balancing rockers: a cradle/balancer

This is a dual purpose item for use in a reha-bilitation centre. The balancer must be quite long if it is to accommodate a sleeping child,

if not, it can be shorter (see Figure 4.38). The rails serve several purposes:

● They hold the side boards together and strengthen them. Therefore, the rails should be as near to the rocker edge as possible where most of the strain is

● They form a base for the bed, therefore, the middle rails should be set level, and

● The top rails are for holding and are not attached to any board down their length. There-fore, they must be extra strong. The bed is a curved board of thin card (say four layers). It can be made and fitted in several ways. If it is carefully watched and pressed the board can be laminated, moulded to the right curve, tied at several points to the rails, and pressed and dried in position. Sandbags and masses of plastic in larger plastic bags are useful in press-ing and drying.

A toy bar can be fitted as an accessory (see Figure 4.40).

## Round rocker

The idea is that the child sits in the middle, holds the hand bars and rocks in various direc-tions. The rocker can also be spun. The model is made by Utility approach one, but the base boards are bent double and not crossed.

Points to note in the construction of the round rocker follow:

● The circle – be sure it is large enough

● The rocking boards – make them slightly

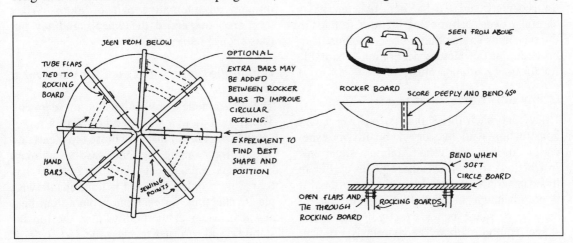

SEEN FROM BELOW

TUBE FLAPS TIED TO ROCKING BOARD

OPTIONAL

EXTRA BARS MAY BE ADDED BETWEEN ROCKER BARS TO IMPROVE CIRCULAR ROCKING.

EXPERIMENT TO FIND BEST SHAPE AND POSITION

HAND BARS

SEWING POINTS

SEEN FROM ABOVE

ROCKER BOARD

SCORE DEEPLY AND BEND 45°

BEND WHEN SOFT

CIRCLE BOARD

OPEN FLAPS AND TIE THROUGH ROCKING BOARD

ROCKING BOARDS

Figure 4.39 *Round rocker*

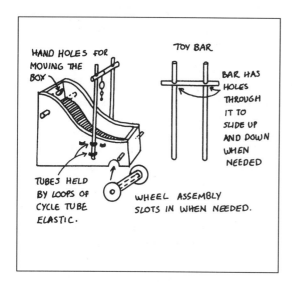

Figure 4.40 *Mobile hammock for hydrocephalic child*

longer than the diameter of the circle. They can, if desired, be cut back to the circle edge later. Cut and score the boards deeply at the centre. Paste the groove. Slowly force the two halves around to the required angle. Tie the boards as follows. At their centres tie opposite pairs together, very securely. Then, tie each board to the circle boards in its correct position, first at its end, then at one or two points near the middle. Fix very firmly with suitable angle piece technology

● The hand bars – these are very strong tubes, bent when still soft near each end, leaving enough to go through the board and be tied to the rocking board. To fix them plan the holes carefully over each rocking board. Cut flaps in the tube ends so that they fit over the boards to be tied. Cut-out picture decoration is suitable for this piece of apparatus.

## Utility approach three

Utility approach three, that is, making a box construction with five or six boards, is especially useful in rehabilitation situations. Instructions to approach three given earlier in this chapter are applicable to any size of box. It is an advantage in rehabilitation situations to be able to make boxes exactly the size and shape required. Hinges are extremely efficient whatever their size, if properly made. Box structures are the main elements in numerous rehabilitation models, including some wheeled apparatus.

## Mobile hammock box for a hydrocephalic child

Elements in the design and construction of this hammock follow:

● The hammock is a belt of cloth held by rods that pass through holes in the box and inside the hammock belt. Its height can be adjusted using a different set of holes in the box side or by a hem sewn into the belt

● The box (say five carton-card layers) is made on the normal pattern and cut away to allow the child to see out and be seen and for ventilation

● The rods are strong card tubes, preferably with a stick bone still inside

● The wheel assembly is the same as for the pushchair (see Figure 4.36)

● Finger-holds for moving the box are slits of a convenient shape and size cut in the back board of the box

● The toy bar must be made of strongly rolled tubes, the top tube bigger inside and out than the others to allow the uprights to be fitted through holes in it without weakening it. Parts with holes must be very strongly bound and layered over

● The bar is adjustable in three ways. Uprights can be pulled higher if desired. The bar itself can be moved up or down. The uprights can be set at an angle if threaded through an alternative pair of loops. When they are not needed the wheels and toy bar rods should be removed.

## Commode and a toilet seat for use over a hole

These two models are similar but not identical. The commode is a six-sided box with a removable bucket or tin inside, a loose top (seat) and a lid fitting over it. The toilet seat has an open bottom and a fixed seat. The toilet seat also has four waterproofed feet and is lined inside with plastic sheeting, for example, from a flour bag, and it is wider at the bottom than the top for stability and in order to keep the feet wide of the hole. A toilet seat can also be made to fit on to a pedestal toilet.

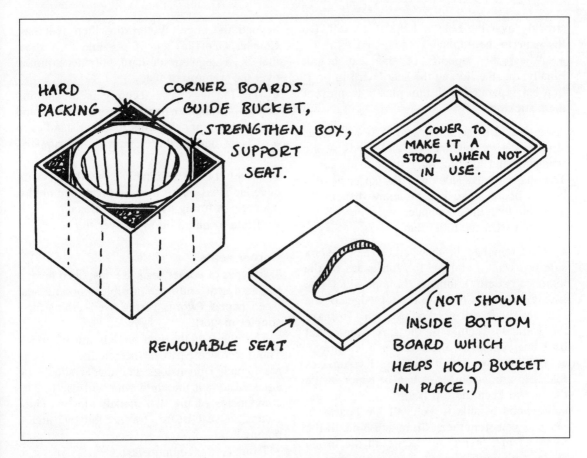

Figure 4.41 *An indoor bucket toilet (a five-sided box with removable top)*

To construct the commode:

• Build as a closed box, with the bucket in place inside and the top resting lightly on it, strapped temporarily in place but not joined properly to the sides

• Remove the top. Take four long narrow boards, press and fit them across the four vertical joining angles inside the box. These are to support the top (seat) and to guide the bucket into its correct position. Fill the space down the joining angles with lightly pasted paper, lightly pressed in, or with fat crushed tubes that fill the space

• Cut another bottom board. Cut a circle out of it to hold the bucket in position and laminate it to the original bottom

• Laminate additional layers of card to strengthen the top. Cut out the seat hole, the right shape and not too big. Tidy and bind

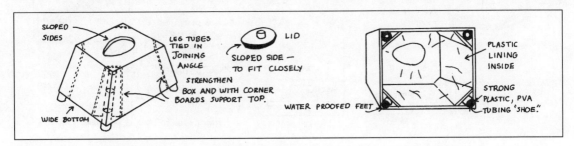

Figure 4.42 *A toilet seat for use over a hole (a wide-bottomed five-sided box, the seat part of the box)*

strongly over the hole and the seat itself. Do the same to the lid, and

• Adjust the supports of the seat board. Finally, dry the lid and the seat board in position but separated with thin plastic to prevent them sticking.

As a structure the toilet seat is not quite as strong as a rectangular box and needs strong strapping and binding over the outside joins. The shape of the sides and the absence of a bottom board make it a bit more difficult to assemble than the commode.

To construct the toilet seat:

• Cut a template the shape and size of the box side you want. Laminate the four sides on the template pattern. Laminate the top, which is a square with sides equal to the top edges of the side boards. It will need adjustment. To make the vertical structure of the box square, cut back one edge of two side pieces as required

• Build the box with a fixed top. Two devices that help are an object or bag of paper inside the box to keep the top from slipping in, and some wooden nails to hold all the boards in place as you strap them. Strap and bind all the joins outside. Invert and secure all the inside angles with angle pieces

• Prepare four strong tubes for legs. They should touch, that is support, the top at each inside corner, and project equally at the bottom

beyond the edge. Waterproof their feet (see Chapter One:17a) and if possible fit a shoe, that is, a segment of hard polythene piping over the waterproof feet

• Tie the legs very securely in the joining angles. Strengthen with crushed tubes and strong strapping, checking that feet stand even

• Check and further reinforce the supports under the seat

• Carefully cut a suitably shaped hole with bevelled sides out of the seat board and bind it strongly. A fitting oval lid is optional

• Build a square lid to fit over the box.

## Corner seats

Two types of corner seats are described here: a standard seat and a collapsible, portable seat (see Chapter Two: Layering over cartons for a simpler model).

The plans of the two models are identical. The difference between them is the way parts are joined. Dimensions and shapes should be adjusted to suit the child who will use it. The components of the two models are two sideboards, a seat board, tray, stabilizer, and a pommel.

To make the components:

• Make an oversize template for the seat, using thick card. Set it up in a corner at the right height for the child, for example on

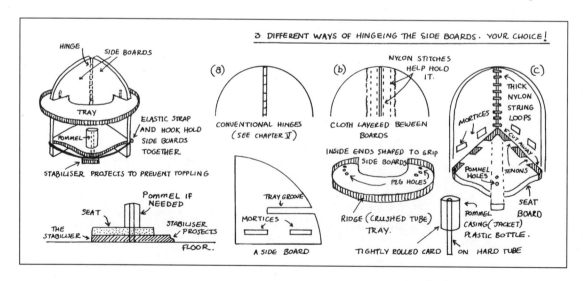

Figure 4.43 *A collapsible and portable corner seat with tray. Three different ways of hinging the side boards are shown*

bricks. With the child in place and allowing for padding, mark and cut the front edge. For the collapsible model, add an extra 3cm to each side for the tenons

● Make the side template by pushing a piece of card with one edge on the floor into the corner between the wall and the seat template. Mark on it the seat level, the tray groove level and the front curve, making it a suitable height for the child
● Make the tray board slightly over-sized, curved like the seat board
● Make the seat support/stabilizer board, which could be 5cm wide, the length of the seat board and as high as the underside of the seat is from the floor
● Laminate the boards with the templates on top, the side and seat boards about 15mm thick.

To build the standard seat, arrange the sides and seat board correctly. Hold and fix them with an elastic belt and wooden nails to start with, then join strongly with angle pieces and layering. Fix the stabilizer under the seat with enough of it projecting to preclude any risk of the seat tipping forward.

To fit the tray for both models, cut the grooves so they grip the tray. Gauge their depth so when pressed the tray touches the child's tummy. Fashion the ends of the tray by cutting and moulding on to them if necessary so they almost hook around the sides. Pierce holes so pegs can be inserted through the tray each side of the side boards to hold everything firm.

Refer to Figure 4.43 for information on how to make the pommel (optional). In the collapsible portable seat version, the two sideboards are hinged to open and close like a book. Three ways to do this are:

● Hinging with tubes (see Chapter Five, and standing board previously described)
● Joining with thick nylon string (stocking) – make the lines for the holes about 1cm in from the edges. Decide on the method of sewing or tying to use. The hinging must be even and tight, and
● Fit a cloth hinge – use a piece of strong thin cloth about 6cm wide. Paste it. When it has stretched, cut it equal to the length of the sides to be joined. Neatly separate two layers of each board to a depth of about 3cm. Paste between the opened layers of one board, insert the cloth, laying it flat. When you are satisfied close the board, press it and sew wide stitches of nylon string through the board and the cloth to prevent the cloth from moving. Do the same with the other board ensuring the boards are held together by the cloth as closely as possible. Press and dry thoroughly before straining the hinge.

In this collapsible model, the seat board is fitted to the sides by tenons that fit into mortises cut in the sides. Work cautiously to get a close fit all around. Fit one side first and when satisfied do the other. The inner tenons may have to be cut away on one side to achieve a close fit.

Mistakes can be rectified by building up parts cut away in error. Finally, bind tidily all the cut edges including the tenons and the holes. Cover the tenons with thin plastic pieces and gently force the seat and sides together for drying.

A stabilizer is normally fixed permanently to the seat board.

A belt to hold the sides together is needed (the tray does this but is not always in place). To make the belt, take a long strip of cycle or car inner-tube elastic. At one end attach a wire hook and make a hole low down in one of the side boards for it. Make a hole low down through the opposite side board and thread the elastic through it. With the hook in place stretch the elastic, tie it as needed to hold the sides firmly. Cut a groove in the front of the stabilizer board where the elastic can be held in place. Fit a belt to hold the tray in if desired.

# Chapter Five: Articles made from thin card boards and tubes

Thin card boards, tubes, or boards and tubes used together, can make a variety of articles. Some articles which have been made successfully are described here. Furniture is dealt with in the next chapter.

## Examples

### Child's cot

The cot is a low bed enclosed by four collapsible sides (see Figure 5.1a). The bed is similar to the junior bed described in Chapter Four, but its top projects beyond the board carcass so it just reaches the cot sides at the level of the bottom rail.

The four sides of the cot are held together by strong bands of cycle tubing placed over the tops and bottoms of each pair of corner posts. There is also a bone-in-a-hole fitting at each corner to stop the posts from slipping about.

The technology for the cot is extremely simple, is rolling tubes (see Chapter One:17) and joining tube to tube at right angles (see Chapter One:19d). However, the components are numerous and their dimensions quite important. Thus, an approximate list of components and specifications follows:

Components for the cot's enclosure are:

- Eight end-posts (say 70cm long)
- Eight horizontal (top and bottom) rails, that

is, four long (say 135mm) and four short (say 75cm), and
- Twenty-six vertical tubes, thinner but still very strong (say 65cm), that is, eight for each long side and five for each short one.

**Note**: post and horizontal rails must be thick and strong.

Components for the cot's bed are:

- Two side boards, the length to fit inside the cot frame, height from floor to top of bottom rail of frame, and thickness approximately five carton cards
- Top board (approximately 30 x 70cm), say four carton cards with two or three thin cards each side, and
- Eight strong rails (65cm long).

**Note**: all measurements given here are greater than necessary to allow a few centimetres to be cut off when tidying ends, edges, and so on.

Although no complicated technology is required, accurate APT-type measurement and careful workmanship are essential so right angles are true, spaces which are meant to be equal are equal, and parts fit properly together. This is achieved not by rulers marked in centimetres but by improvized measures and gauges, and above all, a critical eye. It is a big job.

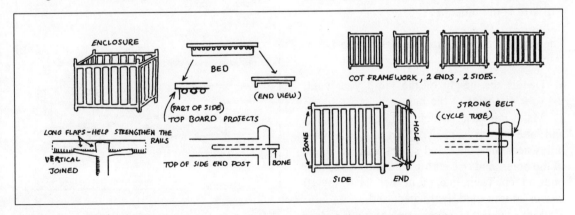

Figure 5.1a *A child's cot*

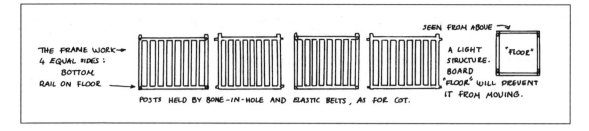

The frame work→ 4 equal sides: bottom rail on floor

Posts held by bone-in-hole and elastic belts, as for cot.

Seen from above →
A light structure. Board "floor" will prevent it from moving.
"Floor"

Figure 5.1b *A play pen*

## Play pen

The technology used to make this play pen (see Figure 5.1b) is the same as for the cot sides. The differences in design between the cot and play pen are shown in the diagrams. In the play pen there is no bed base, so the sides for the child are higher. The pen is square.

The bottom rests on the floor to stop toys slipping out underneath the rail. A base is not essential, but the pen is light and unless it is anchored to something like a table leg, an enterprising child will discover it can be moved on a smooth floor. A flat board base or a mat that fits inside the pen reduces the risk of it becoming mobile.

## Standard lampstand

Study Figure 5.2a. Note these features:

● A large thick and weighted base with feet underneath
● A pillar that fits through the base
● Flex that goes up through the pillar to a bulb holder fixed into its top, and
● A lampshade (electrical items and shade will cost some money).

The suggested procedure for making the lampstand is to:

● Decide the height of the lamp you want, then the diameter of the base
● Make the base, which is three thin cards and one carton card, six carton cards with holes near the edges and stones and sandbags in the holes, and one carton card plus three thin ones on top. Then, make four feet, each, say 10 circles of thin card, laminated, and
● Make the pillar strong, straight, with a clear hole right through it. Thread a string through

the pillar for pulling the flex through later and attach the ends so they do not come out
● To fit the pillar (see Chapter One:19bii, and Chapter Four: Small chair for a child) cut the

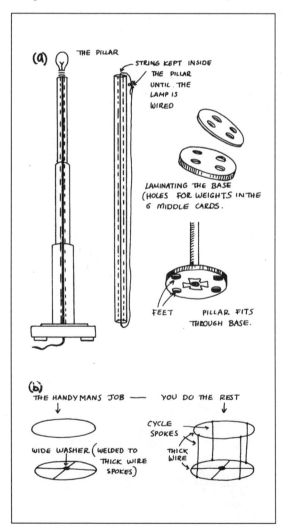

(a) The pillar
String kept inside the pillar until the lamp is wired
Laminating the base (holes for weights in the 6 middle cards.
Feet   Pillar fits through base.

(b) The handymans job — you do the rest
Wide washer (welded to thick wire spokes)
Cycle spokes
Thick wire

Figure 5.2 *A Lampstand (a) and home-made shade frame (b)*

hole for the pillar, and make it fit the pillar. Strap and bind the four feet to hold the base one hundred per cent level. Join pillar through the base, strengthen the join with some collars. Dry the pillar, making sure it is totally perpendicular from all angles, and

● Fit the lamp holder (bulb holder). The holder will carry the bulb and a heavy shade. It must be straight and immovable. One way to do this is to make a strong bone that fits tightly into the pillar and hold the bulb holder. Use the string to pull the flex up through the pillar and bone. Join the holder strongly to the bone, attach the wires and fix the bone with its holder firmly into the pillar. Test the holder is level with a shade.

**Note**: if you are inexperienced with electricity get technical help.

Lamp shades are outside the field of APT. However, if you want to make one, here is a suggestion. Get a handyman to weld two circles of strong wire and place a large washer exactly in the middle of one circle. The washer will fit on the lamp holder. Next, ask him or her to join the washer to the circle by welding four spokes of strong wire to it and to the circle (see Figure 5.2b).

The rest is up to you. Join the bottom wheel to the top by four bicycle spokes equally spaced. Join them by twisting the spoke ends and tying them over and over with nylon string. Get a long piece of white plastic (mealie meal bag) and sew the top of it to the top circle all round, then sew the bottom of it to the bottom circle, seeing its surface is flat.

Make, or order, a long narrow reed mat to go around the shade. Sew it first to the top circle, then to the bottom one. This must be done with great care. The sewing gives stability to the whole shade and makes it straight or crooked, affecting the whole efficiency and appearance of the lampstand.

### Table lamp

Although smaller than a lampstand, a table lamp (see Figure 5.3) must have a heavy base. It could be a jam tin filled with stones, with the pillar in the middle fixed by flaps to the bottom. The pillar card can be rolled in to a

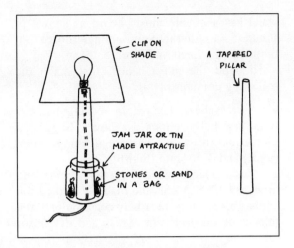

Figure 5.3 *A table or bedside lamp*

tapered shape. Mould and layer over the base to make it attractive.

### Music stand

A music stand must be portable. It is an advantage if it is collapsible. It needs to be light but strong. The music board must be at an almost vertical angle. It is sometimes useful if a music

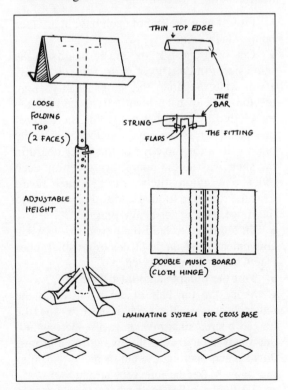

Figure 5.4a *A music stand*

stand has a double music board as shown in Figure 5.4a. Alternatively, a single board can be fitted (see Lectern, Figure 5.4b).

To build the music stand, first make the following components:

• A cross base, layered in rectangular sections and half-sections as shown. Suggested dimensions of a full bar are 40cm × 7mm (wide) and 4 or 5mm (high)
• Music boards, which are fairly wide and high, say 40 × 30cm, and made of two carton cards (pipes alternated) between two or three thin cards on each side. Press and dry absolutely flat
• A two-section pillar (one fitting inside the other) is made by the method described in chapter seven (axles and bearings). Make the wider (outside) tube considerably bigger than the inside one as it will shrink, and
• The bar for holding the music boards, about 10 layers of thin card 30cm × 5cm.

When the components are dry, start work again. To assemble the music stand carry out the following procedure:

• Fit feet near the end of each base board (see lamp stand)
• Cut, bind and tidy the music boards to the same size. Find a strip of strong thin cloth, say 10cm wide. Separate the cards cleanly along the top edge of each board. Paste and stretch the cloth. Lay half of it flat inside the edge of one board. Press the edge together and fit the other half in the top edge of the other board in the same way so the boards are touching each other. Sew nylon stitches through each board near the top edge to give additional strength to the hinge. Dry under heavy pressure
• Fit the ridge to hold the music sheet (when convenient). Use angle pieces or crushed tubes (see Chapter Four: Tray edges)
• Test the pillars and adjust their fit
• Shape the top half of the bar to hold the music boards so the edge is narrow and the hinged boards sit firmly on it. Fit the bar into the top of the narrow pillar by cutting a groove down it and opening the cut to make two joining flaps. Make the join very strong
• To fit the pillar to the base take a strong bone and fit it into the bottom of the pillar with about 10cm projecting. Cut and open flaps at the bottom end of the pillar to fit on to the base. Cut a hole through the centre of the base fit the bone through it. Strap and layer the flaps of the pillar on to the base and the flaps of the bone underneath it, and
• Cut the pillars to their correct lengths. Decide the lengths with the future owner of the stand. Cut the pillars and fit the narrow one in. Decide the positions of the peg holes consulting the owner. With a sharp tool, pierce the first hole right through the two tubes. Tidy the hole by rubbing a smooth pasted stick or pencil through it. Make, say, two other holes in the narrow tube.

**Note**: it is recommended that struts are added, as shown in Figure 5.4a, to prevent risk of damage by improper use.

### Lectern
A lectern must be stronger than a music stand. It should be heavier and more solid and could have a weighted circular base like a lampstand. Figure 5.4b shows how the pillar is fitted to the book board by long flaps.

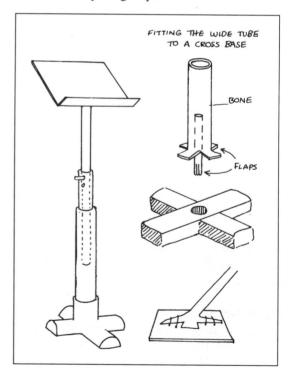

Figure 5.4b *A lectern*

## Boxes made from boards

Standard procedures for construction of boxes and lids from boards were given in Chapter Four for corrugated card (utility-style) items. The example was for a large box with a lid that rests on it and is fitted into it (a coffin). The following example is for a small elegant box with a lid that fits on to it and is attached by a tubular hinge.

### Cassette box (or jewellery box, and the like)

This box features a lid that fits accurately on to it, which can be hinged. The box is made of hard, thin card. You will need approximately six layers of thin card to make boards 3 to 4mm thick.

The process consists of making a closed, six-sided box (see Chapter Four: Utility approach three) and cutting around its sides when it is dry, to make the lid. Although the concept is simple, problems can occur:

• The lid should not be cut off until the box is dry, or it will disintegrate. Because the box is closed it takes very long to dry, and
• You must exert a lot of pressure to cut through thin card boards. If the box is hollow it might collapse.

To avoid those difficulties take the following precautions:

• Build a fairly accurate armature the size of the inside of the box to cut against, for example, one or two bricks enclosed in carefully measured rectangles of card, or a block of polystyrene packing material. Build the box around this
• Do most of the cutting on the boards before assembling them finally. Leave only a little, mainly corners, to be cut after the box has been made. Do an accurate mock assembly first to get the cut marks right
• When building the box and lid, the parts must be one hundred per cent accurate. Wrap the armature in plastic. Join the box boards with strong paper and angle pieces around the outside, bottom and sides. If possible, remove the top and armature to strengthen inside, then replace it

• Cutting off the lid when dry, despite precautions, is likely to be messy on your first attempt. Repair the damage, even rebuild the lid, with confidence and make lid and box match. Dry separately
• If the lid is not to be hinged, build a ridge that will project from the inside of the box all around for the lid to fit over. It could be two thin cards laminated together, strapped and layered to the box inside, and
• If the lid is to be hinged, plan and proceed to instructions on hinges next.

The hinge system is very simple, and efficient. A strong clean tube is rolled and dried. It is cut into segments which are strapped in alternating positions on to the two edges that are to be hinged. The hinged edges are placed together and a hinge rod is fitted through the segments.

Hinges can be made any size. Materials may vary according to the size — thick paper for small hinges, thin card for larger ones. Rods may be thin or thick wire, cycle spokes, wood dowelling, reed or bamboo, rolled card, and so on.

To make hinges from rolled card or paper use the following method:

• Find a suitable rod. Fatten it if necessary to the size you want. Wrap thin plastic around it. Roll a hard tube over it, as long as the sides to be joined. When it is quite dry cut the tube to a few millimetres shorter than the sides to be joined, mark it into an odd number of segments, the two end ones shorter than the others. Number the segments and cut them neatly. Arrange the segments as they will be fitted to the two boards, one board having the odd number segments and the two shorter ones as its end segments
• Tie the segments on their respective boards. Place the boards together. Position the segments correctly. Tie and strap them firmly in position. Align them correctly by passing rod through the hinges, first separately, then together. Dry them the first time separately.
• When they are dry fit the two hinged boards together again. Open and close them. When you are satisfied bind the segments very firmly to the board in every direction. There should be

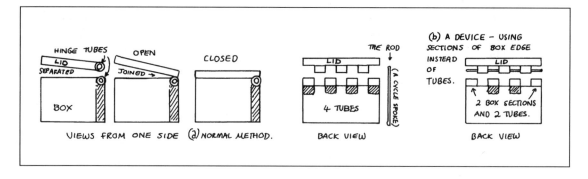

Figure 5.5 *Making hinges from thin card or paper*

very little space between them, but the boards must turn freely. Dry with the boards hinged together with thin plastic between the segments.

**Note**: where exactly the hinges should be attached depends on their function, whether for a box lid, door, and so on, and on the angle of turning needed. For a cassette box lid the side of the box is cut away. Sometimes, hinges are attached as projections to the boards to give a two-way turning angle. To avoid excessive strain on hinges a restraining device, for example a tidy piece of string or thread, may be fitted.

To fit a hinge on a box, for example, a cassette box, miss out some of the tubes. Parts of the box sides where the tubes would have been fitted may be left and their top edges strongly bound to prevent them from splitting open. A long sharp tool (the rod itself, if it is hard wire) is used to carefully and patiently pierce a well-aligned hole through the box edge sections. The result is a strong tight-fitting hinge, after quite a long struggle! A simpler plan is to leave the two end sections of the box to serve as hinge tubes, and use actual tubes for the middle segments.

**Picture frames**

These can be made in many ways. The instructions here are for making a frame with some kind of decoration, and a raised frame near the glass to give the picture depth. The only techniques used are card layering (laminating), binding and paper layering. Unfortunately, whole rectangles of card cannot be used. Frames must be layered with strips, each layer overlapping the corner join of the previous layer. In addition, the grain direction must be alternated and strips of three different widths used. Finally, the difference in width necessitates differences in lengths. Consequently, every frame requires strips of 24 different kinds (see Figure 5.7).

Extreme accuracy, which means measuring in millimetres, is required. Do not be put off by these requirements. Plan to make several frames of the same specifications. After your first effort you will find the process straightforward. By preparing large numbers of pieces of different dimensions the time spent on each frame is not excessive.

When making picture frames two APT factors must be borne in mind. These are:

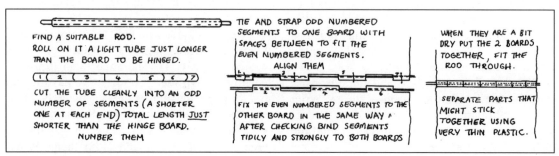

Figure 5.6 *Fitting boxes with lids and hinges*

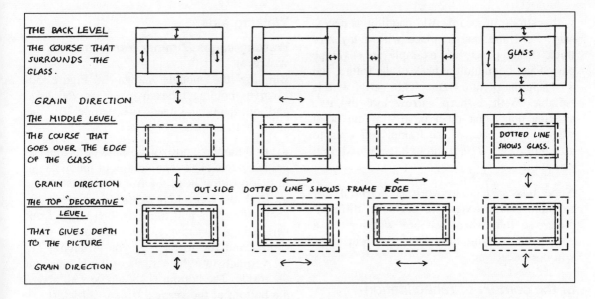

Figure 5.7 *Details of APT three-level picture frame, showing patterns, sets and courses*

- Shrinkage plus layering reduces enclosed space. Therefore, the frame must be measured to fit a glass 4mm bigger than the glass you have, and
- Warping has to be controlled in drying and especially in the very last stages.

The process of making a picture frame starts with the picture. Then, get a piece of glass to fit it. Decide on the kind of frame you want (width, shape and size of raised border).

Next, prepare the glass around which to build the frame, and which is the basis of all your measurements. Either fatten the glass very accurately by adding 2mm, for example, of very narrow card strips, to the sides and two thin cards on top, or make a hard template exactly that size. Wrap the glass very neatly in thin plastic with no loose ends.

Calculate and cut plenty of pieces of card. Keep each set of pieces separately on its own tray (or sheet of card).

Terms used in the construction are:

- Set — the four pieces (two pairs) that make a rectangle of a certain size
- Pattern — one arrangement of the four pieces, and
- Course — four sets of the same size but with different patterns, laminated. As each set has two different kinds of pieces, each course will have eight different kinds. A frame with

three levels to it will need pieces of 24 different kinds.

To build the frame:

- Place the fattened glass (or your hard template of it) on a flat plastic-covered surface. Layer the first course (four sets) closely around it. Repeat until you have reached the level of the fattened glass. Remove the frame you have made. Cover it with a single layer of strong paper. Avoid any lumps or creases. Replace it around the glass
- Layer the second level of the frame, that is the courses that will just go over the edges of the glass and hold it on. One course (four sets) could be enough. You may, if you wish, remove the frame as it now is and layer a few strips of paper to bind the two levels together, but it should not be necessary
- Layer on the third level. Dry for a time, with the fattened glass in place, a weighted board on top, and if necessary, thin boards against the sides
- Strengthen and tidy with a strong knife and layering paper, to produce a strong flat and stable frame. During these stages use the real glass in thin plastic instead of the fattened glass. Skilful drying is the key to success. Decorate before framing
- To frame the picture, see that the glass and picture are perfectly clean. Back the picture

with a strong thin card. Add padding as necessary. Hold and seal in place with a layer of thick strong paper, for example an envelope pasted and bound to the back of the frame, and

● Hang the picture frame. Thin aerial wire is suitable. With a sharp narrow tool dig two slanting holes that meet in a V at the point where, at the back of the frame, you want to attach the wire. Pass it through the V and tie it or knot it.

**Note**: tidy systematic work is essential, for example arrange your 12 trays of different pieces so that when you are working on a certain course you only have the four trays you need near you.

## In the context of rehabilitation

The extreme lightness of tube structures, the relative simplicity of tube technology and the range of useful articles that can be made by tubes and a little board make this chapter a relevant one for rehabilitation workers. This section of the chapter describes a few more articles that can be made with tubes, and some more sophisticated tube technology. Some articles need wheels, which are covered in Chapter Seven.

### Bed sides

These prevent a child from falling out of bed. No precise plan is given here as requirements and beds to which the sides are to be attached vary greatly. The technology for making a cot is relevant.

## Walking aids

### Walking cages (Zimmer frame and fun walkers)

Building the models shown in Figure 5.8 involves holding tubes in place as you bend and join them, and needs two people. To construct both models:

● Roll the three horizontal tubes (U pieces) of graded sizes, bend them and hold them drying in that position. Roll the front verticals
● Roll two more long tubes, to be used soft, about one and a half times as long as the front verticals. Alternatively, you can make them shorter and add to them as you go along. Tie the verticals into the corners of the U tubes on the inside. The bottom U should be well above the bottom of the vertical (this is difficult)
● With the bell-shape of the cage in mind, that is, the front verticals going outwards, make the shape by joining the long tube to one end of the top U piece and bend it to make the back vertical and the bottom rail of the cage, then join it to the front vertical
● When you have fitted both long tubes and shaped the cage satisfactorily attach the other two U tubes to the back verticals you have made. Force and manipulate the cage again into its correct shape, with sides at the correct angle. Leave to dry, held in position
● Drying and watching and manipulating as the cage dries is vital. Tie and strap on diagonal strengthening tubes when you are sure the cage is right. Do not stop checking it. See the bottom tube is straight and stands flat on the floor.

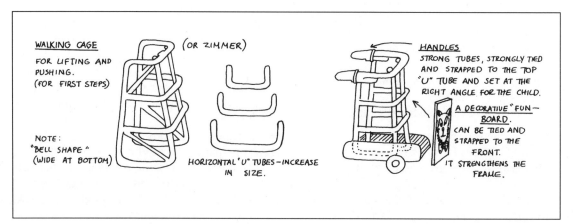

Figure 5.8 *Aids for walking*

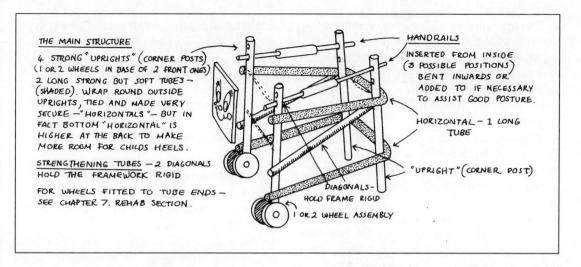

THE MAIN STRUCTURE

4 STRONG "UPRIGHTS" (CORNER POSTS)
(1 OR 2 WHEELS IN BASE OF 2 FRONT ONES)
2 LONG STRONG BUT SOFT TUBES —
(SHADED). WRAP ROUND OUTSIDE
UPRIGHTS, TIED AND MADE VERY
SECURE — "HORIZONTALS" — BUT IN
FACT BOTTOM "HORIZONTAL" IS
HIGHER AT THE BACK TO MAKE
MORE ROOM FOR CHILDS HEELS.

STRENGTHENING TUBES — 2 DIAGONALS
HOLD THE FRAMEWORK RIGID

FOR WHEELS FITTED TO TUBE ENDS —
SEE CHAPTER 7. REHAB SECTION.

HANDRAILS

INSERTED FROM INSIDE
(3 POSSIBLE POSITIONS)
BENT INWARDS OR
ADDED TO IF NECESSARY
TO ASSIST GOOD POSTURE.

HORIZONTAL — 1 LONG
TUBE

"UPRIGHT" (CORNER POST)

DIAGONALS —
HOLD FRAME RIGID

1 OR 2 WHEEL ASSEMBLY

Figure 5.9 *A posture-control walker*

Bind and shoe it with the strongest card or paper you can find.

In the fun walker the two boards (five-layer carton) strapped to the bottom of the cage have two functions. They project forwards, to prevent tipping, and they have grooves into which the wheel assembly (preferably with a PVC tube bearing) is slotted. The wheel assembly can be held in position by strong elastic (car-tyre tube) and removed if the cage is needed as a Zimmer frame. For the handles and front fun board see Figure 5.8. It is possible, and may seem easier, to dispense with the bottom boards and fix the wheel assembly to the top of the bottom rail, or underneath it, but there are disadvantages to doing this.

**Posture walker**

This is a walking cage with wheels. The child gets inside the cage by sitting on the ground and lifting it over his or her head. When the child walks, he or she is obliged to stand fairly straight. The back rail's design helps further.

The walker is a bell-like frame with wide strong corner posts. The corner posts have holes in their upper sections for holding adjustable hand rails and the two front posts have wheels at the bottom. The front posts are set out at a forward angle at the bottom to prevent overtipping. The diagonals give the frame rigidity. A fun board helps to hold the frame rigid and it pleases the child.

The posture walker must be constructed to suit the child and tested by the child during construction. There must be comfortable width and height at the top when the child is holding the hand rail as well as length at top to control the child's posture.

At the bottom of the walker sufficient length for the child to walk freely is crucial. The back rail must be clear of the child's heels. The top back rail should be bent inwards if necessary to prevent the child's bottom adopting a wrong position.

As the child walks forward the frame will tend to lift a little at the back and move forward or turn on its front wheels. The back corner posts will slide along if they touch the floor.

When building the posture walker, as with the Zimmer frame, you must know exactly what features you want and wrestle with your material until you have created them. This is a job for two people. It is a large structure, with numerous features, and must be worked on for some time before it holds together and is manageable. See Chapter Seven for wheel technology.

When building the posture walker:

● Be as sure as possible of all dimensions. Cut a piece of flat carton card the size and shape of the inside of the frame at floor level. Cut out shapes for the posts at each corner. Use this to help construct the frame, together with a similar template of the top of the frame

- Decide whether you will fit single or two wheel assemblies to the front posts
- Make and dry the following components (see Figure 7.9 and Figure 7.10) – two wheel assemblies, four very strong and wide corner posts, two very strong hand rails, rolled on a thin tube
- Number the corner posts and mark where the top and bottom rails will be attached and the levels of the hand rail holes
- Fit the bearings (if required, cut wheel grooves) for the front posts
- Make the other rail components, to be used while they are still soft, which are two long strong tubes (about 130cm) and some other tubes and bones to extend them if necessary, and two diagonal tubes
- Prepare for assembling. Have available strong nylon string loops, strips of cycle tubing for tying key joins, wooden pegs and a piercing tool, two cycle tubes or other strong stretch material to hold and press the structure together. Start by tying the horizontals to the corner posts, outside them
- Do a mock assembly, that is without paste. Test it with the child. Get it right
- Assemble permanently
- Bind and layer over the diagonals joins and do the same with the other joins. Make the frame rigid by tying temporary diagonal tubes where needed. Test with the child walking it. Correct as necessary. Dry held in its correct position. Make holes for the hand rails
- Tidy, strengthen and decorate the structure. The hand rails should project about 6cm at each end. Cut the hand rails to size. Pull them out. Work on all the inside faces of the holes until you can fit the rail by pushing each end into its hole through the inside face. Add more layers of card and paper to fatten and strengthen the middle section of the rail (rails have two horizontal and two diagonal positions), and
- Attach a front fun board, for example, a car or animal face front. It does not have to be thick.

**Flat shoulder crutches**

These are not simple to make. They must withstand pressure from all directions, and misuse, and they are flat. The crutch described here was finalized after much experimenting and served an eight-year-old child (and his friends) very well.

Making the crutch involves going through several stages. Work as much as possible with the crutch flat on the table. Check it often with its user.

To construct a flat shoulder crutch:

- Make the basic skeleton out of two long tubes by lengthening two shorter tubes. Use a long bone (see Chapter One:17) to join them. Ensure the bone spans at least the part of the tube that will be bent
- Mark on the tubes where the hand rail will be. From a point about 15cm below the mark press the two tubes together (do not crush them) and bind them together firmly with nylon string to make one strong leg tube
- Separate the tubes above the join and, still trying not to crush them, bend and fashion them to make the upper section of the crutch. Cut flaps into each end of a suitable hand rail tube and fix it in place. Fit a shoulder support tube in the same way. Hold the upper section pressed together using nylon or elastic belts
- Place a sheet of paper or card under the crutch. Make it absolutely straight and mark its outline on the paper. This will be used frequently to check the straightness of the crutch as you work
- The skeleton is extremely weak and needs a lot of strengthening. Start with the leg and middle section. Roll a number of strong tubes, a bit thinner than the long tubes and use them as required.

Forcibly guide two tubes, one on each side from the foot up, along the join of the tubes, under the string to just beyond the V where they are joined. Crush, press and mould the tubes along the join. Use the extension to strengthen the middle section in any way that is effective.

- The middle part of the crutch needs much strengthening over the bend. Tie straight tube struts, crushed only at their ends, to each tube, one end to the leg and the other to the upper section above the bend. Pack the space so it is enclosed with hard packing, for example thin card. Check for straightness and leave to dry

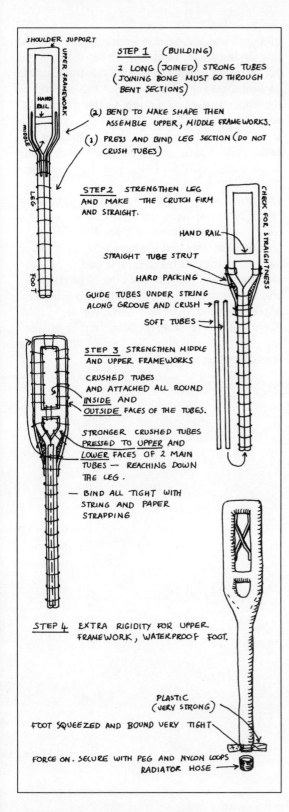

STEP 1 (BUILDING)
2 LONG (JOINED) STRONG TUBES
(JOINING BONE MUST GO THROUGH BENT SECTIONS)

(2) BEND TO MAKE SHAPE THEN ASSEMBLE UPPER, MIDDLE FRAMEWORKS.

(1) PRESS AND BIND LEG SECTION (DO NOT CRUSH TUBES)

STEP 2 STRENGTHEN LEG AND MAKE THE CRUTCH FIRM AND STRAIGHT.

SHOULDER SUPPORT
UPPER FRAMEWORK
HAND RAIL
MIDDLE
LEG
FOOT

HAND RAIL
CHECK FOR STRAIGHTNESS

STRAIGHT TUBE STRUT

HARD PACKING

GUIDE TUBES UNDER STRING ALONG GROOVE AND CRUSH →

SOFT TUBES →

STEP 3 STRENGTHEN MIDDLE AND UPPER FRAMEWORKS

CRUSHED TUBES AND ATTACHED ALL ROUND INSIDE AND OUTSIDE FACES OF THE TUBES.

STRONGER CRUSHED TUBES PRESSED TO UPPER AND LOWER FACES OF 2 MAIN TUBES — REACHING DOWN THE LEG.

— BIND ALL TIGHT WITH STRING AND PAPER STRAPPING

STEP 4 EXTRA RIGIDITY FOR UPPER FRAMEWORK, WATERPROOF FOOT.

PLASTIC (VERY STRONG)

FOOT SQUEEZED AND BOUND VERY TIGHT

FORCE ON. SECURE WITH PEG AND NYLON LOOPS
RADIATOR HOSE

Figure 5.10 *Crutches, which must be able to withstand strain in every direction*

- To strengthen the middle and upper framework, tie strengthening tubes, which have been crushed, on to the upper and lower faces of the crutch as it lies on the table, starting from the top and going down as far as the leg. Tie more crushed tubes to the outer and inner faces of the middle and upper sections, including above and below the hand rail

- Further strengthening of the upper section is essential as it will take a huge amount of strain, and is still only a rectangle. Devise a system of diagonal struts across it near the upper section and out of the way of the hands

- Make the foot of the crutch waterproof. Moisten it and crush the tube ends together until they make one solid cylinder. Bind it tightly all over with nylon string. Leave it to dry. When dry cover it with strong plastic, for example a milk bag, and find a suitable shoe to fit over it. A section of old radiator hose is ideal, which must fit very tightly. Pierce one or two holes and push pegs in, their heads sunk into the rubber hose, their points in the leg, and

- Layer strongly all over the crutch. Do not test it until it is quite dry.

**Elbow crutch**

To make an elbow crutch, four strong, but not very thick, tubes are tied together to make the leg and opened out in four directions to make the upper sections. It is a more satisfactory article to make than the flat crutch because the upper cage-like structure is strong without special reinforcement. Study the instructions for the flat crutch for the general procedure, see below for specific points:

- Roll tubes on a thin roller, make them thick enough to form one strong leg

- Take measurements from the child – from the floor to the height for holding the hand rail, to just below the elbow, that is the crutch length, a comfortable size for the arm opening, and the length and size of the hand rail

- Find a cylindrical object (a bottle is ideal) the size of the required opening, over which to mould the upper section. Wrap it tidily in thin plastic

- Roll the tubes. Tie and bind them to make the leg. Separate the tubes to make the upper section. Shape it over the cylinder you have

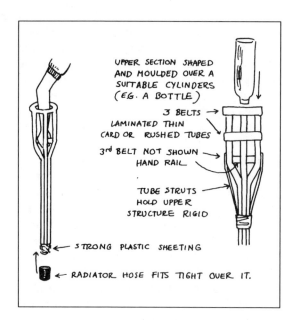

UPPER SECTION SHAPED AND MOULDED OVER A SUITABLE CYLINDERS (EG. A BOTTLE)

3 BELTS →

LAMINATED THIN CARD OR RUSHED TUBES

3rd BELT NOT SHOWN →

HAND RAIL

TUBE STRUTS HOLD UPPER STRUCTURE RIGID

← STRONG PLASTIC SHEETING

← RADIATOR HOSE FITS TIGHT OVER IT.

Figure 5.11 *The elbow crutch*

prepared and leave the cylinder in place for the first drying stage. Wrap and tie belts, for example, crushed paper tubes or about three layers of thin card laminated, around the outside of the upper section at the top, in the middle and near the bottom. Leave to dry

• When it is dry, test with the child, fit the hand rail, attach other belts on the inside against the outside belts and tie and bind them together

• Attach four strong tube struts to each long tube, joining it from the leg section to above the bend in the upper section. Fill the space between the strut and the bent tube with strong packing. Test and leave to dry, and

• Strengthen and tidy the crutch, paying special attention to the inside of the upper section. Make the crutch comfortable for the child. Foam rubber or other padding might be useful. For waterproofing the foot of the crutch, see flat crutch example.

# Chapter Six: Using thin card boards and tubes to make a wide range of furniture

## Classic style

It was in the field of legged furniture that APT first established its reputation and where some of the technology's finest work is still done. In this area, more than in any other, the claim that APT makes articles superior in several respects to equivalent wooden articles, can be justified.

APT articles are light, extremely strong and robust. They cannot crack. Only as the result of severe misuse may joints begin to creak, but they still remain strong despite tipping, over-loading, dropping and other malpractice.

A factor giving strength to all APT articles is the matted-fibre texture of paper and card, as opposed to wood, which cannot split. Other factors that give APT classic-style furniture its special quality of lightness with strength follow:

- Rolled tubes of card are very light but stood vertically they can bear almost any weight
- Tubes incorporated in triangular structures, for example with struts, can withstand stress in all directions
- Joins made with paste and pressure (in this case, joins that are tied tightly together and then bound and layered over tightly with strong paper) are extremely strong, and
- A system (used in all APT legged furniture items) whereby struts are fixed under the centre of the top and attached at the other end to each leg, and the legs are fixed together by a system of rails, which anchors each leg at three different points. This construction makes the whole structure rigid.

**Note**: if there is any risk of a legged article standing on a damp surface, its feet should be waterproofed (see Chapter One:17). The feet of APT articles are very vulnerable to water.

The smaller items described in this chapter could be made equally well and equally strong with paper instead of card, but using card is infinitely easier and quicker.

## Examples

### Small coffee table

By following this example you will cover all the basic technology of making legged furniture. Subsequent examples will be dealt with briefly, mainly by reference to illustrations.

**Note**: for making boards, rolling tubes, joining parts and pressing, see chapter one. Letters in brackets refer to Figures 6.1a and b.

First, make the coffee table's components:

- A strong square board of thin card 10-12 layers thick and with sides about 35cm long. Alternatively, use a sandwich board with two or three thin cards on the bottom face where the legs will be attached and which must be hard. Trim and bind the edges. Use when 100 per cent dry (b)
- Tubes for legs (about 40cm long) and rails (about 6cm shorter than the top board) (c)
- When you are almost ready to assemble the table, roll the diagonals for the central support system. Make them about 10cm longer than the diagonal of the top board (d). Use thin card. Make the diagonals quite strong but not too thick. Bind them with strong paper so they do not come undone
- Make holes and tie the diagonals to the centre of the underneath of the top. Site the holes by placing the supports exactly in their diagonal positions. Make the holes a little way outwards from the angles made where the supports cross (e). Do not damage the top surface unduly when making the holes. Thread a nylon string, double, through each pair of holes (four strings). Press the centre part of one support flat, and tie it down securely by its two strings. To get a tight fit, flatten half of the second tube,

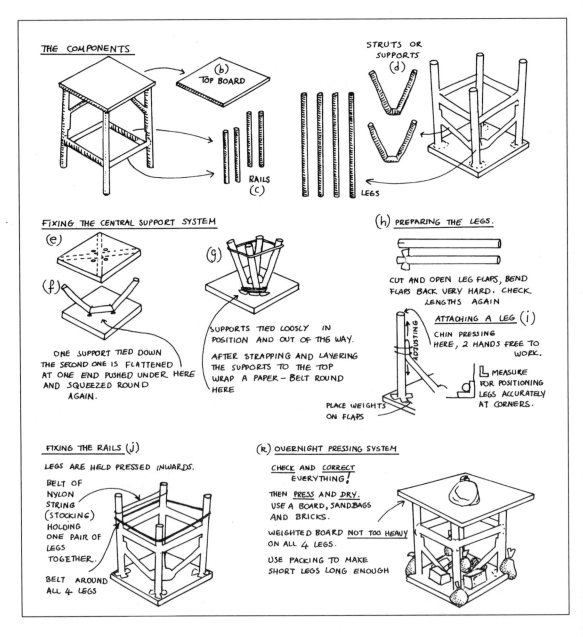

THE COMPONENTS

(b) TOP BOARD

RAILS (c)

STRUTS OR SUPPORTS (d)

LEGS

FIXING THE CENTRAL SUPPORT SYSTEM

(e)

(f)

ONE SUPPORT TIED DOWN
THE SECOND ONE IS FLATTENED
AT ONE END PUSHED UNDER HERE
AND SQUEEZED ROUND
AGAIN.

(g)

SUPPORTS TIED LOOSLY IN
POSITION AND OUT OF THE WAY.

AFTER STRAPPING AND LAYERING
THE SUPPORTS TO THE TOP
WRAP A PAPER – BELT ROUND
HERE

PLACE WEIGHTS
ON FLAPS

(h) PREPARING THE LEGS.

CUT AND OPEN LEG FLAPS, BEND
FLAPS BACK VERY HARD. CHECK
LENGTHS AGAIN

ATTACHING A LEG (i)

CHIN PRESSING
HERE, 2 HANDS FREE TO
WORK.

ADJUSTING

L MEASURE
FOR POSITIONING
LEGS ACCURATELY
AT CORNERS.

FIXING THE RAILS (j)

LEGS ARE HELD PRESSED INWARDS.

BELT OF
NYLON
STRING
(STOCKING)
HOLDING
ONE PAIR OF
LEGS
TOGETHER.

BELT AROUND
ALL 4 LEGS

(k) OVERNIGHT PRESSING SYSTEM

CHECK AND CORRECT
EVERYTHING!

THEN PRESS AND DRY.
USE A BOARD, SANDBAGS
AND BRICKS.

WEIGHTED BOARD NOT TOO HEAVY
ON ALL 4 LEGS.

USE PACKING TO MAKE
SHORT LEGS LONG ENOUGH

Figure 6.1 *Making a small legged coffee table, classic style, step by step*

paste and slip it to its position under the first one. Tie it down. Make it round again (f). Bend the four support arms upwards and tie them in that position. Make the support system really firm by strapping over it in all directions and layering the strap ends to the board. Bind a belt of strong paper tightly around where it joins the board, and strap again over that. Leave a weight on it (g)

• Prepare and fix the legs. Make their lengths

equal. Cut four equidistant slits down into each leg top. Dip in paste. Open the flaps to a right-angle or further. With the legs vertical, press the opened ends flat against the table surface. If necessary, bend the flaps again to ensure each leg is really down hard against the table not rising away from it, and that all legs are still equal (h).

Take the table top. Place it top-side down on the table. Make an L measure to help you

Figure 6.2 *Checking on a level table (a) and at floor-level (b)*

position each leg equally inwards from each corner. Place a leg in position, hold it pressed there with your chin. Release its support. Crush its end and mould it, then tie it tightly, but with one string only, to the table leg. Still holding it with your chin, strap its flaps firmly over and over in various directions to the table top. Adjust the leg angle by moving the support up or down. Put weights on the flap. Fix all legs in the same way (i)

● Prepare and fix the rails (j). Cut them to the right length. For tables with perpendicular legs make rails about 25mm longer than the space between two legs where they join the top. Cut and open flaps (as for legs) but at both ends. Open them pressing two of them right back. When flaps are opened rails should be just too big to fit between the legs where they join the board.

Next, check the leg joins are firm and weighted and do not move when rails are fitted between them. Use nylon string or thin elastic belts to pull and hold things together as rails are inserted, for example hold pairs of legs together above and below the rail. Later, encircle all four legs with a belt of stretchy nylon. Fit the rails one at a time between the legs. Loop the belt tighter as you do so. Use a measure to get each rail at the right height. Then (or when you have fitted all four rails)

tie the joins over in all directions with a long thin string. Press the legs inwards at the level of the rails. Check they have not moved at their table joins

● Do a first check by looking down on to the square made by the rails. Check it against the line of the top's edges. If necessary, press and gently twist the carcass and make any other obvious corrections. Then, place a lightly weighted board across the feet (padding any foot that is not pressed by the board), and, without delay

● Check and correct everything, that is square-up. This is the most vital and difficult part of making APT legged-furniture and when you are rewarded for accurate work. However, for the first table be realistic. Only undo and remake if it is a clear disaster! Be content with less than perfection if necessary. The table will be strong.

To check the coffee table place it on a flat level surface. This is essential. Throughout this stage check the table from a distance of 3 or 4m, from eye-level down to the level of the table. After every check and correction, rotate the table so you see all four sides (and correct them) in succession. You will be surprised!

Check in succession:

● Space between legs. Are they parallel?
● Angle of legs up from the board. Are all pairs of legs at the same correct angle? Check against an upright, such as a door frame, in the room, and
● Height and level of rails. Are they the same?

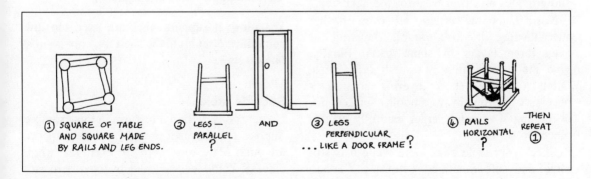

Figure 6.3 *Checking after assembling*

83

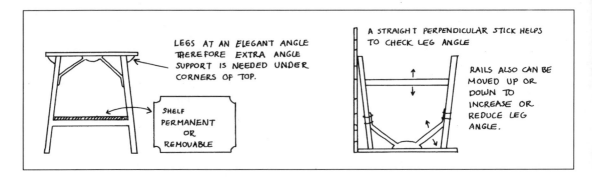

Figure 6.4 *An occasional table, for example for the lounge*

Devices used to correct the structure include: pressing two legs hard together at the joins; taking a rail out and cutting the flap deeper into it (to make it shorter); inserting a thick wedge of card between the rail and the leg (to make it longer); moving a leg where it joins the table top. Ensure supports (struts) are free to move up and down the leg face to help you make adjustments.

When you are satisfied, that is you have done all you can, strap over all the joins very thoroughly. Check the table again, then leave to dry under a system of weights. Figure 6.1k shows a simple way of doing this.

The next stage is tidying and strengthening when the table is dry (Stage Two). This is a very important and time-consuming stage in making legged furniture. Before you start, recheck your table standing on its feet. Make adjustments. Go over the whole article filling gaps and hollows with little wedges of pasted card, or balls of slightly pasted and crushed soft paper. This helps to strengthen the article and provides an easier base for the next step.

Now, layer the article all over, further strengthening it. Use double layering or even three layers in some parts. Finally, give the whole thing a smooth tidy finish. Often a second short layering session is necessary to obtain a smooth surface for decorating. Use some larger carefully shaped pieces to do this.

Check your table once more while it is still moist and soft. Small corrections can sometimes be made by pressing the table in a certain way as it dries again.

### Elegant occasional table

Make this table's legs strong but not too thick. Legs are set some distance in from the edges of the table-top and splayed out. Splayed out legs necessitate:

● Extra supports, for example triangles of card board, strapped firmly against the legs and the table top. The corners will need firm control by weights during drying. They will tend to curl downwards, and

● Care in setting and checking legs at a suitable angle. Checking takes a long time. A stick placed perpendicular at each corner is a good guide. Finally, it depends on your eye and perseverance!

The occasional table's shelf (see Figure 6.4) is optional. The shelf could be four thin cards, laminated. Corners are cut to allow it to rest flat on the rails. The shelf is strapped and layered to legs and rails as part of the structure. The shelf strengthens the whole table.

**Warning**: if support tubes are fixed too low, and rails are set high, the shelf may not go in as one piece.

### Bedside table

No new constructional features in this example. Shelves are strapped to rails. Central supports are high. The top shelf, or even the whole carcass, could be enclosed by boards to stop items falling out. The bottom shelf needs to be strong, about six cards thick.

*The beginnings: students of the United College of Education, Bulawayo with gifts prepared for their Graduation Day speaker, now Vice Chancellor of the University of Zimbabwe. (Table and tray decoration was done with minute paper mosaic pieces).*

*A variety of APT articles and decorative processes. Behind the table: card-layered stools (Ch. 3), a classic style stool and chair (Ch. 6). On the table: a variety of paper layered bowls and trays, and a layered casket; also, at the back, a jam-tin based lampstand and a picture frame (Ch. 5); and, centre, a cassette tape box (Ch. 4) and a garden basket of layered card.*

*A variety of utility articles made with boards of laminated corrugated card. See Chapter 4 for diagrams and notes on all these articles except the footrest (front left corner).*

*The creativity of no-cost decoration: pressed flowers and leaves; magazine cut-outs; tobacco leaf; strips of earth-painted paper; flower cut-outs; earth-paint leaf prints. The green backgrounds are paper from the butcher.*

*Articles decorated entirely with earth paints used in different ways: direct painting, stencils; paper cut-outs, paper strips, mosaic pieces (Ch. 11).*

*"APT articles are made to stand far more than normal wear" (quote from Ch 3: Design). A classic-style table (Ch. 6).*

*The first stage in making any APT article – building (Ch. 1.5). Two utility articles from Chapter 4: round stool (on the table) and armchair. These are ready for stage two – strengthening and tidying.*

*Tables, classic style (made from thin card, Ch. 6). Tops are painted with earth colour, with cut-outs of earth-painted paper pasted on. The carcass is layed over with pieces of wrapping paper.*

*The armchair above (after stages 3 & 4) decorated and finished. Decoration of earth paint – applied directly (Ch. 11).*

*Two classic style chairs (Ch. 6). The original was decorated with a safari suit box lid. The model was unnecessarily large, and a second smaller chair was made, but Commander had to be shortened to fit in.*

*High stools: Contrasts in style: a utility style stool, which is also a set of steps (Ch. 4), flanked by two classic-style stools, for kitchen, lab or bar (Ch. 6). Left and centre: Decoration paper peeled from shoe-boxes.*

*Low round table, classic style (Ch. 6). Decoration entirely earth colour and soot paint. Top cut-outs from earth-painted sheets; carcass painted and grained (Ch. 11). Two layered articles from Chapter 2: hat, now nine years old, of layered newspaper and Inyanga earthpaint; layered bowl background of earth-painted paper mosaic with torn paper flowers superimposed.*

Pre-school room in rural Matabeleland beyond Esigodini, furnished by 'mums' working under APT trainee Mrs Eunice Pinda, 1985.

Children's corner at exhibition during NAM conference. Articles above are described mainly in chapters 7–10.

Some of the 35 pre-school helpers who attended an APT course run by trainer Mrs Muyambo, Chimanimani, 1985.

Animal seats for children, made from mash (Ch. 8) resting on round layered stools, closed pattern (Ch. 3). IRED course, 1987.

APT for all ages (a). Mrs Masona (1984 trainee) with her husband at home in rural Seke, displaying the wardrobe she made there to her own design. It has a strong APT-hinged door.

APT for all ages (b). Gareth Hess, aged five, strengthening with cement bag paper the kaylite body of the car he is making. (Tough cars – Ch. 7).

*Learning APT to solve your unemployment problems. Two men at the latest course (see Foreword) working on a coffee table, classic style (Ch. 6) and two small chairs, utility style (Ch. 4).*

*Some articles for rehabilitating the handicapped. (Ministry of Health organized two courses in 1988). From the left: corner seat; standing board; floor hammock for hydrocephalic child; wheeled walker. Decoration mainly peeled off shoe and shirt boxes.*

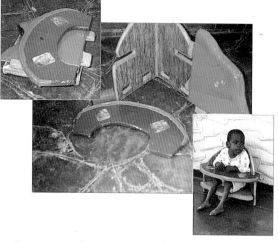

*Corner seat, above, dismantled ready for folding and carrying on a journey.*

*Home pushchair (Ch. 4). Some features to note: PVC tubing 'shoes' to prevent leg wear (one only visible); wheel-assembly removed and resting across handles at back; grooves for inserting wheel-assembly (front); side pockets for oddments; hinged and adjustable reading and writing board and unfastened foot strap!*

*Solar cookers (eleven years old) in action (Ch. 10) bottling fruit and heating milk and coffee. Note curved (cracked windscreen) glasses and two-tier shelf to reach hottest part of stove. Hinge for reflector on stove left. Reflector not used.*

*A day's fruit bottling (canning) – any jar with a good lid-seal can be used – resting on thermo-box next to the oldest (1983) solar stove with fixed (car window) glasses.*

APT - A Technology Appropriate to the Nineties.
Poster at International Environment Expo 1993.

Articles from Ch. 3. (Layering card over moulds).
The four different patterns of stools/tables. L to R:
square open, square closed, round open, round closed.
At the back two moulds.

Two coffins (adult and child sizes) showing some
constructional details. (Ch. 4 – approaches 2 and 3
combined). Note: rails hold sides and support bottom
board. The coffin is a box. The lid rests on and fits into
it. Note also in adult coffin: top side-locking tubes;
ropes through handle tubes go through bottom
support tubes.

Stages in making an APT article (Ch. 1.5). Left: 1 –
building; centre: 2 – strengthening and tidying; right:
3 & 4: decorating, finishing. Examples: ball (Ch. 8); bowl
(Ch. 2); cross-based stool (Ch. 4); classic table (Ch. 6).

Articles from Ch. 2 – approaches 1 and 2. Layering
to cover armatures. Two sewing baskets (shoe boxes),
one showing components; card holder (cereal box). On
tray (paint drum lid) are three thermo holders for
water, milk and coffee drink. (Ch. 10 – Solarware:
Accessories).

Lusaka Workshop for Disabled People aims to enable
them to make a living by producing top quality
APTware. (1992). Participants are seen making
their first piece of APT furniture – a cross-based stool
(Ch. 4).

*Harare Hospital grounds – 1990. Six mothers of cerebral-palsied children worked seven Thursdays to make these wheeled pushchairs to enable their children to sit up and see the world and other people face to face, like normal children – Ch. 4 (R).*

*Workshop at HEARU Centre, London – 1991. Primary health care and rehabilitation workers from many countries go there every year. Participants shown here with their work came from Egypt, Kenya, South Africa, Solomon Islands, Uganda, Botswana.*

*J.J.C.H. Harare. Integrated Pre-school. Disabled child between two able children enjoys a ride on an APT rocking horse. (Ch. 4 – Rehab.)*

*Kenya workshop (Eldoret) 1992, for community and rehabilitation workers. Participant working on a wheeled pushchair for a disabled child – Ch. 4 (R).*

*Left: Jairos Jiri Children's Home, Harare. Disabled child on an APT round rocker – Ch. 4 (R). Right: self-propelling trolley (Ch. 7 – Rehab.) Note: in the model shown here the front wheel assemblies are fixed to the top surface of the trolleyboard.*

*Some APT rocking apparatus. Top of picture, items standing normally. Below, items tipped to show some details of construction. The items are rocking chair, horse and round-rocker (Ch. 4 – Rehab.)*

Two APT 'toilets' – Ch. 4 (R). Left: commode with removable receptacle, fitting seat and lid. Right: seat for use over a hole. (Note: fitting lid, plastic lining, waterproofed feet).

Four models from Chapter 5. Standard lampstand (different in some details from the Ch. 5 model); bedside lamp (base is jam tin weighted with stones); picture frame (three-level); music stand. Also classic six-legged table (Ch. 6).

From Chapter 7 – toy cars of two types. Back: four 'quality cars' i.e. recognizable models, with some careful detail. Front: three small tough pre-school cars and components of another one.

APT posture-control walking frame (Ch. 5). Note: front corner posts fitted with two-wheel wheel assemblies; adjustable handrails with three possible positions.

Models from Chapter 6. Desks, double and single, one adult chair, two-legged (classic style) stools.

An independent standing board and tray, based on an original model by Mrs Archie Hinchcliffe. It is slightly different from the model shown in Ch. 4 (R).

*Mobility apparatus with wheels – Ch. 7 (R). Top: standing normally; below: tipped to show some details of construction. Front: floor raft/prone board; back, l to r: self propelling trolley; cart with steering; tricycle 1 – steering bearing is a tube; baby walker; tricycle 2 – steering bearing of laminated cards.*

*Children enjoying mobility apparatus.*

*From Ch. 9: Dolls' house, type B, with roof removed for play. Furniture is of two main types: clay armatures layered over with paper (lounge and dining room suites and beds); modelled card layered over with paper (cupboards etc.) Toilet and bath are cut from plastic bottles.*

*Items from Ch. 8 – Mainly mash. L to R: two dolls seated, one on a mash stool and holding a mash ball; front: one doll dismembered to show parts, including a limb-hook; three glove puppets; mash animal seat.*

*Items from Ch. 9. L to R: shapes in spaces, and, front, graduated squares on a pole; creative playshapes, and, in front, puzzle in frame, and building blocks.*

*From Ch. 11: Earth paints, making and using them. L to R: raw materials – soils and rocks; grinding them; sifting the powder; powder paint stored in bottles; some tools: foam rubber brushes and sponges; grainers; two approaches to painting: directly onto objects; painting and graining sheets of paper for use as mosaic pieces or cut-outs.*

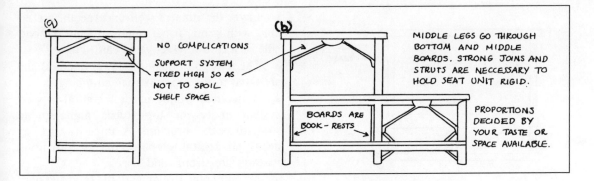

Figure 6.5 *Bedside table or cabinet (a) and a telephone table and seat (b)*

## Telephone table and seat

There are some new features in this example, which are:

- Legs that go through boards
- Two long boards which actually hold two articles together (table and stool), although in fact it is the subsequent addition of struts and much strapping that makes the whole thing rigid, and
- Possible modifications to plan. The table could be made shorter and lower.

If the table is large and the shelf is likely to carry heavy things it should have supports underneath.

When constructing this piece of furniture note:

- Fit legs to the top. Make holes in shelves and fit them to the legs before you fit the rails that will support them
- When fitting the rails and the boards that rest on them, work with the structure standing the right way up. Be very careful as you turn it over, and

- The ends of the book shelf could have vertical boards fitted to enable books to stand.

## Nest of two tables under a mother table

This item is designed so:

- The long top is given extra support along each side
- The front legs have no rails and are therefore reinforced down most of their length
- The small tables, not the mother table, must have splayed legs, and
- There must be adequate room under the mother table for the small tables.

## Table for small children

No new technology is employed in the design and construction of this article. However, remember:

- The table must be very strong. It may be used as a lorry, a stage, a boat, a house, the right way up or upside down
- The table cannot have the usual low rails that strengthen the legs. Rails must be high, so support is given to the legs by long tubes from

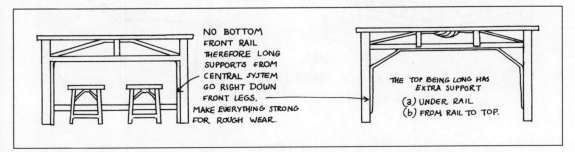

Figure 6.6 *A nest of two tables (a) and a child's dining table or play table (b)*

85

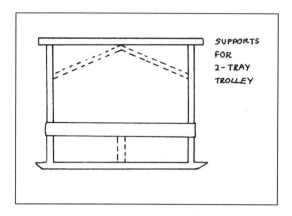

Figure 6.7 *A tea trolley on runners*

the central support system and long struts from the centre of the high rail

• The top has extra supports under its side and ends, for example small tube segments resting on the top rail, and

• Decide where to place the rails by seating a child at the table and checking knee room.

## Tea trolley (with runners instead of wheels)
Special construction points follow:

• Curve the runners underneath at the ends for smooth running

• Layer the runners well underneath, preferably with strong paper removed from the outside of a carton (corrugated card) box.

• The legs go through the lower board(s) and are fixed to the top by strong strapping

• A two-tray trolley needs a central support system under the top (tubes high up) to strengthen the structure. A three-tray trolley needs no central support systems, providing its trays are strong, and

• Assemble the trolley with the trays in board form. Fit the edge ridges later (Chapter Four: thick board tray).

## Low round coffee table with six legs
Design and construction follow:

• This is an easy and pleasing article to make. The design can be adapted to make oval- or other-shaped low tables with six legs

• The table is low because six tall splayed legs look ugly

• The large circular top needs much support. Six legs (not four) can give it stability

• The technology and procedure is the same as for the four-legged table, with small common-sense modifications here and there, and

• Make the tubes strong but fairly thin to give an elegant appearance.

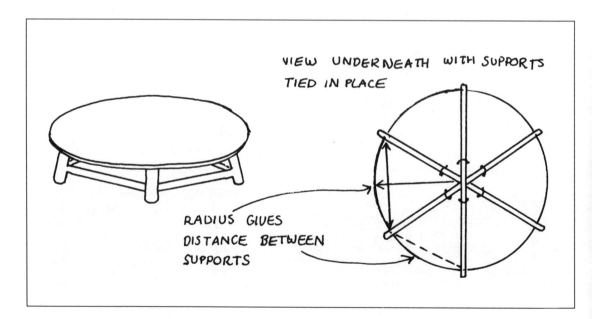

Figure 6.8 *Six-legged round table*

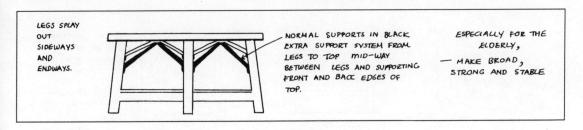

Figure 6.9 *A single (kitchen) step for reaching high shelves*

## Steps

Steps are potentially the most dangerous articles described in this book. They must, of course, be strongly made with no possibility of any part giving way. That should not be a problem. The danger is in poor design, for example a top that is too small or a base that will allows the steps to tip.

Legs are splayed out to increase stability. Both steps have additional support systems for boards that are going to be stood on. Supports for the boards are fitted between every pair of adjacent legs.

### *Single step*

This is a useful item for the kitchen or anywhere high shelves have to be reached. If the steps are used in a bathroom the feet should be waterproofed (see Chapter One:17c).

Optional additions to this design include:

● The bottom shelf, which adds strength and is also useful, and

● Fairly thin boards, enclosing three sides, add strength and provide useful storage space. These could be tied to the rails and legs and strapped and layered over.

### *Double step*

Key design and construction factors follow:

● Attractively decorated this item is more than a pair of steps. It can also be very useful as a set of shelves or a pot stand and can be part of the general furniture of the room

● The construction is the same as for the telephone table, but it is better if all four long legs go through the boards

● The back legs must splay out most, and

● The bottom front rail and board are not steps, because people tend to treat them as such the front rail, and all the lower rails should be set almost at floor level.

### Footrest

This is one of the few models that has had to be modified. It was found that a footrest that only carries two legs gets very rough wear. The user pushes and pulls it with his feet, he tips it and wriggles his legs on it, as well as sitting on it at times.

The model shown in Figure 6.11 is strongly built. It has a sloping and curved top on perpendicular legs. There are struts to the top sides from the legs, as well as to the central support system. The footrest's front struts are attached

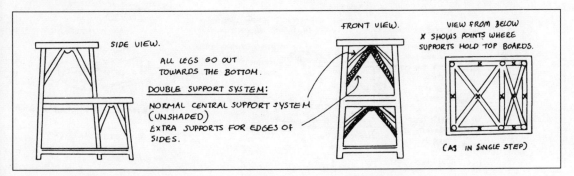

Figure 6.10 *A double step*

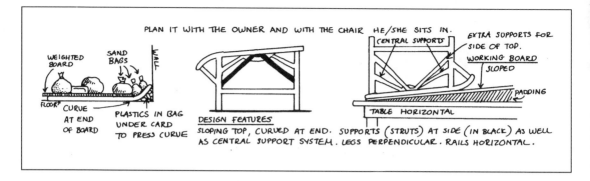

CENTRAL SUPPORTS

EXTRA SUPPORTS FOR SIDE OF TOP.

WORKING BOARD SLOPED

WEIGHTED BOARD

SAND BAGS

PADDING

FLOOR CURVE AT END OF BOARD

PLASTICS IN BAG UNDER CARD TO PRESS CURVE

TABLE HORIZONTAL

DESIGN FEATURES
SLOPING TOP, CURVED AT END. SUPPORTS (STRUTS) AT SIDE (IN BLACK) AS WELL AS CENTRAL SUPPORT SYSTEM. LEGS PERPENDICULAR. RAILS HORIZONTAL.

Figure 6.11 *A foot rest – plan with the owner and the chair that he or she sits with it*

to the front legs (not to the rail between them), and support the curved end.

The footrest's construction details follow:

• The curved board is made mainly of thin card that has the grain crosswise. It is pressed on a surface that has a rising curved part at one end. This could be made by plastic bags or a loose bag of sand with some cards on top, pressed in between the surface and the board. The front part of the board is weighted with loose sandbags, and

• The footrest is built on a slightly sloping surface with some similar kind of support for the curved end. The slope must be right for the legs to be fixed in a perpendicular position. The rails are horizontal, that is parallel to the table level.

• A footrest needs a soft upholstered top, or a cushion.

## Two-piece high-chair unit

The chair is attached to the table by four car inner-tube belts that slip on to the ends of the

runners. The chair and table can be separated. The tray is removable.

There must be no risk of the table tipping over so legs are splayed out a bit, but not so much that they are a nuisance and unsightly. The chair's legs should splay out slightly. The chair's structure starts from the runners, held together by rails and footrest. The uprights pass through the seat board to form the back posts and to support the arms. The tray (layered paper or laminated card) has so-called bones on each side which fit into the arm tubes and are held in by pegs.

Elements in the high chair's construction follow:

• Dimensions depend on the future user

• Start with the runners. Lay them on the table. Decide the correct space between them. Strap the two cross rails and foot board to the top of the runners at suitable points. Square up the base

• Make holes in the seat board corners. Tie

A LOW CHAIR

(CHILD AT TABLE LEVEL)

CHAIR FIXED ON TABLE BY SLIP-OVER CYCLE ELASTIC BANDS

TABLE LEGS SPLAYED OUT.

– DETACHED FROM TABLE –
(CHILD AT GROUND LEVEL)

REMOVABLE TRAY

UPRIGHTS GO THROUGH SEAT, THEY SPLAY OUT.

RUNNERS

JOINING RAILS AND FOOT REST ON RUNNERS.

DETAIL OF "SLIP-ON" TRAY FITTING

CHAIR ARM TUBES

STRONG CLOSE FITTING "BONES."

TUBES CUT FROM ARM TUBE.

Figure 6.12 *A high chair*

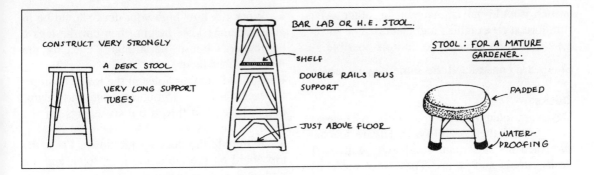

Figure 6.13 *Stools*

the uprights to the runners at suitable points. Slip the seat down over the uprights to the correct points and keep it there by strapping below and above it. Strap the uprights at their correct angle to the runners

● Fitting arm rails and the seat back is straightforward (see example of legged chair in this chapter for details of back and fitting)
● The system for fitting the tray to the arms is illustrated in Figure 6.12. A good strong fitting is essential
● The tubes strapped under the tray that hold the bone can be cut from the arm tubes if they are long enough. The bone must fit closely into the arm tube. The bone must be strong, the arm-rest tubes strong, the tray tubes (and bones) must be perfectly aligned with the arm tubes. The tray board sides should project over the bone so they rest on the chair arm tubes when the tray is in place.

## Stools

People sitting on stools move a lot, they twist around and may tip the stool. Feet feel for a rail to rest their weight on. Remember these facts when designing and making stools.

Key elements in the design and construction of stools follow:

● Stools must be stout. Tubes and boards must be thicker and stronger than for tables
● There must be struts and supports wherever special strength is needed, for example, underneath the top and under rails where any feet might press, and right down the legs
● Rails which are likely to be used as steps or footrests should be double in addition to having struts. Stool bases must be wide, and the tops small, without being too small and uncomfortable. This means that legs must splay out, sometimes beyond the line of the top edges

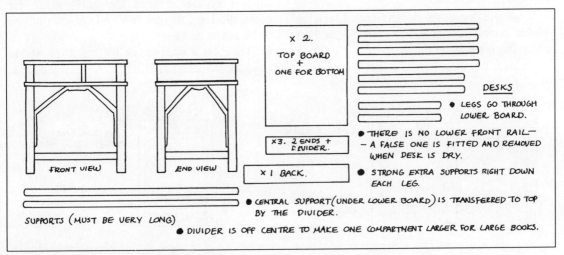

Figure 6.14 *A scholar's desk (single)*

89

(which should never happen in other APT furniture such as tables and chairs). The lower rails should be as near the floor as possible.

Stools are constructed the same way as tables.

## Desks

Desks are much needed in schools. APT desks have proved their viability. A Harare teacher furnished his classroom completely with APT desks, stools and tables. They were made by grade six and seven pupils.

Compared with normal desks the APT desk is a luxury item and can have any extra fittings that the owner desires. Making a desk is a big job, but not particularly difficult. It incorporates a few new features which will be dealt with in some detail.

A scholar's desk is designed so that (see Figure 6.14):

- The top is a box. This strengthens the whole structure. It has a large compartment (for large books) and a smaller one
- The central support system is under the box, but its support is transferred to the top through the divider in the box. The struts join the legs high up (to make leg room) but run right down the legs to add strength, and
- There is no (permanent) front rail, but, to make construction easier a temporary one is built and removed when the desk has been finished.

To construct the desk:

- Make and dry all the components. Make the two big boards identical. Make the other four boards the same height

- Work out how high your desk should be to give adequate knee height, then cut the legs a bit longer. Choose the strongest ends for the feet. Number them
- Cut and number holes in the lower board to fit each leg, say 15mm in from the edges. Pierce holes and thread the six strings for the central supports
- Assemble the desk upside down. Place the top board on the table, top side down and the bottom board on top of it
- Cut leg flaps, but on back rails push two adjacent flaps up into the tube, and in front rails, one (this allows vertical boards to be pressed hard against the rails with no flaps obstructing)
- Push each leg end through its hole in the bottom board, stand them all correctly on the top board. Press the side boards into place against the legs, and the divider in its place near the middle. Press the bottom board down on to the side boards. Tie a nylon string around the desk to hold the side boards in place. Get the legs as straight as you can. Place a slightly weighted board across the feet and weights on the bottom board above the divider. Then, adjusting, correcting and pressing as you work, strap the flaps to the top board. Using angle pieces, strengthen all the angles where boards join. Use crushed tubes and card pieces to join all the tubes to the side boards. Strengthen all the outside joins
- Check that all is correct then fit central support system. Extend the tubes to go far down the legs, fit four low rails (the front one to be removed later)
- Time for a final check of this stage. It can

LONG STRONG SUPPORTS FROM CENTRE.

SIDE AND BACK RAILS ONLY.

SYSTEM FOR PRESSING A DESK.

Figure 6.15 *A double desk*

90

be useful to check the desk standing the right way up, but turning it over requires great care as the top is only fixed on with pasted paper and card

● Press and dry the article. Dry upside down with as much pressing as possible, for example,

weights all over the top board and on a board over the feet. The best system is to build up with packing on the top board, inside the box, until you can press in boards that will support the lower board underneath. Then, press the lower board in the normal way, and

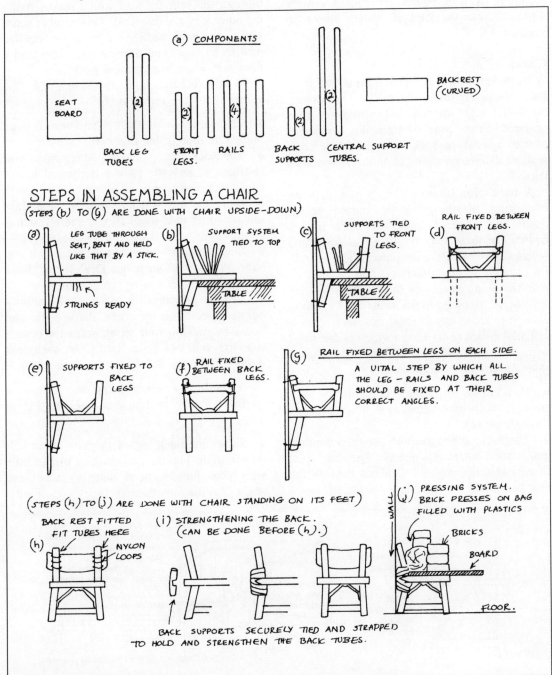

Figure 6.16 *Chairs*

- Tidy and strengthen (Stage Two). As usual, check and correct again afterwards. Dry inverted, with weights on the top board.

## Double desk

Construction of this desk presents no new problems. It is a bigger job, but not more difficult. Note the support system shown in Figure 6.15.

## Chairs

What makes a chair different from a stool is its back. Backs are there to support, if necessary, the full weight of the body from the hips upwards. From time to time this weight is exerted against the back to tip the whole chair with all the person's weight on to the two back legs.

A back also turns a child's seat into an interesting plaything to be turned upside down and climbed upon, or built into a house. For these reasons do not make chairs where stools will serve the purpose just as well, for example in play centres.

If chairs are necessary design them so they discourage tipping. Make chair backs strong enough to stand any use and misuse.

The standard chair design which is described here and also illustrated in Figure 6.16 meets these requirements because:

- It is made of strong components very strongly built (including two tubes that go through the seat board
- The back, although short, provides comfort and support where it is needed. The short back discourages tipping as it is fixed through the seat board and very strongly reinforced, and

- The back legs in particular are set out at an angle which makes tipping more difficult.

## Small child's chair

In some respects chair-making is easier than table-making because the two legs that go through the seat are firm which makes fixing the other legs and rails easy. On the other hand, setting the back and legs at an angle requires new techniques, and fitting back pillars and a back rest board is additional work.

To construct the child's chair, first make the components (see Figure 6.16):

- The seat – children's chairs need large seats. Use nine or ten thin cards
- The back rest – bind its edges when you laminate it. Dry the back rest pressed into a slightly curved shape
- Rails and legs – if possible, find a slightly thinner roller than usual so you can roll extra-strong tubes without making them extra fat
- Back supports – use old tube off-cuts if you have any (say 12cm long). Dry all the above components before using them, and
- Central supports – make these shortly before assembling the chair. Prepare the seat board by making four string holes for central supports and two holes to fit the back legs tightly. Make the holes 1cm from the edges.

Next, build the chair using the following method (letters in brackets refer to Figure 6.16):

- Soften the back legs with paste about half way from the bottom and, crushing them a little with your fingers, bend them to a suitable angle. Put the legs through their holes. Find a

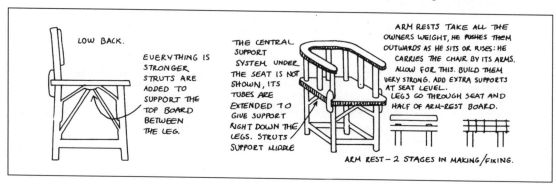

Figure 6.17 *A railed chair for an adult (a) and an office chair (b)*

Figure 6.18 *Children's armchairs – two models by Timothy Gono*

straight stick and slip narrow bands of strong elastic (cycle tubing) over the tube and stick so they are held in that position during the next step (a)

● Place the seat board on the table with the leg upwards and the back rest pillar down against the edge of the table. Fix the central support system to the seat board with its tubes held loosely together (b)

● Proceed to fix all the legs, rails and supports if possible in this (easy) order: front legs to boards; front supports to legs (c); front rail, low, between front legs so they go out at a slight angle (keep weights on leg flaps) (d); back supports to back legs so that they go out backwards and a little bit sideways (e) and back rail between back legs (f)

● Last, fit the side rails (g) and adjust everything holding it in position with bricks or other weights. The legs must go slightly outwards on three sides, further outwards towards the back, but check that the back pillar also can go a little bit outward and backwards. You may have to twist the whole tube in its hole to do this. Strap over all these joins

● Now, either leave the chair for a time, having corrected everything and placed a weighted board on its feet, or stand it on its feet (screw a temporary bone into any short leg to make the chair stand flat and level). Do the two remaining steps with a weighted board on the chair seat

● Fit the back rest (h). This involves further bending of the back pillars and checking the effect of this on the angle of the back legs. Tie the board on by the method shown, and slip small tubes under the strings before strapping and layering them (see armchair arm rests in Chapter Four), and

● Fit the supports over the bent section of the back tubes (i). Cut deep grooves into the supports as wide as the thickness of the board. Paste them so that you can mould them a bit. Push them into position against the leg tube. Push some slightly pasted paper down into them against the seat board on both sides. Crush and mould them a bit at both ends to make a good fit, then bind them around over and over with strong nylon string. Strap and bind all over checking for the last time that all is really right. Leave to dry with a weight system that presses the seat board to the legs and also presses the back rest board over all its surface, and which also holds it in its correct position (j).

### Legged chair, adult size
When building this chair:

● Do not (as you did for the child's chair) make the seat board larger than necessary in any direction
● Add extra supports mid-way along the side and front edges, and
● Keep the back as low as possible, say less than half the length of the legs.

### Office chair
The office chair's carcass structure is similar to the adult-size chair, but all the leg tubes go through the seat board and through the lower half (say ten layers) of the arm rest. The middle uprights fit into sockets cut in the arm rests and the seat board.

As in the case of the armchair described in Chapter Four, the arm-rest board must be very strong and strongly attached. It is made in two sections. After the middle uprights have been fitted another six or more layers of thin card are added and the whole of the board is bound over and over with string before being strapped and layered. The seat board between each pair of corner posts is supported by struts based on the legs (see Figure 6.17b).

### Television or reading armchairs for children (two models by T Gono)

In model 1 (see Figure 6.18) all the leg tubes go through the seat board. Back tubes could go through arm rest (see model 2).

In model 2 strong tube supports go through the seat board and are joined to make one tube where they are strapped under the arm rests.

The back is very strong (approximately ten cards) because it only has end posts to hold it.

**Note:** proportions shown in Figure 6.18 assume there will be seat cushions. If not, arm rests may need to be set lower.

## In the context of rehabilitation

The lightness with strength of classic-style furniture makes it particularly suitable for use in rehabilitation situations. This chapter has described numerous models which as they are or with modifications would be useful in some circumstances.

# Chapter Seven: For play and early learning (1). Wheeled toys and playthings made from paper and card

APT structures are extremely strong but, as with many toys, wheels can break. When that happens the whole toy is useless. People practising APT who have made wheeled toys can easily repair or replace wheel systems. In fact, well-made wheel systems can stand up to a lot of wear and misuse. Notwithstanding, our advice is not to make APT wheeled articles for sale to the public.

APT's slogan **Small is Strong** is particularly true of wheeled toys. Heavy bodies put extra strains on wheel systems. Long axles may bend and cause wear at one point inside the bearing. Large wheels work loose on their axles more easily (the lever principle). Small light cars can be thrown with little risk of damage, whereas dropping a heavy car could cause some damage to its wheel system.

Wheeled-toy-making is precision work. It demands much care and skill as well as a thorough understanding of APT materials and some basic mechanics. There is no room in wheeled-toy-making for approximate work and hoping that something second-rate will do because it will not.

Make your wheel assembly first and give it a thorough test. If it is not satisfactory, correct it or make another one. By doing this you will avoid the worst and commonest mistake, that is assembling the parts (wheels, axle and bearing) before all of them are 100 per cent dry. If this is done the toy will not last more than a few minutes.

## Wheel assemblies

In APT, wheel assemblies usually consist of two wheels (or sometimes only one) that are fixed to an axle which rotates freely in a tube (the bearing). The instructions that follow are for the simplest wheel assemblies. For those interested, the rehabilitation section at the end of the chapter contains more advanced wheel technology needed for heavier and special equipment.

To construct a wheel assembly, first build the wheels. These are made out of laminated circles of thin card (although the card should be as thick as possible). A small wheel should be about 5mm thick, bigger wheels may be as much as 20mm (40 or more cards). Press very hard and dry. Rub the edges so they are quite round. Bind with several layers of strong paper. If tyres (sections of inner tube) are to be fitted, do that now.

The next stage is making the axles and bearings (see Chapter Five: music stand pillar). Brief instructions are given here. Use thin card. Tear off the front and back edges to help you get a very tight roll. Wrap a layer of thin plastic on to the roller. Roll the axle. Wrap on another layer of thin plastic, then roll on to it the right amount of fattening paper or card, then another layer of plastic. Roll the bearing on the fattened axle. Pull the bearing off. Dry them both completely.

Test when dry. (To be satisfactory the axle and the inside of the bearing must be perfectly smooth, and the axle must turn quite freely in the bearing.)

When all the parts are quite dry, assemble the components.

Make the holes in the wheels to fit the axle ends. Specifications for the holes are: dead centre of wheel with perpendicular sides, a tight fit, but not one that crushes the tube end.

Fit one wheel to the axle. Check your bearing is the right length and your axle free of any paste. Pass the axle through the bearing and fit the second wheel so that there is a gap of 1 or 2mm between wheel face and bearing end.

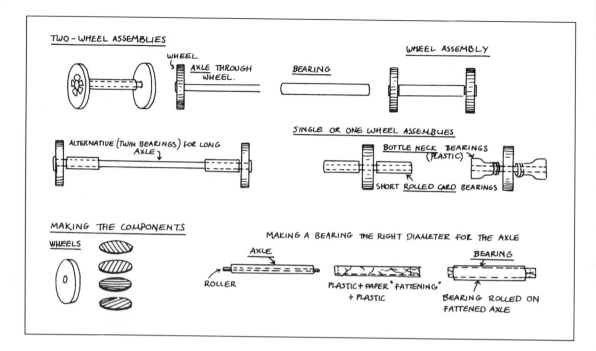

Figure 7.1 *APT wheel assemblies and how to make their components*

Check that wheels rotate at right angles to the axle, and dry them, flatten and seal down end flaps.

When fixing a wheel assembly to the underneath of a vehicle the specifications are for a strong, immovable fitting placed so the wheels do not project beyond the car ends and the bearings project slightly beyond the chassis at the point where they fit. This is so the wheels rotate without touching the car body.

To obtain an immovable fitting cut a groove across the chassis for the bearing to lie in. Tie the bearing firmly in place and strap it over strongly in all directions. Check that your bearing is not crushed down on to the axle as the strapping dries. This happens if the bearing is too thin.

Dry with car upside down.

Certain problems can arise, such as the axle will not turn. This sometimes happens if the fit is tight and the assembly is a long one. It will always happen if the parts did not dry. Sometimes it can be cured by carefully cutting away the centre part of the bearing. The axle may then rotate freely in the two end sections of the bearing. Some APT engineers prefer to make their long assemblies with two end bearings instead of one long one (see Figure 7.1).

## Making wheeled toys

### Toy cars

For the purpose of this manual, toy cars are divided into two types, which are:

● Tough cars for small children, that is small, low, solid minicars, maximum length 25cm, and

● Quality cars, that is cars made by older children or adults for themselves or someone in the family who wants a larger car and who will take reasonable care of it. These cars are recognizable by shape and detail as a certain model.

Both types consist of a strong board (the chassis) in the middle, with two wheel assemblies fixed under it and a body built on top.

It is essential that the chassis projects slightly at the front and back, like a bumper. The wheels must be housed under the body to protect them so spaces must be cut in the chassis, and probably in the body, to house the wheels comfortably and allow them to turn freely.

To make a tough, small toy car, first decide on the size. Then, follow this method:

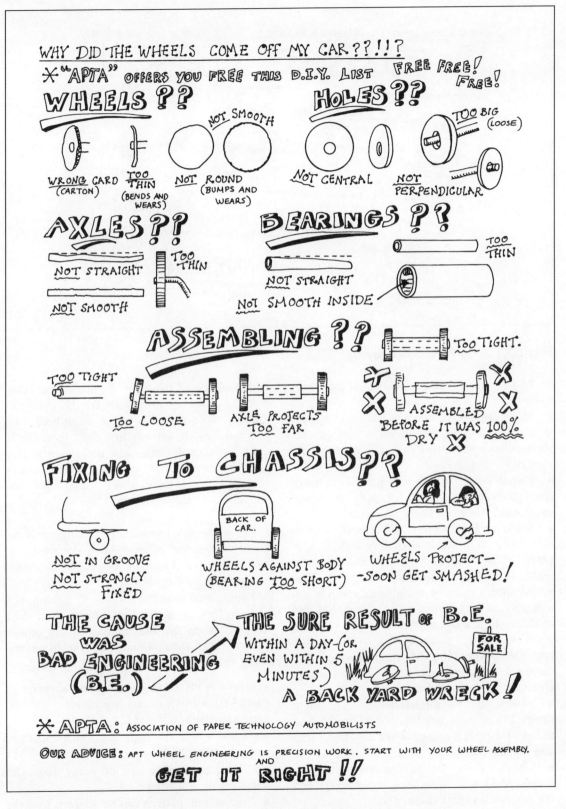

Figure 7.2 *APT wheel assembly problem-solving*

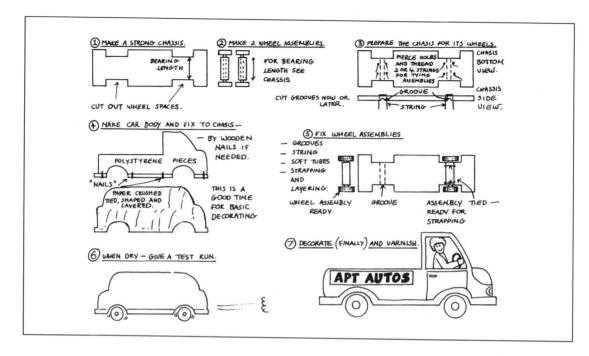

Figure 7.3 *Steps in making a toy car*

• Make a strong chassis and cut out the wheel spaces

• Make two strong wheel assemblies. Wheels at least 5mm thick and at most 3cm in diameter. Assemble when all components are very dry

• Pierce holes and thread pairs of strings through the chassis ready for tying the wheel assemblies on (when the time comes)

• Build a light car body. Either build it on to the chassis or make it separately and tie it in place when completed. It may be the same width or slightly wider than the chassis. The wheel spaces must be quite large enough. An armature of polystyrene packing material, cut to shape, or one of crushed dry paper makes a good light body. It can be tied to the chassis and the whole thing skillfully layered and moulded to make it the right size and shape. Decorate the body and chassis

• Attach the wheel assemblies. Tie them firmly in the right position. Check by testing the car the right way up. When satisfied, strap and layer the assembly very firmly in place.

• Check again. Do any necessary adjustments. Make sure the wheels rotate freely and are protected from knocks, and

• Complete decoration.

The method and structure of a quality car is the same as described previously for the small car. Quality cars are usually larger. Their bodies are carefully modelled in thin card (corrugated card for large models). The bodies are stuffed with dry paper or light packing material to give them solidity. If they are see-in cars with plastic windows the body shell has to be extra-strong.

For modelling techniques see Chapter Nine. Figure 7.4 shows patterns for making tidy car body shapes, and neatly constructing the wheel spaces in a card-modelled body.

Four useful standard ways of making box shapes for car bodies are shown in Figure 7.4. Notes on the illustrations should enable you to make them. Find your way of assembling the shapes. A few hints are offered:

• Have ready some sticky paste, supplies of pasted strong paper, and if possible some air-mail newsprint, unpasted

• Score where the flaps bend and fold them very sharply

• The cab template has too many flaps. Cut some off as you work

• The saloon pattern can be adapted to make almost any shape of car, and

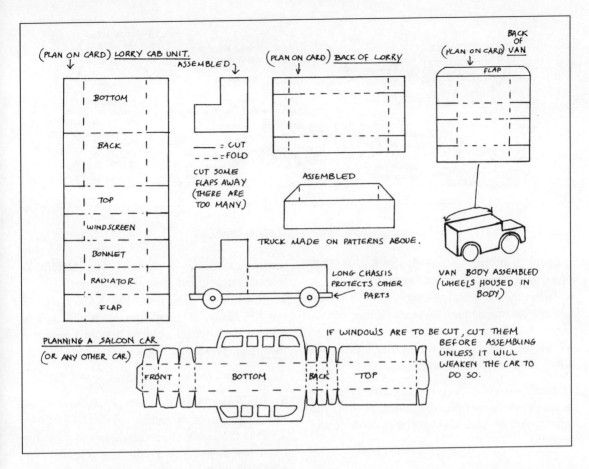

Figure 7.4 *Some car bodies, built on a base of card*

- The process is not complicated but demands patience and careful finger work. A clean plastic-covered brick on each side of the body to hold the sides up helps a lot. Stuff crumpled paper or polystyrene inside the body to prevent the sides and top from being pushed inwards.

Instructions and diagrams in Figure 7.5 describe how to neatly cut and fold the card of a carefully constructed body to make spaces for wheels in the sides of the body so they are fully protected. Construction points for housing wheels in a body made of card follow (letters in brackets refer to Figure 7.5):

- Cut a shape of card (b) (an approximate semicircle) the size and shape of the space you want to make in the side of the car (a). Be sure it is big enough

- Mark the two end points of the bottom of

that shape on the bottom edge of the car where you want the wheel space to be

- Make three cuts to form a flap, one between the two points you marked, and one at each point going inwards into the bottom as deep as you want the wheel space to be. Fold the flap up sharply inside the body (c)

- Make cuts with scissors in the side of the car, as illustrated, the cuts spreading outwards to make a rough semicircle. First, bend all those flaps sharply inwards. At the point where they are just above the flap in the bottom bend them back again so that their points point to that flap (d)

- With strong paper and paste fix the shaped piece of card to the bottom flap and fix the very points of the side flaps to the shaped piece of card to make the wheel space that you want (e). Layer with a little paper to hold it all together

- Let it dry till it has stuck well then work on

99

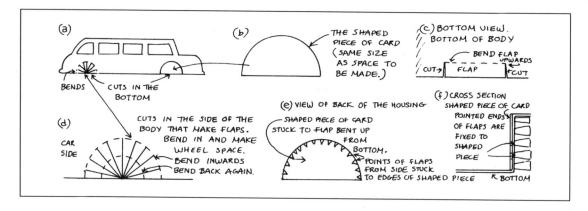

Figure 7.5 *Making wheel housing in the side of a card-bodied car*

it again to strengthen and finally tidy it. Dry, pressing it to maintain the shapes

● After the car wheel assembly has been fixed and the car stands on its wheels further adjustments may be necessary, and

● Throughout the operation the rule is to solve each problem as it comes!

Housing wheels in polystyrene-based bodies is a straightforward process. Simply cut the spaces and remake their surfaces with strong layering.

**Baby-walker**

Design points to note when making a baby-walker are:

● It should be suitably large and strong for the user, not too short

● Decide the height of the handle by trying it with the child before fitting it. Most APT technicians prefer a perpendicular handle. It must be strong and strongly fixed, and

● Balance is important. The walker should not tip easily. It should be longer than it is wide – back wheels can be attached near the back end, projecting a little backwards.

To construct the baby-walker:

● Build the body as a rectangular five-sided box. (Figures 4.23a and b)

● Plan the join in the handle tubes so that they form the cross-piece at the top (Figure 7.6). Make the join by crushing the tubes as necessary and binding them together first with string then with strong paper strapping, and

● Fix the handle. As well as making flaps at the bottom, adding a strut and tying these tubes in place, wedge some off-cuts of carton board into the triangle between them as you strap and layer them to the box.

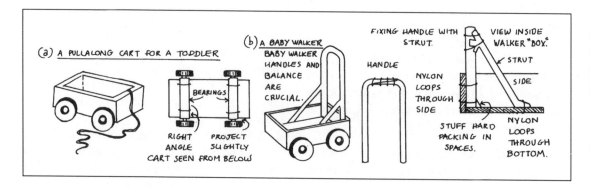

Figure 7.6 *Carts and walkers*

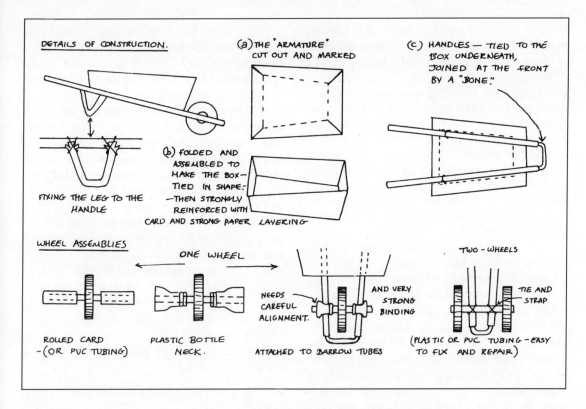

Figure 7.7 *Barrow for a small child (built on an armature of carton card)*

## Wheelbarrow for a small child

Real wheelbarrows have two bends in their tubes, but bends weaken card tubes. The straight tubes make the handles low. Therefore, the wheel has to be fairly small. All these features, that is straight tubes, small wheels, short legs, help make the barrow strong and construction simple.

Do not make large barrows, which would be taken by older children for rough work outside or used to carry other children. APT barrows are not made for that.

The barrow can be thought of as a car, that is a chassis (the long tubes), with a wheel assembly (and two legs) fitted underneath and a box body on top. The box body is a piece of corrugated card made into an armature the shape of the barrow box, strapped and layered over to make it strong (see Chapter Two: Second approach to layering). The two long tubes (the handles and the chassis, are joined at the narrow end by a bone which is bent into a U and then strengthened.

Choose whether you will fit a one-wheel or a

two-wheel assembly. Fitting a single wheel between the tubes and repairing it are not very easy jobs. A simple alternative design illustrated in Figure 7.7 shows how a two-wheel assembly can be used. Whichever system you choose, if you can find plastic bearings, for example PVC piping, use them instead of card. For a single-wheel assembly, hard plastic bottle necks can serve as bearings. Short card bearings must be made very strong or they will get crushed on the axle as the strapping over them dries.

To make the wheelbarrow:

● Make your components for the wheel assembly. Dry them and (whichever system you use) fix one wheel to its axle. Let it dry again

● Make the box. Take a thin card sheet and experiment until you get the size and shape you want. Then make that shape with a piece of carton card, cutting, scoring, moulding, tying and strapping with strips of strong paper (doubled) until you are satisfied with its shape. Then, with thin card and paper layering

101

make it into a strong box, with a flat bottom, higher and narrower at the front than the back

• Roll two strong tubes and a bone that will fit into them

• Do a mock assembly with the box upside down, the two tubes lying across it. Place your wheel assembly where it should go, adjust the tube positions as necessary. Note that for a one-wheel assembly the tubes must allow space in the front for the top of the wheel to rotate between them. Therefore, the tubes must not be too close together. For a two-wheeled assembly the wheels rotate outside the tubes, so the tubes must be close together

• Tie the tubes firmly in place and then join them at the front with the bone

• For a two-wheel assembly, tie a strong narrow board on to the tubes first. Fix the wheel assembly on to the board strapping it all firmly in place so the wheels turn freely and the front of the tubes do not touch the ground when the barrow is pushed about

• For a single-wheel assembly decide by experimenting exactly where the bearings must be so the wheel turns freely and does not touch any other part of the barrow. Then, tie the bearings firmly in position with the wheel in place. Check again. Strap the bearings securely in position and layer very strongly over them

• Roll two strong tubes for the legs and plan their position and shape. The legs should be joined under the handles where they go under the box. The legs should also be a strong V-shape with long flaps at suitable heights to set the handles at the right angle, equal in shape and position. This should be very firmly attached, and reinforced with layering of strong paper over their feet, and

• Dry upside down.

## In the context of rehabilitation

Mobility, which is a high priority in rehabilitation work, often involves wheel systems. Experience with APT equipment quickly shows that because of their lightness and smooth texture APT models slide easily along a smooth floor. The tea trolley in Chapter Six uses runners instead of wheels and this sliding ability should be exploited and the parts touching the floor suitably toughened.

This chapter has described small models for use as toys. However, some of the models could be modified for heavier use. The wheel systems described in the chapter are simple but have proved their viability.

Rehabilitation situations often require larger apparatus which must bear quite heavy loads and therefore demands more sophisticated wheel technology. Such apparatus has been made and used mainly in well-controlled centres. Further trials, experiments, improvements and new models are needed.

A number of the prototypes so far developed are included in this section because rehabilitation workers are renowned for their eagerness to try out new equipment and modify it if it is going to meet a patient's need. Many rehabilitation workers are more competent technicians than the author and will improve on these models.

Facts to remember about wheel systems include:

• Small wheels and assemblies can be very robust

• Larger wheels and assemblies are necessary for most large items

• Larger wheels give a smoother ride for large vehicles

• Larger wheels can more easily work loose on their axles than smaller ones

• The thicker the wheel the stronger its hold on the axle

• The greater the weight carried the more friction there is in the bearing

• Friction hinders movement and causes wear

• APT material is flexible, not rigid. In long assemblies, the axle will bend slightly inside the bearing and cause friction that could cause wear and seize-up. Two shorter bearings, one at each end, might be better

• Plastic tubing, for example, PVC or segments of small bottles or bottle necks, used as bearings causes less wear on axles than card bearings

• Sooner or later a well-used wheeled article will need repair. When installing a wheel system make it easily removable and replaceable, and

• When a wheel system breaks down, study it carefully, try to identify the cause and eliminate it in the future.

Figure 7.8 *Insertable/removable wheel assembly (a) and groove for removable wheel assembly (b)*

## Examples of larger wheel systems and steering systems

**Note:** because people already fairly experienced in APT are the ones likely to tackle these models instructions are brief and describe what is being aimed at and some of the steps that have to be gone through, rather than detailed advice about how to do everything.

### Insertable/removable wheels

These types of wheels can be used for a pushchair, hammock box, and the like. The apparatus is made to stand correctly without them. The wheels are for moving it from place to place and should be taken out when they are not required, which reduces wear. An advantage of making wheels removable is the ease of inspection and repair.

Note that:

● The bearing should be strong and rigid. PVC tubing is ideal.

● It can be layered over with paper and shoulders built onto it if necessary to prevent it from slipping in its grooves. The bearing's

length must be calculated to keep the wheels clear of the apparatus

● The grooves need to be carefully sited and of suitable depth for the apparatus to stand or be balanced and moved as desired. They should be a good fit for the bearing

● An elastic belt under which the assembly is slipped is a useful device for keeping it in place, and

● The apparatus and its wheel assembly should have a common mark for identification.

### Single-wheel assemblies and fitting them

The only system recommended is for a wheel to be fixed on an axle and not to rotate on it. It is very important that the axle hole in the wheel is central; the fitting on the axle very firm; and the wheel quite perpendicular. The bearings must be fitted immovably to strong bases or in compact housing (see example of single wheels fitted to tube ends).

### Steering columns

Making a steering column is basically simple. Incorporating one in a model is more compli-

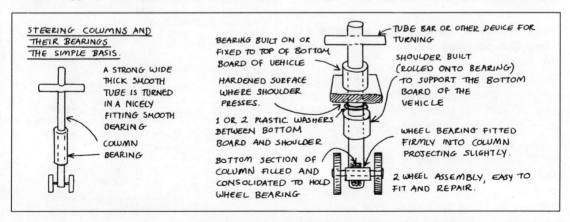

Figure 7.9 *Steering unit for tricycle, using a tube as a bearing*

103

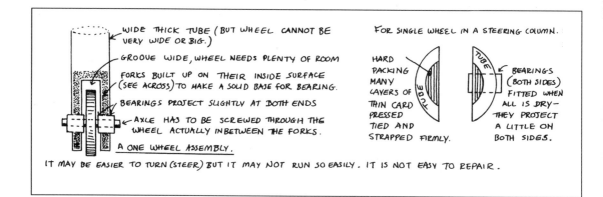

WIDE THICK TUBE (BUT WHEEL CANNOT BE VERY WIDE OR BIG.)

GROOVE WIDE, WHEEL NEEDS PLENTY OF ROOM

FORKS BUILT UP ON THEIR INSIDE SURFACE (SEE ACROSS) TO MAKE A SOLID BASE FOR BEARING.

BEARINGS PROJECT SLIGHTLY AT BOTH ENDS

AXLE HAS TO BE SCREWED THROUGH THE WHEEL ACTUALLY INBETWEEN THE FORKS.

A ONE WHEEL ASSEMBLY.

FOR SINGLE WHEEL IN A STEERING COLUMN.

HARD PACKING MANY LAYERS OF THIN CARD PRESSED TIED AND STRAPPED FIRMLY.

BEARINGS (BOTH SIDES) FITTED WHEN ALL IS DRY— THEY PROJECT A LITTLE ON BOTH SIDES.

IT MAY BE EASIER TO TURN (STEER) BUT IT MAY NOT RUN SO EASILY. IT IS NOT EASY TO REPAIR.

Figure 7.10 *Alternative single-wheel assembly*

cated (see Figures 7.14, 7.15 and related models).

The column has to hold a wheel assembly at the bottom. It usually has to support the weight of the vehicle on a shoulder built on to it. The column has some turning device (wheel or bar) at the top, and must stand the strain of being twisted while bearing weight. The column must be a wide, thick and very strong tube (factory-cloth centre tubes are sometimes suitable). It must be smooth outside. The bearing must be smooth inside. It can sometimes be lined with a plastic cylinder, for example, a bottle.

### Self-steering wheels (castors)

These have been made as small wheels securely fitted into a short column, with the column fitted into a bearing with a closed dome (plastic) top. The self-steering wheel could not be set at an angle and did not swivel under weight. More experimentation is needed.

### Wheel systems fitted to the bottoms of tubes (for steering columns, chair legs, and so on)

There is sometimes a choice between one and two-wheel assemblies. In both cases the tube must be wide and strong and made very solid where the bearing(s) are to be fitted.

For a single-wheel assembly a wide groove has to be cut in the base of the tube and the resulting forks built up to be very firm and solid, for example by laminating pieces of thin card to make the insides level and layering it over (see Figures 7.10a and b). The bearings are then fitted and the fitting of the wheel

to its axle should be perfectly prepared. The axle is then passed through the bearing and screwed through the (pasted) hole in the wheel when it is in its groove. Strengthen the fitting by suitable means.

A single-wheel is easier to steer than pair of wheels. The fitting for a two-wheel assembly at the base of a tube is straightforward. Repairing it is not a problem (see Figure 7.9).

### Steering bar or board

This is the simple system used on some home-made go-carts. The wheel assembly is fitted to a board of some kind. The board is fitted under the front of the cart where it is narrow, so it can be turned at a central point, steered by the feet or a rope, or even the hands.

The APT steering board must give good

AT EACH END CARTON CARDS ENCLOSE TUBES, PACKING IS ADDED TO MAKE ENDS STRONG FOR HOLDING THE HANDLE BAR AND BEARING.

TUBE HANDLE-BAR

3 STRONG TUBES

CARTON CARD AND PACKING

Figure 7.11 *Steering unit for car or trolley*

104

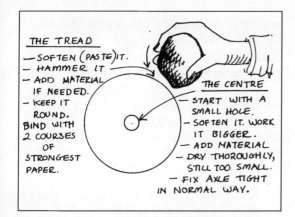

Inside the figure:

THE TREAD
— SOFTEN (PASTE) IT.
— HAMMER IT
— ADD MATERIAL IF NEEDED.
— KEEP IT ROUND. BIND WITH 2 COURSES OF STRONGEST PAPER.

THE CENTRE
— START WITH A SMALL HOLE.
— SOFTEN IT. WORK IT BIGGER.
— ADD MATERIAL
— DRY THOROUGHLY, STILL TOO SMALL.
— FIX AXLE TIGHT IN NORMAL WAY.

Figure 7.12 *Hardening tread and centre of a thick wheel of corrugated card*

support to the bearing but have a hard, slightly raised surface (hard card, with a wide plastic washer fitted over it) at the centre. In APT steering board systems:

• The underside of the board against which the bearing will turn must be similarly hardened
• The wheel bearing should be well embedded in its board to minimize rocking
• The board will have a fairly short column fitted to it very strongly, and
• The column will fit through a close-fitting hole in the vehicle board and a short bearing built on to the board to reduce rocking (see Figures 7.9b and 7.11).

### Large, thick wheels of carton card that can be rotated by the driver

This type of system is used, for example for a self-propelling trolley. The wheels should be at least 4cm thick and pressed extra hard. Their surfaces are hard enough but their inside texture has to be compacted and hardened at two points, that is around the rim and around the axle hole. This can be done by two methods. To harden the rim, first moisten it with paste. Hammer it all around with a heavy instrument, (but keep it round). Mould and press the rim smooth, bind thoroughly with two courses of extra-strong paper.

Fit a tyre if possible (wide section of a suitably sized motor inner tube). To harden round the rim hole, pierce a small hole for the axle, paste it and work it larger by any

means, adding extra hard material if necessary. Finish with a hole that is slightly small but which has hard sides. When dry fit the axle, forcing in extra packing where there is room.

## Examples of models using wheel systems

### Hobby horse

Some children ride sticks calling them bicycles or horses. A hobby horse has wheels, handlebars and a head! It should be as simple, that is, as much like a stick as possible. The middle must be very strong and the top and bottom parts made wide and strong enough to hold handlebars and a wheel assembly, respectively, as these will bear a lot of strain and rough use.

The centre of the hobby horse is made of three long tubes which extend to both ends. The ends are thickened with layers of carton card, reinforced with hard packing.

To make the hobby horse:

• All the tubes need to be strong, made on a fairly thin roller. A plastic bearing tube is preferable. Wheels are thick, of medium size
• Laminate two pairs of end boards, making a safe estimate of their size. They will be cut after fitting. Lay the three tubes on the table, bind them together with nylon string, strengthen them with crushed tubes (see flat crutch Figure 5.10 and Figure 7.13), and layer all over them

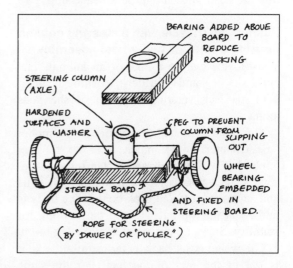

Figure 7.13 *A hobby horse*

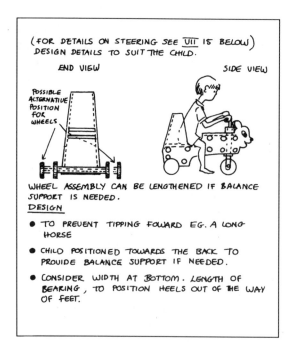

(FOR DETAILS ON STEERING SEE VIII IS BELOW)
DESIGN DETAILS TO SUIT THE CHILD.

END VIEW                    SIDE VIEW

POSSIBLE
ALTERNATIVE
POSITION
FOR
WHEELS

WHEEL ASSEMBLY CAN BE LENGTHENED IF BALANCE
SUPPORT IS NEEDED.
DESIGN

● TO PREVENT TIPPING FOWARD EG. A LONG
  HORSE
● CHILD POSITIONED TOWARDS THE BACK TO
  PROVIDE BALANCE SUPPORT IF NEEDED.
● CONSIDER WIDTH AT BOTTOM. LENGTH OF
  BEARING, TO POSITION HEELS OUT OF THE WAY
  OF FEET.

Figure 7.14 *A push-along tricycle*

● Plan (with the child) where the handlebars and wheels should be
● Tie the pairs of end boards together each side of the tubes, mark where the handlebars and bearing will be fitted. Make the boards immovable using some wooden nails. Force in suitable packing where necessary to make the space between the boards very solid, and
● When dry fit all the accessories, not forgetting the head, or it might be a head lamp!

**Push-along tricycle with a steering column housing a one- or two-wheel assembly**

The tricycle can be a bike or an animal. The child sits or stands astride it, pushing it along with his feet, steering it as he or she goes along.

This item is a Utility approach two model (see Chapter Four), much like the rocking horse, but with wheels and a steering column. Two shaped boards are held together by rails and support a seat and back board. The body is narrow at the top but wider at the bottom, for stability. Sides are cut away to make leg room.

The wheel is set back as far as possible so it is out of the way of the feet. For the same reason, unless a long bearing is needed to provide extra stability, the wheels are close to the side boards (Figure 7.14).

For details on the steering column and bearing, refer to the beginning of this rehabilitation section. The wide, hard steering column tube fits closely through a hole in the seat board. A shoulder of thin card will be rolled on to the tube and its bearing built round it during the construction process.

To make the tricycle:

● Assemble the body. Fit the back bearing. Check with the child, make any adjustments, strengthen and dry
● Find or make a steering column
● Decide on a one- or two-wheel assembly. Make components, do a trial fit of the whole assembly. Fix the bearings in the column, and
● Calculate and mark on the steering column where it will have to support the seat board. Roll well-stretched thin card on to the column to make the shoulder. Make a close-fitting hole through the seat board. Fit the column through it and arrange it in its correct position.

One way of making and fitting the upper bearing is to:

● Cut many squares of carton card the width of the seat board. Cut holes through them the size of the column. A quick way to do this is to bind a pile of squares together dry and cut the

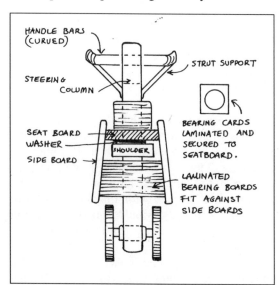

Figure 7.15 *Steering column and bearing*

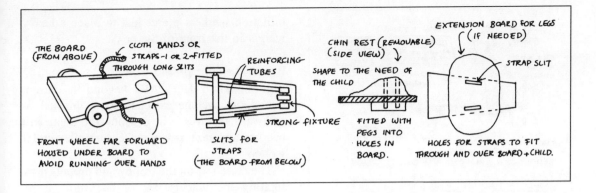

Figure 7.16 *Mobile prone board (floor raft)*

holes all at once with a tool like a chisel. They may then be pasted together, lightly pressed and be applied as one block

● Cover the upper section of the column with thin plastic

● Manipulate the bearing boards over the column, press them into place on the seat board. Tie and strap the boards in position and let them dry. Withdraw the column. Strengthen the bearing

● If you have not already fitted a front board between the side boards do so now

● The bearing underneath the seat board must be fairly long and rigidly fixed, with the column in place. Once the bearing is fixed the column cannot be withdrawn because of the shoulder around it. The lower bearing is made in much the same way as the upper one but the cards are cut so that they rest against or are pressed in place against the front and side boards. This makes them rigid. A thin plastic can be wrapped over the lower part of the column and pulled out when the bearing is a bit dry. When building the lower bearing, space has somehow to be left to allow the shoulder to rotate, and

● Fit the back wheels and axle, front wheels and axle, and handle bar. The handle bar should be curved to prevent the child from being too far forward. It will need strut supports. Add extra card layers around the handle bar to strengthen it and its joins with the steering column.

### Wheeled prone board (floor raft)

This is a strong board with tube reinforcement underneath, which is narrower at the front to allow free arm movement (see Chapter Four: Standing board type A and Figure 4.31). The front wheel is fixed under the board as far forward as possible.

The child propels herself or himself, and changes direction by pressing with hands against the floor. Two accessories may sometimes be needed:

● A chin rest, moulded to suit the child, fitted with pegs that go into the board, and

● If the legs would otherwise fall off and drag along the ground, an extension board, placed under the child, and extending beyond the prone board edge.

### Wheeled walker

This chapter has described a baby-walker, which is a toy for a child. A rehabilitation wheeled walking aid is made in the same way but must be strong. It may be necessary to design it to prevent it from tipping easily when weight is put on the handle. Extending the side boards backwards is one way of doing this. The angle at which the handle is set is another factor to be looked at, but many reha-

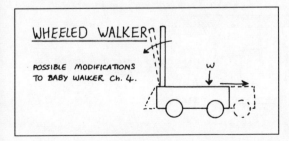

Figure 7.17 *Wheeled walker*

107

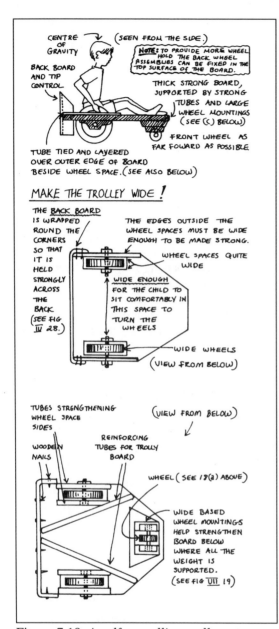

Figure 7.18 *A self-propelling trolley*

bilitation workers prefer just to place a heavy weight in the front of the box.

## Swivel/self-propelled trolley

This model stretches APT beyond its current boundaries and necessitates some unusual or awkward features. The reasons for them will become apparent as you make the trolley and it works.

The child sits on the trolley and propels it by rotating the wheels. He or she turns it by shifting weight to lift the front wheel slightly off the ground, while turning one wheel more than the other.

Note the following features in Figures 7.18 and 7.19:

• The shape is short, that is, long enough for a seated child, but wide. The child, as he or she sits, is quite wide. The wheels must be in a comfortable position, not right against the child. The wheels are wide. They need grooves that are at least 20 per cent wider, and outside them the board must be wide enough to support the bearing

• Two large thick wheels protruding far enough through the board for the child to rotate them efficiently. In the model shown, the bearings are under the board. (The trolley has also been made with the bearings tied and strapped on top of the board. The engineering was rather more difficult but it worked well with more wheel protruding

• One smaller wheel on a wide high mounting, which is under the board and right in front, and

• A wrap-around back board that serves as a back support (with a cushion) above the board and a tip-control board below.

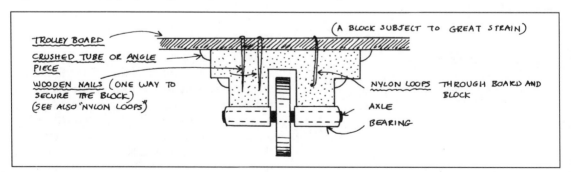

Figure 7.19 *Front-wheel-bearing mounting for trolley*

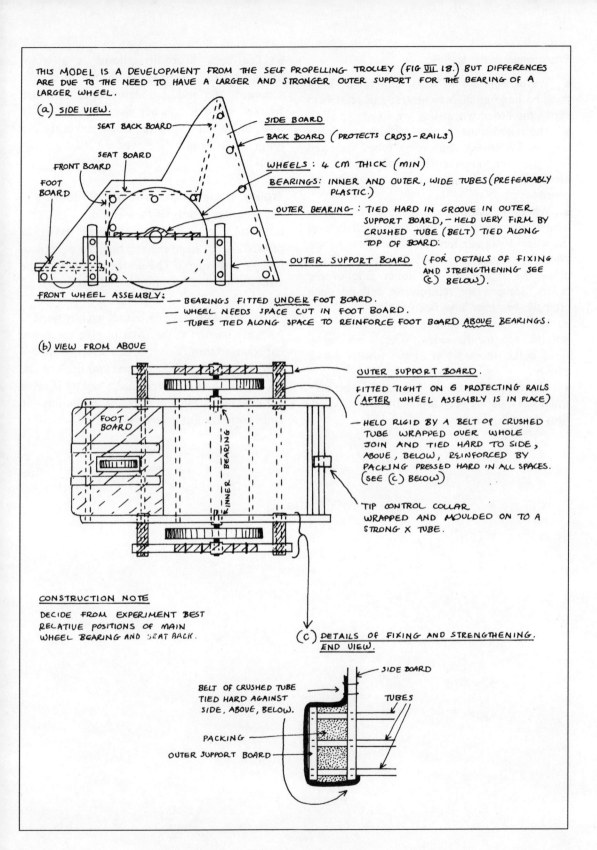

THIS MODEL IS A DEVELOPMENT FROM THE SELF PROPELLING TROLLEY (FIG VII 18.) BUT DIFFERENCES ARE DUE TO THE NEED TO HAVE A LARGER AND STRONGER OUTER SUPPORT FOR THE BEARING OF A LARGER WHEEL.

(a) SIDE VIEW.

SEAT BACK BOARD
SEAT BOARD
FRONT BOARD
FOOT BOARD

SIDE BOARD
BACK BOARD (PROTECTS CROSS-RAILS)
WHEELS: 4 CM THICK (MIN)
BEARINGS: INNER AND OUTER, WIDE TUBES (PREFERABLY PLASTIC.)
OUTER BEARING: TIED HARD IN GROOVE IN OUTER SUPPORT BOARD, — HELD VERY FIRM BY CRUSHED TUBE (BELT) TIED ALONG TOP OF BOARD.
OUTER SUPPORT BOARD (FOR DETAILS OF FIXING AND STRENGTHENING SEE (c) BELOW).

FRONT WHEEL ASSEMBLY:
— BEARINGS FITTED UNDER FOOT BOARD.
— WHEEL NEEDS SPACE CUT IN FOOT BOARD.
— TUBES TIED ALONG SPACE TO REINFORCE FOOT BOARD ABOVE BEARINGS.

(b) VIEW FROM ABOVE

FOOT BOARD
INNER BEARING

OUTER SUPPORT BOARD.
FITTED TIGHT ON 6 PROJECTING RAILS (AFTER WHEEL ASSEMBLY IS IN PLACE)
— HELD RIGID BY A BELT OF CRUSHED TUBE WRAPPED OVER WHOLE JOIN AND TIED HARD TO SIDE, ABOVE, BELOW, REINFORCED BY PACKING PRESSED HARD IN ALL SPACES. (SEE (c) BELOW)

TIP CONTROL COLLAR WRAPPED AND MOULDED ON TO A STRONG X TUBE.

CONSTRUCTION NOTE
DECIDE FROM EXPERIMENT BEST RELATIVE POSITIONS OF MAIN WHEEL BEARING AND SEAT BACK.

(c) DETAILS OF FIXING AND STRENGTHENING. END VIEW.

SIDE BOARD
BELT OF CRUSHED TUBE TIED HARD AGAINST SIDE, ABOVE, BELOW.
TUBES
PACKING
OUTER SUPPORT BOARD

Figure 7.20 *A self-drive wheelchair*

When making the trolley:

- The wheels are at least 4cm thick. They must be large enough to protrude at least 6cm above the board when they are fixed
- The board must be able to bear an adult's weight. Two main reinforcing tubes are fixed from the back to converge near the front wheel block. The block also gives support to the board
- Wheel mountings of thick card slightly longer than the spaces are fixed each side of the wheel spaces underneath the trolley. Tubes, which have not been flattened, are attached along the spaces on the upper side of the board. Some extra reinforcing can be done after the bearings have been fitted
- Wheel spaces need to be wide. Wheels must not rub against the sides. Wheels are wide, tyres make them wider. Few wheels rotate evenly
- The front wheel does not have to be very small but must be very firmly fixed to a broad, firm mounting, and

- The back board/tip control is a wrap-around board. It might be shaped to almost a point at the middle underneath to minimize friction when it touches the floor. It would have to be built up to be thick and solid – a lump – that would slide over the floor without breaking.

## Trolley or cart with front-wheel steering

See steering boards or bars earlier in this section and Figure 7.11. No specific design is offered. Apart from the steering, no new technology is involved. The design depends on the size and kind of disability, and ingenuity, of the child.

Trolleys with steering boards usually need to be fairly narrow at the front to give the board bar room to turn. The simplest steering control is by a rope attached near the two ends of the board held by the driver on the trolley if he or she is being pushed, or by someone pulling the child from the front.

# Chapter Eight: For play and early learning (2). Puppets, dolls, animal seats, etc., using mash or layered and moulded paper

The purpose of this chapter is to describe making articles with mash, a process that has not yet been properly dealt with in this book. The reason for postponing the topic until now is that in APT mash is used almost exclusively to make toys. The advantages of mash are set out below.

However, people experienced in APT often abandon mash and create the articles described in this chapter and many others by the method of layering and moulding paper and card described in Chapter Two: Second approach to layering. Moulding paper and card requires more APT knowledge and skill than moulding mash, and without this results can be disappointing. However, individuals experienced in APT prefer paper moulding because it is quicker, the drying is faster and simpler and the end result is comparable to the mash article and lighter.

This chapter is devoted to mash and makes few references to the alternative paper-moulding method. Those who want to use it will know how to interpret mash instructions for their different way of working.

## Mash

### Advantages

The advantages of mash are numerous. It can be made from any waste paper and card and from very small pieces. When all other forms of paper and card are short, mash can be made and used. It is one of the easiest ways of making solid things from paper. Even young children can do it.

Mash is the easiest way for anyone to mould irregular shapes, such as animals, people, and so on. The technique is similar to clay modelling, which most people have done at some time. It is the easiest way of moulding features – you just squeeze, pinch, and work with your fingers or a small tool. Quite often you are surprised when something different from what you were trying to create is born between your hands!

### Disadvantages

However, there are some disadvantages to mash. It dries very slowly and needs constant attention and corrective measures during drying. In wet weather it may grow a coat of mildew, (which will disappear after a little exposure to sun). Large articles take proportionately longer to dry.

Mash is a heavy material when wet and if applied thickly or to large flat surfaces it may tend to fall off, in which case it must be strapped back again. Mash made with a lot of *sadza* may be attacked by weevils. This condition can be cured by putting the article for a time in a solar oven.

### Approaches

In theory, mash can be used in all the three approaches to paper layering described in Chapter Two. In practice it is mainly used with approach two, that is, making an armature and moulding on it the creature or object of your imagination. This approach is essentially creative, and using it you can make a whole range of articles for children and for use in play school.

Mash has a limited but valuable use in that it is possible to build up the material without interior support. Very small puppet heads can be made in this way by small children. Low shapes can be created on a flat base, for example, the high ground of a relief map, the build-

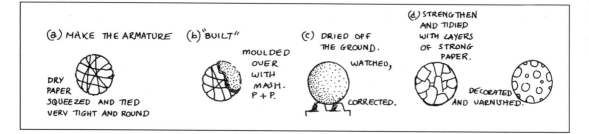

Figure 8.1 *Stages in making a mash ball*

ings in a development project or the raised edge around a board tray (see Chapter Four).

## Small ball

First, refer back to Chapter One and Chapter Two: Second approach to paper layering, to remind yourself of the procedure.

To make a small ball using mash (letters in brackets refer to Figure 8.1):

• Make the armature. It should be 2cm or so smaller than the object you will make. Squeeze some waste, preferably hard, paper into a tight ball, and, while a friend holds it, tie it around and around in all directions to make a hard round ball (a)

• Apply the mash. Make your hands and the ball sticky with paste or *sadza* and press on small pieces of mash until the whole thing is covered. Remember the APT rule, **Paste + Pressure = Stick**. Squeeze the whole thing in your hands pressing the mash more firmly to the armature and making your ball really round (b)

• Put it to dry so air circulates all around it. Watch it, turn it, press it and correct it frequently as it dries. It will take more than a day (c). If the mash persistently falls away from the armature as you make it, take it all off, see what the trouble is and start again. Most often the problem is the mash is too wet or not sticky, or the armature is not hard.

• When the ball is quite dry improve its shape by any suitable means and cover it with three or more courses of strong layering paper (d), and

• Decorate and varnish (e).

## Glove puppets

Glove puppets are made by the same method as the small ball. The puppets consist of a head moulded on an armature with a tube in the centre for the fingers that control the head. A glove dress is made. The neck is fixed to the puppet neck by a strong elastic. The puppet neck has a ridge around it that prevents it from slipping off. The thumb and one of the fingers fit into the puppet's hands which are sewn to the sleeves of the dress.

Playing the puppet is an art learnt by looking at your puppet in the mirror and slowly discovering its expressions as you manipulate its head and hands with your fingers. There are different ways of holding a puppet (see Figure 8.2) and each puppeteer has to decide which to use before making the armature for the puppet. Puppets may be played with the first finger only in the head, or with the first two fingers, or with all three middle fingers. The latter is the traditional Russian way for playing large puppet heads.

To make a puppet, first decide on which fingers you will play your puppet head. Make a strong short tube to fit loosely on to those fingers. A toilet roll is not strong enough. The tube must be long enough to reach up almost to the top of the puppet's head and should project 5cm below the chin to allow plenty, that is too much, room for the neck and ridge.

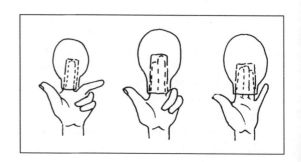

Figure 8.2 *Different way of playing puppets*

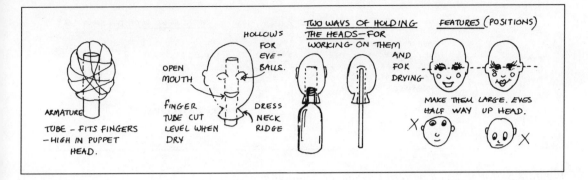

Figure 8.3 *Puppet head*

Next:

• Make the armature, but not too big. Make it a bit like a head with a chin, and not too thin in the face. You need not cover the neck tube, it can be moulded over with mash as it is

• Mould the head and a short neck. The ridge can be a belt of rolled paper moulded over, either now or during the drying period. Make the basic features. This is delicate work. Three things can help you – transfer the head to a bottle or to a stick that can be fixed in a bottle so you have two free hands to work with, on the whole add little bits of mash to make features, and make some kind of small plastic tool to help you mould the delicate parts of the features

• To make the eyes, start by moulding two hollows where the eyes will be, not higher than half-way up the head. Later, make two small balls of mash and press them in the right places in the hollows. Finish the eyes in the last stage (final decorating)

• Make the nose not too long or big, unless you want a comic effect

• The mouth is important. Do not make it too small. It must be open because puppets talk. Shape a mouth by digging into the mash with a tool. To make it smile make the corners curl a little upwards. Add lips if necessary. Finish off by adding teeth in the decorating stage

• Make ears small and flat against the head, unless you want a comic effect

• The chin makes a lot of difference to the face. A puppet needs a chin. Add mash as necessary to make chin and cheeks

• It saves trouble if you make foundations for the puppet's hair at this stage, for example, use little balls of mash, or make marks in the head with a suitable tool to represent hair. Real hair can cause problems

• The neck-ridge (see Figure 8.3) is a sharp ridge to hold the dress. Take care not to make the ridge too high or the dress neck opening may not be big enough to go over it

• To make the hands construct short, very thin rolls of card or strong paper, with the finger end part cut away a bit so it is thinner. Make each roll on the finger or thumb that will play it. They must fit loosely. Be sure the hands face the right way when on the respective fingers. It is easy to make a mistake. Fashion the hands by crushing, cutting, shaping, adding to, and layering over until you are satisfied. When dry pierce the wrists with about six holes for sewing them into the sleeves

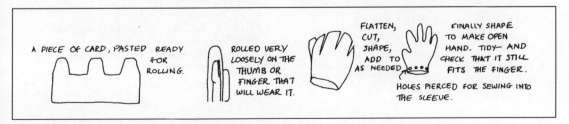

Figure 8.4 *A way of making the hands*

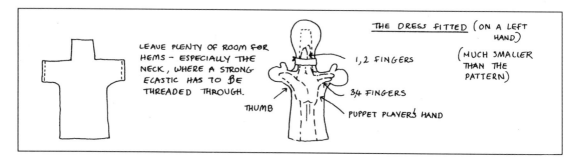

Figure 8.5 *Rough basic pattern for puppet foundation dress*

• The basic dress is a simple garment. You may if you wish make other clothes to suit a character. The basic dress is a glove. The neck of the dress fits over the neck of the puppet, and the puppet's hands are sewn in the sleeves. Your hand is the body of the puppet

• The dress hardly has any sleeves; they are more like arm holes with a little extra cloth to make a hem, to which the wrist of the puppet hand will be sewn. Each hand must be sewn on in the right position for clapping hands or holding things. The body of the dress must be large enough for your fist to work in. The neck band through which the rubber tubing will be threaded must be big enough to go over the neck ridge. The hem must be wide enough to allow cycle-tube elastic to be threaded through it. The neck itself should not be long. The elastic (cycle tubing is best) must be tightly tied, and

• Decorating the puppet is extremely important. Suggestions on decorating faces are given in Chapter Eleven: Decorating puppets and dolls. Ultimately you learn to decorate by experience, rather than by reading.

*Animal puppet heads*
These are a delight to children. They are made in the same way as human puppets but on differently shaped armatures. With a little ingenuity, and the use of cloth hinges, animal puppets can be made with ears that flap and mouths that open and close.

**Dolls**
APT doll-making is skilled work. You need to be a bit of an artist as well as a technician. It is the face that determines if the doll is liked or rejected. The face is the hardest part to make and decorating it is one of the most challenging tasks because no bought materials may be used. Read Chapter Eleven: Decorating puppets and dolls for more information.

Before deciding to make a doll, try to build and decorate a head and face. If you are fairly successful proceed to make a whole doll.

This section describes how to make a head with shoulders to sew on to a cloth or soft body as well as how to construct a complete mash doll with moving head and limbs. Small

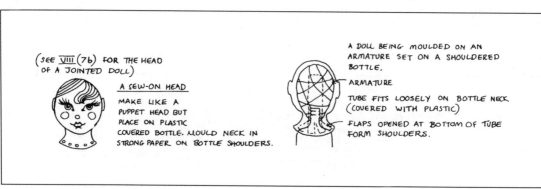

Figure 8.6 *A doll's head, for sewing to a soft body*

children love cuddly dolls and for them the soft-bodied doll is best. Older children prefer dolls with moving parts.

## Sew-on doll's head
To make this type of head:

- Select a suitable bottle – one with shoulders of the right size and shape
- Make an armature in the same way as for a puppet but to the following specifications – a tube long enough to reach nearly to the top of the head and protrude below the chin far enough to make flaps for the shoulders on the bottle, and a round full face
- Cover the top of the bottle with thin plastic. Open about eight flaps in the tube about 1cm below the chin and fit it loosely on to the bottle neck. Press the flaps hard down on the bottle shoulders. Strap and layer them on top and underneath to make a strong foundation for the mash
- Mould in the same way as a puppet head but make all features except the eyes small. Make the mouth slightly open, smiling, showing gums or perhaps two small teeth, and
- Making a mash doll's face is an on-going process. Lay good foundations, even for the mouth parts in first moulding. Return to the face to improve it during the drying stages. It will only be finished in the final decorating stage (see Chapter Eleven).

## Jointed doll
This doll consists of a body made with hollows (cups) where the head, arms and legs will join it. Holes are pierced through the body between the pairs of cups, and through the neck cup. The head, arms and legs have strong spiral-based hooks embedded in them where they join the body. The part around each hook is built up to a dome so it can rotate in its cup. Strong cycle inner tube is hooked to each limb on one side of the body and stretched through the body to hook on to the opposite limb. The tubing joining the arms is hooked up through the neck hole and the head is hooked on to it.

Instructions and suggestions will be given on how to make a jointed doll. These should help you avoid pitfalls and enable you to complete your doll. However, the operation, particularly after you begin to fit the doll together, requires imagination and ingenuity rather than the ability to follow precise instructions.

Make the doll by the following method:

- Make five hooks from strong wire. The spiral must be fairly flat, the hook is at the end of a short stem and bent right around, leaving only 3mm or so between its end and the stem (see Figure 8.7)
- Make the armatures small and fairly thin, but hard. The exception is the body, which should be fairly soft so it can be crushed and shaped as you mould and because holes have to be pierced through it. Applying mash will make all the parts much fatter and a bit longer. To get the proportions right, start with the head. Do not make the body more than twice as long as the head. Arms when in sockets should almost reach the bottom of the body. Legs are a fraction longer

To construct the head make an armature as for a ball (not a puppet). Tangle the hook deep and strongly in the armature. Make the armature for the body a bit like a baby's body in shape, but most of the shaping will be done during the moulding stage. Make the armatures for the limbs. The part on the outside of the limb where the limb will join the body must be flattened a lot (otherwise the limbs will be so thick that clothes will not pass over them). Make the limbs slightly bent. Use some strips or pieces of card to make the lower ends of each limb. It will be easier to fashion them into feet and hands

- Mould the parts in this order. First, shape the head (see Sew-on doll's head for advice). The doll's neck must end in a rounded shape with the hook in the middle of its lower part to fit into the cup in the body. Next, mould the body – you will have to come back to it again after this first moulding. Make the body a nice fat baby-shape, but also do anything you can to it that will begin to shape cups for the arms and very narrow lower part where the legs will fit. Mark the navel to help remember which is back and front. Check that the body is the right length. If it is not, correct it now.

Finally, make the legs and arms. As you mould check them from time to time with the

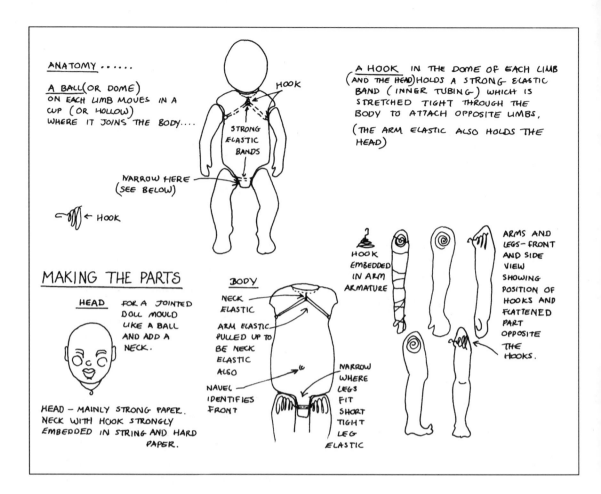

Figure 8.7 *A jointed doll and how to make its parts*

body. Adjust the body cups or the limb domes to get a reasonable fit, but you will have to make further adjustments as they dry. Check the limbs' lengths, thickness where they join the body and the angle of feet and hands when the limbs are in their cups

● Put the parts to dry. Attend to them constantly, squeezing if the mash is separating, sealing cracks, and improving the limbs, especially the hands and feet. Do anything that seems necessary to improve the head. Strengthen all over. Only when it is completely dry and the hooks very, very firm can you do a trial fit and begin the next series of adjustments.

● To assemble the doll's parts for the first time, you need bands of wide elastic (cycle tubing segments 3–5mm wide) and a homemade hook with a strong handle to help you pull very hard on the elastic. Press the parts in

place. Screw them if it helps to get a better fit. Pierce and rub pencil-sized holes through the body between the limbs and one down from the neck-cup to the arm-elastic hole. Make any adjustments to domes and cups that are obviously necessary

● Do a trial assembly. Get a friend to help you. It will be a struggle. Hook the elastic to one limb, and with a tool pull it through the body and hook on the opposite limb. The leg elastic will probably have to be doubled (making four strands) to get it tight enough. Finally, hook one or if possible both strands of arm elastic up through the neck hole and hook on the head (making sure it is the right way round). Sit your doll up and take a critical look at it

● Correct and adjust the doll. From now on you have to solve your own problems. We can only mention some of the things you may need

116

to do to the parts and how you can do some of them. You will do them in the order you think best either with the doll still assembled or with the parts disconnected again.

Do any alterations with paper, not mash. The body may be too long for the doll to sit properly. You may have to cut some of it away and remake it or repair it with paper. The dome cup joins may not be right. You may have to cut them, or add more paper to build up some parts, or it may be enough to soften them with paste and, with a plastic separating them, press and rotate the dome in the cup. The limbs may be too fat where they join the body. Softening and hitting or pressing them may be enough or you may have to cut them and remould over the cut. The limbs may not be at the right angle when they are rotated, or feet or hands may be at the wrong angle. This may necessitate building up or cutting either the limb or the body. You will certainly have other problems but by this time you will have learnt so many ways of correcting things that none will be too difficult for you. Before decorating the doll it must be very smoothly covered all over. Details on the face, hands and feet should be made as perfect as you can make them

● Decorating is essential. Remember the success of all your labour depends on the finished appearance of the doll. Keep in mind all the time a picture of the parts, and particularly the face as you want it to be, and work until you have achieved it. Chapter Eleven offers suggestions on decorating dolls, and

● If the doll is likely to be sucked by its owner it should NOT be varnished unless you have nontoxic varnish.

## Round stools made from mash

First, refer back to Chapter Three: Round, closed stools, for background information. When it is dry, the mash stool is layered over with paper. The finished stool is as strong as a card one, heavier and not as tidy in appearance. It is harder to make, and takes a long time to dry. But it is a stool you can build, without carton or card, from scraps of paper. Mash stools should be made as low as possible. The top and base may finally be 15 to 20mm thick.

To make a round, closed stool from mash:

● Mould the base on a flowerpot or similar article

● Mould a top using a container with a low circular wall, such as a baking tin, or a board with a circle of wide hoop iron resting on it

● Make plenty of stiff mash, with *sadza* or thick paste

● The technique of applying the mash differs from what you have done previously. There is no armature to build on, only the plastic-covered mould. The finished article must be as solid as possible and the mash 15 to 20mm thick. Being heavy the mash tends to sag down, crack and even fall off. You can do two things to deal with this problem – press the mash hard as you apply it and repeatedly press it tighter during the drying process, and put some paper strapping temporarily over difficult parts to hold them together. Aim at getting surfaces as smooth as possible when moulding and drying to reduce work later

● Remove the components from the moulds as soon as it is safe. Mash articles will probably have to spend two or three days still on their moulds before it is safe to remove them

● Correcting the parts during and after drying is an important part of the process. Do it any

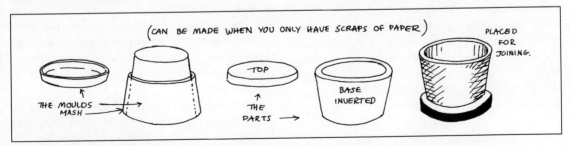

Figure 8.8 *A mash stool*

way that seems suitable. Correct the straightness of the stool base – top and bottom and the surface of the stool's top. If parts have to be patched or built up do it with slightly pasted soft paper screwed and rolled in your hands (instead of using proper mash which takes too long to dry) and layer over with strong paper

• Join the base to the top. Strengthen and tidy. The parts are assembled with the top upside down on the table. The joining areas must be very thoroughly moistened with paste before actually joining, and

• After joining, the stool should be pressed for a day or more under a fairly heavy weighted board. The strengthening of joins and edges is done with doubled strong paper. The rough mash surfaces of the stool can be made smooth by pasting them and rubbing them for some time with a hard tool such as a stone. The whole stool must finally be layered over with several thicknesses of strong paper before it is decorated.


*Children's animal seats from mash (or layered paper)*

The advantages of mash seats are that they can be made when you have no card or carton, and can be very strong and attractive. It has to be said that you have to be a master of mash to make them, as the mash falls off some parts even more than it does from a stool. The problem can effectively be dealt with by strapping difficult parts with strong paper as described above. These seats are made in a similar fashion to the door-stop (Chapter Two: Second approach to paper layering). The main difference is that in the case of children's seats the armature, which is wrapped in plastic, is eventually removed so that the seat is hollow and light.

Armatures can be made in many ways. The normal way is to make them of tightly tied paper, but it takes a lot of paper and time. Figure 8.9 shows an armature contrived with plastic containers (the carton is stuffed with paper to make it solid. The nose is a piece of card tubing).

The specifications of the armature are:

• It should be of the right basic shape

• The main part of it must make a comfortable seat for the child

• The back end should be slightly raised

• It should not be too large as it will have 2 to 4cm of mash or paper moulded on to it

• Its sides should be almost perpendicular

• It should be wrapped in plastic to facilitate its ultimate removal from the animal, and

• Like all armatures it must be hard so you can press against it.

Before applying the mash see previous examples of problems and how to deal with them. With animal seats you must also think of the parts which will have to be especially strengthened, especially the neck at the top and underside where it joins the body. Strengthen the armature with paper strapping now and in the strengthening stage. Give it extra support so that it is quite firm as it dries.

The drying stage determines if the model will be successful. Care and action during drying is the deciding factor. The following suggestions are offered:

• You cannot move the seat for some days but must continually press and strengthen it

• The armature must be removed as soon as you can lift it without damage to the neck. To lift it, lay the armature upside down in a nest of crumpled paper and remove it cautiously bit by bit, pressing the mash sides between your hands to repair and strengthen them. The animal may seem worse but in fact it is better. Now, it can begin to dry properly. Removing the armature may be spread over a few days

• When the creature is strong enough suspend it carefully on a bed of netting (an orange bag) but still attend to it as necessary every day

• Eventually, the animal will all hold together but will have many cracks. You will be able to set it upright to see what adjustments and improvements need to be done. Do them with tightly crumpled pasted paper rather than mash, and strap them over with layered paper. Do repairs from inside the body as well as outside and

• Only when the mash is absolutely dry begin the overall strengthening with several courses of two or three layered strips of paper outside, and one course inside. During this strengthening stage you can improve the features and

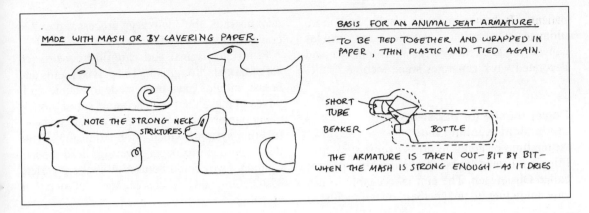

Figure 8.9 *Animal seats for children*

make your seat look like an animal. Decorating completes the process.

**Note**: It is much easier to make the seat by layering four layered strips of paper instead of mash. If you use mash only, make animal seats when the weather is fairly good for drying. Nevertheless, mash seats, when finished, are as good as paper-layered articles, except they may be attacked by weevils in some environments.

## Layering paper over clay models

See Chapter Three: Third approach to paper layering. This can be done to make, for example little people, animals, farm and home articles for imaginative play.

Let us say again that because of the simplicity of layering paper over clay, the widespread ability of people, and children in particular, to mould clay articles, and because of the nature and quality of the articles that can be made, at no expense, layering paper over clay is a technique that should be used much more than it is. See Chapter Two for information on how to layer over clay, but note:

● In this method the clay figure does not remains strong inside the paper. It may break into several pieces. However, the clay model provided the shape for the first layering and remained inside to give a solid base for the paper. Eventually, it is a paper-made article that you create. Ensure your layering covers every part of the figure in order to make a complete and strong shell around the clay

● Layering, especially the first few courses of it, must be done with the smallest possible pieces of paper (assuming that the model is a small one)

● Some clay models need sticks to support certain parts, such as neck, legs, and so on. This is an advantage when it comes to layering the first courses on to the clay

● This is creative layering. The characteristics of the creature do not come automatically from layering over the clay, you have to recreate them by your layering, and

● Children like to play with things that can stand by themselves. Persevere, even if it means making feet extra large or adding a stand, until your little people and animals can stand by themselves.

## In the context of rehabilitation

You will have identified in this chapter several articles that would be useful in rehabilitation situations. Animal seats, for instance, could be modified for use by a child who needs to sit astride something in a certain position. The seats can be fitted with wheels. Adapting tools or other utensils to help a child grip has been mentioned in chapter two.

### As therapy

Moulding mash, like moulding clay, can be very relaxing and therefore therapeutic. It stimulates creativity and has been found to be a useful activity for retarded and mentally ill patients. Moulding paper presents more of a challenge and is suitable for more confident

119

patients. It brings quicker results and more ultimate satisfaction as quite large articles can be made in this way. Well-finished and decorated work generates some income.

## Papier mâché (or paper-layered) anatomical teaching aids

At the time of going to press exciting possibilities in this area are being explored in a project called Obsteteach. The aim is to enable health care midwives to make their own models to demonstrate the delivery process, possible complications and aftercare.

From an original and carefully constructed set of models, comprising the pelvis, foetus and breast, moulds have been made to enable midwives to make their own accurate set of models using papier mâché or paper layers. If successful, this system (which is an extension of the third approach to paper layering, described in Chapter Two) could be used to make a variety of teaching aids where accuracy of detail is essential.

# Chapter Nine: for play and early learning (3). Dolls' houses and early learning apparatus

## Dolls' houses

These are realistic little houses with one or more rooms housing furniture and little people for young children (not infants) to play with. Without their contents the houses are of little interest to children.

Two types of dolls' houses are described: type A, which is a box with a front that can be removed and high walls; and type B, which is a box with a roof or ceiling that can be removed and low walls.

Parents, teachers or elder brothers and sisters are likely to make these houses and they will know what detail they are prepared to include. For example will there be hinged doors or just doorways, one room or eight, curtains and lights? Box-building technology has already been dealt with (see Chapter Four: Utility approach three). The points that follow refer especially to dolls' houses and to details which otherwise might be overlooked.

Key elements in the design of dolls' houses are that:

- The house must be strong. Children will lean, even sit, on it
- It must be slightly heavy. If it is too light a small knock could upset furniture
- It must be squarely built with flat floors, or items will not stand straight in it
- Children must be able to see and have enough room to put their hands into the rooms without knocking things over. For these reasons the walls of a type A house should be higher than normal and the walls of a type B house should be low
- The edges must be strongly bound and the front or top of the house, where the front wall or the ceiling (roof) will fit, must be level, and
- The rooms must not be too small. Better to have fewer larger rooms than many small ones.

When building the dolls' house:

- Build it up from carefully cut boards following the usual system (see Figure 4.23)
- Use two-layered corrugated card (more card will be added when fixing the parts together)
- Plan the house carefully
- If possible, mark the doors and windows. Cut some before you assemble the house, if it does not weaken the boards too much
- Doorways are essential. A front door (hinged) is also necessary. Hinges for doors do not have to be very sophisticated. The doors will not be opened and closed very frequently. It will be sufficient for most doors if the hinges are made just by cutting away a little of the card facing where the hinge will come and crushing and bending the carton to make a hinge. For the front door if the above system is not good enough make a cloth hinge (see Chapter Five: Music stand)
- Use angle pieces of thin card for all joins. If possible, measure each piece so that it covers the floor and wall until it meets another piece. This avoids unevenness, and
- A roof looks nice, but a gable roof is an expensive luxury and can be a nuisance. Close type B with a strong flat roof or just a ceiling. Both kinds of closing boards (front or ceiling) need to be held in place. The system shown in Figure 9.1 is simple and effective. Closing boards should fit against the outside walls (or the top edges of them) and not be held between them. Strong small blocks should be fitted to two opposite ends of the inside of the closing board so that when the front or roof is closed the blocks just touch the walls. Pierce holes through the walls and into the blocks so that a wooden peg can be pushed through the wall into the block to hold the board in position.

Furniture must not be too light. The method recommended for making it is to make the

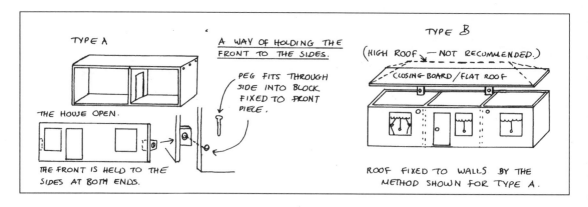

Figure 9.1 *Two types of dolls' houses*

articles in clay and layer them over with paper (see Chapter Two: Second approach to layering, layering over clay articles and the end of Chapter Eight). Little people (dolls) need to be a bit flexible, so they are often made by layering over an armature of knotted string.

**Note:** it may seem easy, but it is, in fact, very difficult and unsatisfactory to convert a ready-made carton into a dolls' house.

### Small or medium-sized buildings with closed windows and doors for creative play made by modelling card

This section describes how strong wood-like but light buildings for farm or home play can be made by modelling them in thin card (or carton in the case of larger models), strengthening them with more card, if required, and strong paper layering (see Figure 9.2).

Card modelling requires the ability to work accurately. Making one house properly takes time. This may not always be a disadvantage. In a well-organized group where the relative size of buildings, and so on, can be controlled, it can make an exciting group project. But for a serious and accurate plan, say of a new school project, it would probably be better to construct the buildings on templates of carton card and build them up with carton layers, or polystyr-

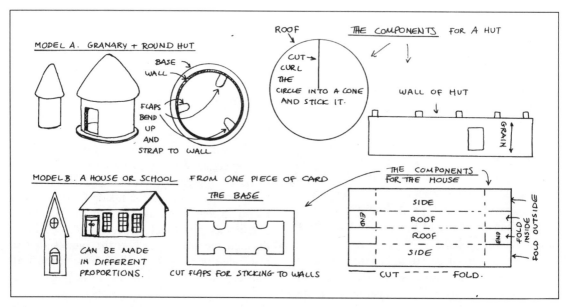

Figure 9.2 *Small buildings for play* (models A and B)

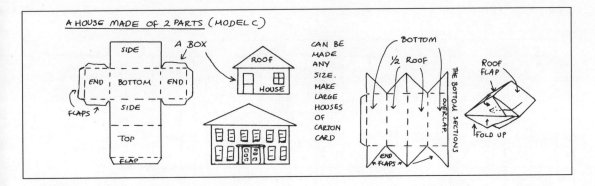

Figure 9.3 *A house made of two parts (model C)*

ene, then layer them over and stick them in position on the ground-plan board.

Three simple plans are offered, each involving bending or folding card. Each plan can be modified by the positions of the folds. Each can be made small or medium to large in size. Carton card should be used for large buildings. They all need strong card bases. In some models, a floor is incorporated in the initial building. For medium-sized buildings the base should be made of carton card.

Refer back to Chapter One: Cutting and folding. Also, go back to Chapter Two: First approach to paper layering, layering over a weak or unwanted article, for building and strengthening techniques.

In models A and B the base, although made separately, is essential. It is the floor of the house and holds the walls in place.

Construction details for model A are:

● The shape of the roof depends on how you cut and curl your card. Expect and control a slight problem as you curl the card. Because of the grain direction it will not curl evenly or stay the right shape to begin with
● Fitting the walls by flaps to the roof is a bit tricky. Invert the roof cone in a tin. Have some very sticky strapping to hold the flaps firm. Let it dry before proceeding to the next step
● Fit the walls to the base by flaps cut in the base which stick to the inside walls. Stand the house, very round, on the base. Mark on the base the outline of, say, three flaps that will be cut, and where they will be bent up. The size of the flaps must be such that the hole they make in the base will allow your finger to go through it, and

● Cut the flaps and paste them to the wall, pinching them between your fingers (inside) and thumb (outside).

Model B is the simplest model to make. By adjusting the widths of wall and roof, buildings of different sizes and proportions can be made. The roof, which finishes where it is folded to make the wall, does not look good. It can be made to project by pasting a rectangle of carton card cut to the right shape and size, on to each of its sides. Do this after you have strengthened the house a bit. Fix the base as for model A.

To construct model C:

● First, join and strap firmly the bottom, ends and sides. Pinch the corners to keep the box square. Fill the box with soft paper before you join the top so that when you want to press things the box has some padding inside to make it more solid
● Make the house's roof. There are other ways of making gable roofs but the model illustrated in Figure 9.3 makes a strong roof from one piece of card. Pinch along all folds to make it a good shape. Join the roof by the bottom flap and the flaps at one end. Put some soft paper inside the roof unit and then close the opposite end
● Join the roof to the box. This should not be a problem, and
● Strengthen the buildings very thoroughly, working in at least two stages with drying in between.

## Coloured shapes for play

Much early learning consists of playing with shapes of different sizes and colours, by

123

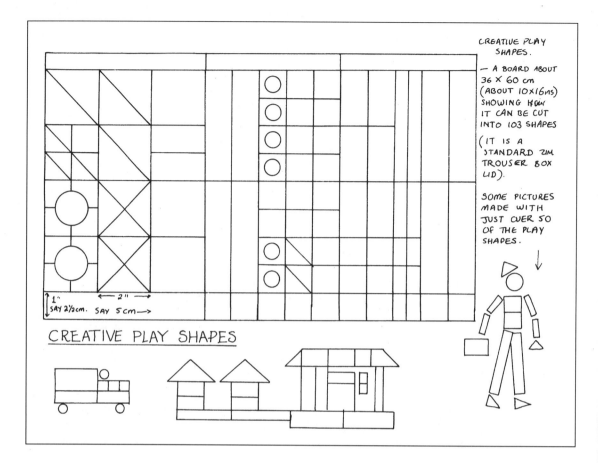

CREATIVE PLAY SHAPES.

— A BOARD ABOUT 36 X 60 cm (ABOUT 10X16ins) SHOWING HOW IT CAN BE CUT INTO 103 SHAPES

(IT IS A STANDARD 2IM TROUSER BOX LID).

SOME PICTURES MADE WITH JUST OVER 50 OF THE PLAY SHAPES.

1" SAY 2½cm.   ← 2" → SAY 5cm →

CREATIVE PLAY SHAPES

Figure 9.4 *Creative play shapes*

placing or fitting them together. APT makes such shapes, but to be of use large numbers are needed. Each shape must be cut, bound and decorated on several sides as well as on both its surfaces.

The work involved in making these shapes is considerable. Much time can be saved or wasted according to how you organize the work, for example, the planning of how the shapes will be cut. One long cut can give sharp sides to ten or more shapes as Figure 9.4 shows.

Flat shapes are made from laminated boards and should be as accurate as possible. For some apparatus they need to be almost perfect. The best board is made from thin card, say six to eight layers of shoe box card. Shapes cut from such boards have hard sharp edges and do not lose their shape when layered over, but they are extremely hard to cut. Therefore, the shapes are often made the quicker and easier way, from

laminated sandwich board with one or two thin cards each side of one, two or three carton cards according to the thickness desired.

The shapes must be very tidy before binding. They must not have a lot of binding, but it must be carefully done so that they finish as neat shapes with straight edges. Plan your binding efficiently, for example, decorate similar shapes at one time. Work out the best way of tearing your paper for covering that shape and tear several pieces together.

Finally, press the shapes between two flat surfaces and decorate with brightly coloured papers.

## Examples of apparatus made from coloured shapes

### Sets of shapes for creative play

Some play shapes apparatus, although it looks impressive to adults and attractive to children, actually holds children's attention for no more than two minutes. Creative play shapes are an

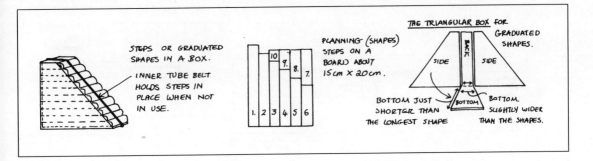

Figure 9.5 *Graduated shapes in a box*

exception. At first, children need to be shown ways of using the shapes. After that, if there are plenty of well-made shapes and a group is playing together, the youngsters get quite absorbed. Figure 9.4 shows how the shapes can be used to make pictures. Older children also enjoy using them making geometrical patterns.

Figure 9.4 illustrates how one board of about 36 x 60cm (10 x 16in) can be planned and cut into more than 100 useful shapes.

**Note:** with all shapes apparatus (and puzzles) if a piece is lost do not abandon the whole thing. Make a replacement shape.

### Graduated shapes in a triangular box (steps)

For these steps:

● Make a strong board big enough for all the box parts. Do not cut it yet
● Decide the size of the biggest step you want. Knowing that each step should be a regular measure (say 1cm) shorter than the one below it, work out how many steps you will make (at least ten) and plan (actually draw) them on a piece of thin card.
● Use this piece as the top card of your board. Laminate the board which could be a sandwich of two carton cards with the templates on top
● When the steps board is dry cut out the steps. Test them for accuracy. Correct them if necessary
● Bind, strengthen, tidy and decorate, and
● Make the box so the steps fit into it a little bit loosely, and the ends of the steps just stick out. Correct the steps or box as necessary.

**Note:** when the steps are not being used hold them in the box in order by a belt of car-tyre elastic (Figure 9.5).

### Squares on a pole (i.e. peg)

This is a building game for children. Square shapes of decreasing size are stacked on a pole (see Figure 9.6).

Key elements in the design and construction of this game follow:

● Unless there are at least seven squares the game will not be very useful for a normal child
● Plan everything first. Decide the size of the smallest square that can have a big hole in the middle. Draw on a card-measure the lengths of the sides of the other squares you will make each, say 1cm bigger than the other
● Make the parts. Draw shapes accurately (and so save unnecessary cutting) on a template of thin card
● Make a sandwich board as for the steps (see Figure 9.5) with your template on top
● Make a stronger and thicker board for the base, 1cm bigger than the largest square
● Roll a very strong peg at least 1cm in diameter
● When the base board is quite dry make a hole right in the centre. Fit the peg tight and straight so that the end can be opened and strapped to the underside of the board (see Chapter Five: Lampstand, fitting the pillar). Add card underneath as necessary to make the board stand flat
● When the squares board is quite dry cut out all the squares very accurately making their sides quite perpendicular. Pile them in their order. Correct them if necessary. Bind the edges
● Strengthen the squares all over by layering

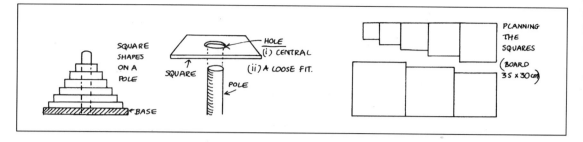

Figure 9.6 *Squares on a pole (peg)*

paper over them. Decorate with bright contrasting colours, still checking their shapes and sizes
• Making the holes requires much care. The holes must be dead centre and the squares should fit slightly loosely on the pole. Cut the hole so that it just fits over the pole, then see on what sides adjustment is needed. Make the adjustment by rubbing with a stick the side of the hole that needs to be enlarged. Bind the base sides tidily. Layer the base all over with decorating paper.
• Wrap the pole in a thin tidy coat of plastic. Tidy your holes again with the tool and see that all decorating paper is stuck down tight near the holes. Place the squares in order on the pole with a thin sheet of plastic separating each one from the next. Dry them like that for a time, twisting each square a little now and then. Finish the drying with the squares separated, and
• Cut the pole so that it projects only about 10mm beyond the top square. Make the top round. Layer over it.

### Shapes that fit into spaces on a board
The technique described is very simple but effective. It can also be used to make a simple picture frame or tray. The board is made up of two boards, which are only joined in the last step. They are made, tidied and decorated separately, and the shapes are actually cut out of the top board, tidied and fitted before the boards are joined.

The advantages of this procedure are two-fold: ease of working – it is so easy to bind edges when you can hold the frame in your hand and get at both sides of it; and efficiency – edges that will not come unstuck are vital for the success of the apparatus where pieces have to be pushed in and pulled out. Edges made by

this method are well-made and can be thoroughly checked before the boards are put together (Figure 9.7).

To make the shapes into spaces apparatus first plan the items. Think of the children. how many shapes will make a suitable game for them? What kind of shapes will appeal and be suitable for them? They could be objects like bananas, oranges, pumpkins, and so on and do not have to be geometrical shapes. There should be at least 10 shapes, preferably 16, otherwise the game is too easy for a normal child.

Use the following method to make the shapes into spaces apparatus (letters in brackets refer to Figure 9.7):

• Decide on the shape and size of the board you want. Make a thin card template of it. Decide the shapes you want. Cut them out in paper. Arrange them on the template leaving plenty of room between them. When you are satisfied stick them down (a)
• Make the two boards (sandwich boards as in the squares on a pole example). Use your template as the top card on what will be the top board (b)
• Tidy and decorate the bottom board with an overall colour (c) as it is visible at the bottom of the holes for the spaces, then put it aside
• Calculate and then cut out the shapes from the top board. The shapes you cut and the holes you make as you take out the shapes have to be tidied and bound, which will fatten them. To make them fit, either the holes must be cut bigger or the shapes made smaller. Look at the board to see if there is room to make the holes, or some of them bigger. Look at the shapes and see which ones could be made smaller and decide what you are going to do for each shape. Then draw a line either 3mm

126

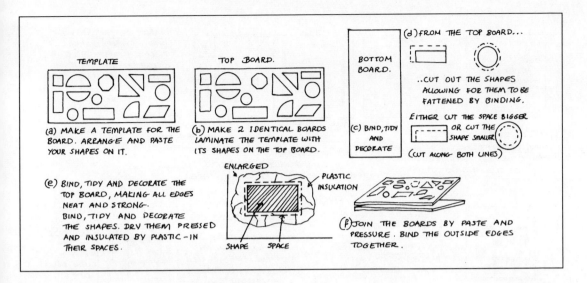

Figure 9.7 *Shapes in spaces apparatus*

outside the hole outline or 3mm inside the shapes. Start with one shape. Take a very sharp knife. Cut along both lines and take out the pieces (d)

● Tidy the hole sides and decorate them with the paper you will use to decorate the top. Strengthen and tidy, bind and decorate the shape all over. When it is finished it must fit loosely in the hole and be taller than the top board so children's fingers can pick it up easily. Try it, with plastic in between, in its hole. When you have got it right press it under a weight in its hole separated by plastic (e)

● Using the experience you have gained cut out, tidy and decorate all the rest and finish by decorating the top board, and

● Join the two boards with paste under the top board and binding around the sides (f). Press under plastic with a weighted board on top.

## Jigsaw puzzles in frames

The frames help children to do their puzzles and help take care of the pieces. The puzzle described here is a simple puzzle of a few rectangular pieces. The method is basically the same as for the shapes in spaces example, but there are some special techniques needed because of the picture.

To make a framed jigsaw:

● Find a suitable picture, that is one that will interest children and with clear detail in it that they can recognize

● The picture dictates the boards' size. Make them at least 8cm wider than the picture on all four sides. Make the boards. Tidy and decorate the bottom board and put it aside

● Straighten, bind and tidy the edges of the top board

● Place the picture in the centre of the top board and draw around it. Draw a second line 6mm outside the first line all the way around. This is to allow for the fattening of the frame and of all the puzzle pieces. Cut out the central piece (the picture board) then cut along the other line and take out the pieces to enlarge the frame

● Bind, strengthen, tidy and decorate the frame using a colour that suits the picture

● Now, work on the picture board. Draw lines to divide it accurately into a suitable number of equal pieces. Mark each piece with numbers in sequence. Turn the board over. Mark the back with the same numbers each exactly opposite the number on the top. Do not layer over the bottom numbers

● Cut the picture board into pieces, accurately following the lines. Bind and tidy each piece, keeping the top surface flat

● Rearrange the pieces in the frame according to their numbers. Fatten or reduce them so that they fit loosely in the frame

● Paste the frame underneath. Place it on the bottom board. Bind its outside edges and leave

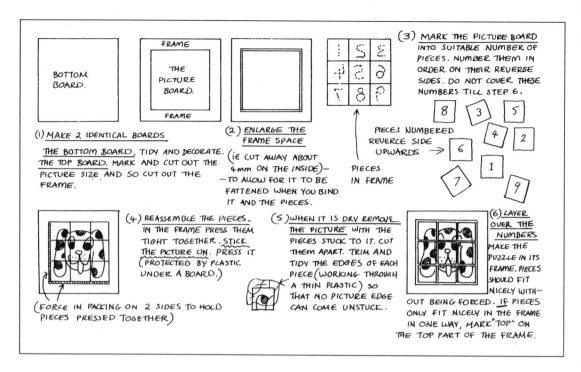

Figure 9.8 *A jigsaw puzzle that fits into a frame*

it pressed to dry for some time, with or without the pieces on it

● Paste the picture on to the pieces. Do this when the frame is completely dry. Place the pieces in the frame in position. Press some very narrow pieces of hard card into the frame to force all the pieces close together

● Paste the picture on both sides. Leave it to stretch between pasted plastic for some minutes. Lay the picture in position on the pieces, pressing it through the plastic. Leave it to dry

● When the picture is firmly stuck, remove it from the frame with the pieces stuck to it, and, with a very sharp knife, cut the picture neatly into its pieces, following the lines

● Layer over the numbers at the back of each piece

● Finally, stick the edges of each piece of the picture down firmly so they will not come unstuck. Take care not to damage the picture surface. A good method is to put paste under all the loose edges, to tear a little into all the corners, and then to put the piece inside a thin transparent plastic bag to work on it, pressing it, and leaving it for a while with the plastic

wrapping the picture edges close around the sides

● If you have not been quite accurate you may find that the picture only fits properly in the frame when it is the right way up, in which case mark the top in some way to help children not to force pieces in

● If you are making a collection of pictures for a group of children make them all in frames the same size so they can be kept, the pieces in place and the frames strapped in a pile, with a card lid over the top one.

## Building blocks

It is an advantage if the blocks are not too heavy and also not too light. APT building blocks are ideal in this respect. They are also made mainly of APT rubbish, that is of pieces of carton cards too small to use in other ways, and which do not make good mash.

Building blocks are really three-dimensional creative play shapes. Like the flat shapes described in the jigsaw example they are excellent apparatus. With encouragement, children in groups can play with them for a long time. But there must be plenty of them. Therefore,

128

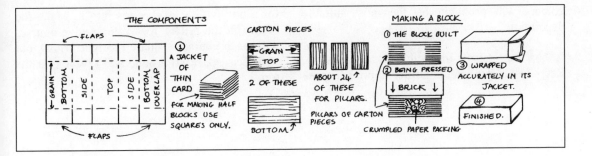

Figure 9.9 *Building blocks made of carton waste pieces and a quarter sheet of thin card*

they are best made by a group of workers. An ideal situation would be for a school class to make them for their younger brothers and sisters' play school.

Key elements in the design of building blocks are:

• The blocks consist of one or two carton cards (grain lengthwise) for a base, a rectangular pillar of carton scraps at each end, one or two top cards, paper stuffing between the pillars to give support, and a standard-size jacket of thin card which wraps the carton structure into a tidy uniform-sized block

• An ideal set of blocks will include some half bricks (made in the same way) and one or two beams (that is long pieces the width of a brick but made of three or four layers of carton card), and

• Whole bricks will, as far as possible, be all the same size and two half bricks equal to one whole brick.

A description of how to make a standard block follows:

• Think and plan first. Blocks are only useful if there are plenty of them and they are the same height and width and of only two different lengths. They have to be made by factory-style methods, so plan and make your first block with this in mind. Correct the system as you work so it is right for mass production, by you or anyone else

• Decide on the finished dimensions of your block and make a jacket of thin card to the pattern shown in Figure 9.9, but with your measurements. Make and keep a copy of it

• Cut the carton as follows – two or four cards for top and bottom like the jacket bottom, but perhaps 2mm smaller with the grain lengthwise. Then, cut a large number of pillar cards; width and pipes are not very important but they should be as long as the width of the top card (not longer)

• Place the bottom card(s) on the table. Avoid pasting the middle area

• Build up a pillar of the small pieces at each end until it is a third higher than the finished block height. Work quickly pasting the pieces with your hands as you build the pillars

• Place the top cards on the pillars

• Tidy the outside edges of the pillars to make the carcass the right shape

• Place a brick on it, balancing it carefully. Press it down slightly and leave it pressing for four or five minutes. Press it down further if necessary to reduce the carcass to the right height for the jacket

• Remove the brick. Encircle the ends where the pillars are with long strips of strong pasted paper. Stuff crumpled soft paper into the carcass between the pillars

• Place the jacket on the table, paste it on the top surface only

• Wrap the carcass in it, further correcting its shape by any means you like as you do so. Finish with a solid, tidy, correctly shaped block. To help you achieve this you may decide to tear off one or two of the end flaps. You will also need to press the sides flat and pinch along the angles to make them sharp. A rounded block is useless for building

• Layer all over with strong paper. Somehow maintain its correct shape until it is dry, and

• Decorate attractively. Very large amounts of colour will be needed. Different earth

129

colours will probably be the most suitable decoration.

A box for storing the bricks is a necessity. Refer to Chapter Four: Utility approach three for a box with a lid that fits into it. Make the box to fit the bricks, for example, five courses with each course a square of eight bricks, but with 2cm space all around and say 5cm at the top.

# Chapter 10: APT solarware. Making cookers, fruit dryers and hot boxes from corrugated card and junk car glass.

## Using APT solarware and recipes

The topic of APT solarware is specialized. Therefore, a separate chapter is devoted to it. Making the solarware described here requires no new skills, although some techniques are modified slightly.

APT solarware is probably unknown to most readers. To use it effectively requires understanding and the ability to adapt to unconventional ways of food processing and cooking. Therefore, the second part of this chapter describes ways of using APT solarware effectively, without knowledge of which you may contravene the second rule of APT and produce an APT article that is not useful.

The terms solar oven or cooker are used interchangeably. A water heater is a cooker adapted to accommodate water containers. A fruit dryer is a ventilated cooker with a movable single glass top.

Although APT solarware is marvellously useful it demands attention during the day. Stoves must be turned to follow the sun. At the first onset of rain and at nightfall they must be protected by a covering of plastic. A clear plastic cover may be left permanently on the stove. You cannot just go out all day and leave your slow cooker to look after itself.

## Solar ovens and heat conservation

Solar ovens embody the principles of heat conservation. The ovens are boxes with glass tops, constructed and decorated to receive and conserve maximum heat from the sun.

Solar ovens catch the sun because:

● They have glass tops which must be kept clean
● The top is set at the most effective sun-catching angle (which varies according to latitude), and
● The stove is rotated to follow the sun.

Solar ovens conserve the sun's heat because:

● They are absolutely air-tight
● The walls and bottom of the box are made of very thick carton card
● The little pipes of imprisoned air in the card help to make them heat-proof. The heat cannot escape
● The top consists of two layers of glass with about 1cm between them so they also hold air motionless and let very little heat through
● The walls and bottom of the box are lined with black paper, and, if it is available, with film wrapping paper that is black on one side and aluminium coated on the other. The effect

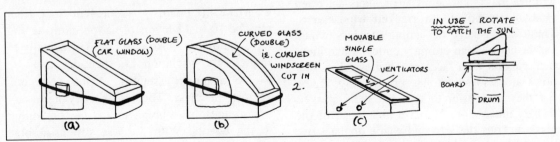

Figure 10.1 *Cookers or water heater (a and b) and a dryer (c)*

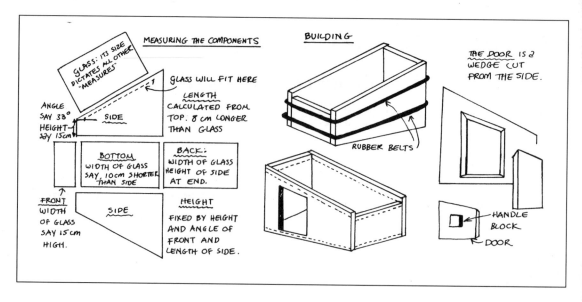

Figure 10.2  *An APT cooker or water heater*

of the black is to absorb the heat while the aluminium reflects what has been absorbed

● The door is a tightly fitting bung, held in place by an elastic strap, and

● One or two pieces of metal, for example flattened tin which is painted black, are used as hot plates either on the stove floor or as shelves that lift containers into the hottest area of the stove.

## Making a solar oven

The following are not step-by-step instructions. They should make your objectives clear and enable you to carry out the various processes in the order and way that seems right in your case. (Refer to Chapter One: 18 and Chapter Four: Utility approach three, boxes.)

First, get two pieces of glass as nearly the same size as possible. Old cars are the best source of supply. The glass, unlike normal window glass, is tough. Car breakers are often glad to get rid of old cracked windscreens. These are usually of laminated glass which can be cut with an ordinary cutter. Make identical cuts on both faces of the glass. Car windows are also sometimes given away. Being flat they are easier to use, but their glass is usually uncuttable. The size and shape of the glass dictates the size and shape of the stove you can make, which can lead to some odd-shaped but still efficient cookers.

Make templates for the sides and bottom of the box in the following order:

● The two sides – take a fairly long piece of card. At one end mark the height of the front (about 12 to 15cm). At that point draw a line about 33° from the horizontal to mark the angle at the top. To mark its length lay an edge of your (shorter) piece of glass along that top edge and add another 8cm to it. From that point you can drop a perpendicular to the bottom edge to mark the length and shape of the side pieces

● The bottom piece – make it the width of the glass, and about 8cm shorter than the side pieces. The bottom will be enclosed by four sides

● The front and back pieces – these will be he same width as the bottom and will get their respective heights from the two ends of the side pieces

● Make the boards – about 4cm thick (that may be 10 to 12 layers of carton card). If you have the option make pipes run horizontally to improve the insulation. Let them dry, and

● Do a mock assembly testing your box against the glass. Then, make any necessary adjustments by rubbing or cutting or adding to the boards. With the box still assembled decide which side the door will be and plan the door. If it will not weaken the board you could cut it now. Otherwise cut it when the box has been properly assembled.

Specifications for the door are: edges cut at an angle, to fit tight (wedged); near the back; and near or level with the bottom (to facilitate cleaning) and as high and as wide as possible (to accommodate tall bottles and wide pots). Corners may be angular or round.

*Making the oven door*
Make the oven door now or later. To construct the door:

• Cut the door out in one piece as cleanly as possible. Do this only when the board is really dry. Use any suitable tool that you can find, a thin saw knife or a pruning saw is ideal
• Paste the cut edges of the door and the hole. Rub them smooth with a rough tool, for example with a stone. Lay some soft slightly pasted paper on the edges, all around, to provide padding. Then, layer them and bind strongly with paper, building edges up where necessary to make them fit
• Wrap the door in a thin plastic bag, lay some more plastic around the hole. Then, force the door into its proper position and leave it pressed in that position for some time
• When convenient remove the door and dry it and the hole, exposed to the air. Replace the door later on so that it dries with a perfect fit
• The door handle is a block of carton tied and then strapped in place in the centre of the door. It serves two purposes because it is a handle and the elastic belt that encircles the stove passes over the handle which holds the door pressed into the hole. Therefore, the handle should be conveniently large.

**Note:** before you finally assemble the stove decide how you are going to fit the pieces of glass, that is will they fit into grooves or be held pressed against the sides of the stoves? Read on for details.

*Fitting the oven glass*
This is the most crucial part of stove-making. The process is explained at this point because some of it may be done at this stage, some during assembling and some after. Instructions are in general terms. You will have to interpret them to suit your stove which may have flat or curved glasses and be rectangular or trapezium-shaped according to the shape of the glass you have.

Specifications for fitting the pieces of glass follow:

• The smaller glass, if one is smaller, is the bottom piece
• Glass must be held quite firm as the fitting must be leakproof
• The ideal space between the glasses is 8 to 10mm all over, but this accuracy is not usually possible. If the glasses are two halves of the same windscreen they may almost touch at one corner and be nearly 20mm apart at the opposite corner, and
• The sides must finally be higher than the glass all round so that if a large object is placed on the stove, or if the stove is turned upside down (and it will be as it is made) the glass will not be touched.

Two alternative methods are used to fit the glass. Either very narrow grooves are cut and rubbed with a pasted tool and the glass is fitted into them, or the stove is assembled so that it tightly holds the glasses at certain points. In both these methods crushed tubes of pasted paper (paper putty) are pressed in along the angles where the glass joins the stove side, below and above the glass. The stove must be made leakproof on both sides of both glasses.

Two other devices are sometimes used to supplement these methods. First, at two or more points edges of the glass may be rested on or let in to the top of the stove wall which is then built up to enclose and overlap the glass. This applies particularly to the top glass. Second, where there is a corner of the stove which it is difficult to cover with one or both the glasses, the walls near the corner are built up from below, even from the bottom if desired, to close the gap and support the glass. The building up does not need to be very strong. It can be done with crumpled paper layered over or with layers of corrugated card.

When you have made all the preparations and are satisfied with your mock assembly, paste all the joining parts and assemble the stove. The order in which you do the operations is for you to decide, but on the whole, the sooner you can get one glass (at least tempora-

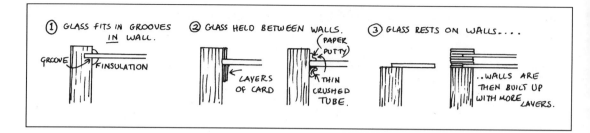

Figure 10.3 *Three ways of fitting the glass*

rily) in place, the better. With the glass in, the stove is stable and can be pressed, turned on its side, and so on, with no fear.

Construct the oven as follows:

● Hold the walls tight together by strong elastic belts, or by whole nylon stocking
● Plug all corners and any gaps with slightly pasted soft paper
● Strengthen all joins, outside and in, with angle pieces wrapped around or pressed tight in all joins
● Make and fit the door (if not done already)
● Colour all the inside of the stove black, by applying a layer of black card or strips of black paper or soot paint. Make the inside of the door black
● Fit the glasses. If possible, leave a small stick, say 5mm diameter, between the glasses at the top corners which, when removed, will leave air holes between the glasses. Also ensure that the top surface of the bottom glass and the bottom of the top glass are perfectly clean before they are assembled. Once in place the surfaces between them cannot be cleaned again

● Tidy the stove. Strengthen all over the outside with at least two layers of strong paper
● Drying may take two or three days. It should be done in the shade. The door must be left open. For a day or two there will be steam condensing between the glasses. The little stick referred to above is withdrawn to leave an air hole or small holes must be pierced from outside at the top into the space between the glasses. The holes must be closed when the stove is quite finished and has dried in the sun for a few days.

## Water heaters

Water heaters and cookers are made in the same way, but the water heater is a larger and designed to hold and expose to the sun a number of water containers. The door needs to be large and in some cases, for example if your vessel is a 20-litre drum, it has to be specially shaped.

In most water heaters a back high shelf is needed to lift the back row of containers as high as possible. This shelf could be made as part of the stove. However, there is one danger in water heaters, which is that more than in any other stove leaks and spills are likely. A built-

Figure 10.4 *Water heaters*

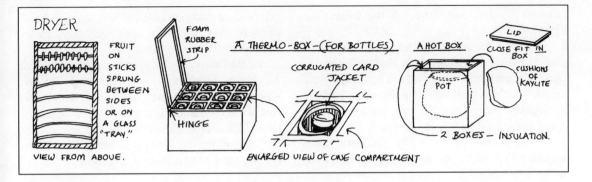

Figure 10.5 *Dryer (a) and Heat- or cold-conserving boxes (b)*

in shelf has to be very strong to prevent its surface becoming uneven.

A water heater should be as efficient as a cooker but because of its large size it heats up more slowly, and because of the amount of water it has to heat it does not normally heat it to boiling point.

## Fruit dryers

A fruit/vegetable/meat/fish dryer must not get too hot and must have air moving through it. Therefore, an APT dryer differs from a cooker in the following respects (although it can be used as a cooker on hot sunny days):

● Its walls are only about 2cm thick
● It has only one glass, which is movable
● It has ventilation holes at the bottom that can be closed, and
● It does not need a door (but some people like their dryer to have a door so they can use their dryer as a second-class cooker if necessary).

Details of modifications for dryers are:

● The loose glass – plan this so it rests on and completely covers the top, so insects do not get in at night. Also plan the glass so it can slide open (sideways or at an angle) for ventilation and be completely removed to put things in and out. The simplest plan is to make ridges around the bottom and one side of the stove to prevent the glass from falling off, and to have a device for lifting and wedging open the top edge. Because the top of the box is not held firmly by two fixed glasses (as it is in stoves), be sure that your box is really strong at all its corners
● Ventilation holes – should be right at the bottom, preferably one or two on each side; the size of a cream carton so that you can use a cream carton as a bung, and
● Drying rod ridge – drying rods are often just bent and sprung between the two sides, but it is better to build one or two ridges on each side and parallel to the bottom, so rods can rest on them as well.

## Thermo boxes, hot boxes and cold boxes

Thermo boxes keep water hot. Hot boxes keep food hot. Cold boxes keep food cold. They work on the same principles as the stoves in that they do not let heat out. However, in these boxes the heat is in the food in the containers and does not come directly from the sun.

A further difference is that whereas in stoves we try to keep the heat in the stove itself, in the boxes we try to keep the heat right there in the food inside the containers and prevent it from even getting into the boxes. Nevertheless, the boxes are heatproofed.

The aim of the boxes is to keep the contents as hot as possible for as long as possible. Indeed, water kept in a well-made thermo box, if it is put in almost boiling, is still warm the next morning. Unlike the stoves, the more hot bottles the thermo box has put into it the better it will work.

*Thermo box for bottles*
This box uses corrugated card to retain heat. To make it:

● Plan a conveniently sized box, for example to hold four rows of three bottles. Compartments are approximately one-third larger than a bottle. Make the box with corrugated card

135

(carton) dividers joined by halving joints (see Figure 4.4 )

- In each compartment fit a roll of corrugated card (card on one side only) that will form a jacket for each bottle to fit into. The jacket itself should fit closely into its compartment, and
- Make a lid from about four layers of laminated card to fit closely into the box top. Hinge it if desired (see Figure 4.24). Strips of foam rubber attached to its lower edges can help make a heatproof fit.

*Thermo box for cans*
Make this in the same way as the box for bottles. Adapt the compartments to accommodate cans.

*Hot box (for food)*
It is better if the box is made as heatproof as possible, although the main components are the cushions. The cushions must be large enough so that the bottom one can be made into a nest in which the pot sits, and the top one cover the pot's top and sides.

The best filling is Kaylite, broken into the smallest possible pieces to make crumbs or powdered into snow (the commercial product). Crumbs are probably best made by breaking odd pieces of Kaylite with the fingers. Other methods seem to spread crumbs everywhere. If Kaylite cannot be found, straw or wood shavings or crumpled paper, or even newspaper or cement bag wrapped thickly round the pot without being made into a cushion, will work quite well. A blanket could also be used.

Plan for an insulated box by making two boxes. One must be large enough to hold the pot and the cushions. The other should be about 4cm bigger all around than the smaller one, and a little bit taller. The smaller box fits inside the bigger box, resting on and pasted to its bottom, but with a space around it. Fill the space with insulating material (as for the cushion above).

Heat tends to escape mostly from the top the box. Make a lid that fits well into or over the box (see Chapter Four: Lids). A carton card lid, for example four layers thick, would be suitable if the food inside is also insulated.

To use a hot box efficiently, the containers should be removed from the stove when they are boiling and put quickly and without being opened into the box and the box closed immediately.

An alternative and less efficient way of using Kaylite cushions is to stuff them into the stove where the food is, and to try to wrap them round the container. It improves heat conservation if the cushions and boxes are warmed by the sun before the containers are put into them (or for cold boxes, if they are cooled).

*Cold box*
There is no difference, theoretically, between a hot box and a cold box. Both are made to maintain temperatures. However, there is a practical problem. Cold items are likely to cause moisture, even liquid inside the box. Such items should be made quite safe by being wrapped in strong plastic bags.

## Accessories for APT solarware

### Turning bases
The stove must not rest on damp ground. It must be raised. A 40-gallon drum is an excellent base. However, stoves, especially if they are full of water bottles, must not stand on sharp drum edges or small bases that only support in the middle. They should be set on flat boards that rest on the base. Two stoves can share a board, provided the doors are on opposite sides. It will probably then be found that the board, and not just the stove is the item that turns on the base.

### Hotplates
These are used for cookers and water heaters. They can be flattened rectangles of tin from large cans, painted black and laid as the floor of the stove or on the shelves.

### Stove blocks
Rectangular closed boxes, for example made of carton card, stuffed with paper, strengthened and layered over with black paper, to hold hot plates or containers as high as possible in the stove.

### Reflectors
Large reflectors, made from tin foil on strong cardboard boards, outside the stoves proved to be a lot of trouble in windy or wet weather, and

when the stove had to be turned that the author no longer uses them. However, recent experiments have shown that an octagonal reflector, its boards set outwards at 60°, placed on the stove and directed at the sun, collects much heat, very rapidly. Small reflectors, cut from the shiny tin of 5-litre oil drums, can be bent to shape to form a reflector that stands against the back, behind cooking bottles and jars, and seems to increase the heat a little.

### Cooking containers

Cooking pots black on the outside heat up very quickly and are excellent for stewing. Transparent glass containers, jars for stewing and wine bottles for water are extensively used and have three advantages. They heat up very quickly, take up relatively little floor space, and you can see what is happening to their contents as they cook.

Cans and drums hold more water but are difficult to handle. They may damage the stoves by spills and leaks and by their weight.

Whenever possible, containers should be filled almost to the top. For small amounts use small containers. Reasons are that on the one hand, since heat goes upwards, the top part of the container gets hottest, but if it is empty much of that heat will get lost. On the other hand, liquids expand as they are heated and containers filled to the brim will spill over long before they boil.

### Equipment for dryers: rods (sticks) to hold fruit; glass bottom for the dryer; and dried fruit containers

The rods must be springy so they are held between the dryer's sides. Bamboo is ideal. A piece of glass, such as a car window, to rest on the bottom or on blocks and to hold fruit that cannot be hung is useful. Screwtop jars or plastic bags can keep dried fruit airtight.

## Using APT solarware

### Care for solarware

#### Solar ovens and water heaters
Neglect of solar ovens soon reduces their efficiency. Care includes:

- Protecting items from rain and damp. Have a waterproof plastic handy and an elastic belt to slip over it. Cover solarware with this hood before it rains or night falls, or better, use a permanent cover of clear plastic
- Keeping glasses clean
- Cleaning up any spills as soon as they happen, and
- Repairing, for example if papers lift or leaks show, as soon as possible.

Use a solar oven to maximum effect by:

- Opening it early
- Turning it frequently
- Keeping shelves and hotplates clean
- Putting food as high as possible in the stove
- Using a hot plate on the floor of the stove as well as on blocks (shelf)
- Using suitable containers (see accessories earlier in this chapter) with lids
- Not overloading the item. Too much food means slower cooking, and
- As soon as the sun leaves the stove remove from it any food or water you want to keep hot and put it in a thermo or hot box.

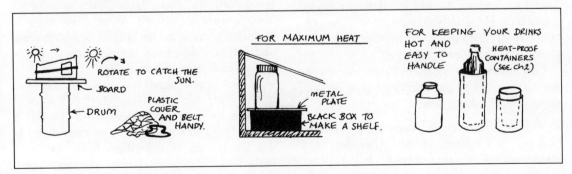

Figure 10.6 *The cooker in use*

137

## Dryers

To ensure maximum use from dryers:

- Always close at night to keep insects out
- Check ventilation frequently, and
- Do not leave the lid on for too long, otherwise your fruit will get baked instead of being dried.

## Cooking and recipes

There is not one answer to the question everyone asks, how long does it take for things to boil? On a good day a small jar or bottle of coffee, milk or water, if put out at sunrise, should boil by 10.30am. The same drinks put in on the hotplate at 10.30am should boil within an hour, because the stove takes time to warm up and so does the sun. On a fairly cloudy day things may not boil at all, but if they have been in the stove all day they may well have cooked.

Temperatures inside the stove often rise well above boiling point. The containers, and if glass containers, their contents also, receive their heat from the sun striking directly on them and from the hot metal plate on which they are standing. In the very early hours of sunlight the sun strikes bottles more directly than when it rises higher. For these reasons it is important to put bottles and jars in the cooker as early as possible. If a bottle has not quite boiled by noon it is not likely to do so until about 2.00pm when the sun will again strike the sides of the bottle directly.

As much of the heat is developed in the actual containers and contents, it must be imprisoned there by loose lids and not allowed to escape into the stove and out from there. Therefore, baking should be done in closed containers. The disadvantage is that if the container is completely closed moisture does not escape and the food is not crisp.

That information should help you to use your stove efficiently to perform the following, and many other cooking tasks:

- Boiling, for example, water for tea, coffee. Making coffee from grains (cheaper than instant coffee). Heating milk
- Doing any slow cooking, for example, stews, soups, vegetables, fruits, rice

- Warming up any food, such as rolls and the like
- Slow baking, for example apples, potatoes (under jars), and biscuits (which will be very hard), and
- Making *sadza*, although you will have to discover which is the easiest and best way of doing it.

## APT recipes for preserving food

*Fruit and tomatoes (bottling or canning):*
The APT no-cost method of bottling is different, and far simpler than the usual method. Therefore, it is explained here in some detail. Be sure your jars have good seals. Card washers are no use. They should be replaced by home-made washers cut from the hard plastic of an ice-cream container or some similar material. Hard plastic lids are excellent.

The best way to add sugar is to keep ready-mixed syrup of sugar and water and to boil the food in this. Other methods waste time and heat because you have to open the stoves, take the bottles out and put the sugar in, stir it and spoil the fruit, then put it back in again.

First, pack the washed fruit fairly tightly in bottles. Pour in the syrup leaving a space of 2cm at the top. Put the lids on loosely and place in a hot part of the stove. Exactly when you screw the lid down after the fruit boils depends on the fruit and how well you want it cooked. When the fruit boils, either screw the lid down immediately or remove it to prevent boiling over and continue cooking it.

When screwing the lid down protect your hand with a cloth, take the bottle out and when it has stopped boiling screw it down fairly tight and leave the cloth over it as a precaution. In fact, explosions have never been known to happen. What does happen, harmlessly, is that the liquid starts boiling again after it has been screwed down, due to the increase of pressure inside.

Do not screw down any more as the fruit cools. When the bottle is cold, if you wish to check it press or tap the centre of the lid. It should feel and sound tight. Look inside up at the top to see that washers have not been sucked in, or lay the bottles on their sides. If all precautions have been taken failure is very unlikely.

## Jam and jelly-making

You must have a flexible approach. Depending on the weather, two days or even six may be needed to make jam, jelly or syrup. The full method for jam-making is not explained, just the APT modifications of it.

One APT method is to start with the fruit in the jam jars in which it will finally be preserved. Another way is to start off in a large pot and only put the fruit into the jars some time after you have put the sugar in and dissolved it.

Cooking the fruit from the start in the small jars means quicker boiling and, without opening the stove, you can monitor the boiling. But it does mean that, as the fruit level goes down in all the jars, the contents from some jars have to be poured into the others to fill them up.

To make jam, jelly and syrup put the washed fruit in containers with no, or very little, water and boil it for some time – it may be more than a day. When it is thoroughly soft and boiling pour in the sugar and stir as needed to dissolve it. Continue boiling for some time – possibly more than a day – until the contents are the consistency of jam.

## Fruit syrup (cordial)

Most fruits make delicious drinks (cordial). Mulberries, guavas, mangos and grapes sometimes ripen in large quantities at once but must have a lot of juice. They are particularly suitable for cordial-making.

The syrup must be corked or screwed down in containers. Screw-on-top wine bottles with extra plastic washers added are suitable, as are wine bottles with corks that have no holes in them. But wine bottles hold a lot of cordial (which has to be diluted). Smaller containers are more suitable for families. Sauce bottles, which often have good seals, and jam jars are convenient sizes.

You must decide on the amount of sugar to use. It depends on the fruit, and the sweetness desired, but a fairly large amount (possibly one-third of the volume of the liquid) may be needed.

To make fruit cordial put the fruit in jars. Crush it down. Add more fruit. Crush it and continue until the liquid is near the top of the jar. For guavas add a little water. Boil thoroughly for one or two days. Strain and squeeze it by handfuls through a cloth (see jam and jelly-making). Boil again. Add and dissolve the sugar. Screw down cautiously when all the sugar is dissolved and the liquid is boiling. Cordial frozen in ice trays makes delicious lollies.

## Drying fruit

Drying vegetables or meat is done in much the same way as drying fruit. Almost any fruit can be dried. When dried it can be kept almost indefinitely, preferably in a screw-top jar or wrapped in plastic.

Dried fruit can be sucked or chewed like sweets and is more nourishing than bought sweets. Or it can be soaked in water overnight, which will soften it and bring it almost back to its original size, then stewed with sugar like fresh fruit.

The main advice about making dried fruit is to learn to dry by drying and testing your results.

The dryer is made so that any fruit that can be pierced and hung on sticks is dried in that way. Smaller fruit, or fruit that is too soft, can be dried, or at least started off, on the glass tray. The process may take two or three days or more than a week. It is best if you can start the fruit off at least on a sunny day so that its surface dries quickly. After that, the dryer should be put out for as long as possible every day. Even on cloudy days drying continues.

Decide:

● Should the fruit be sliced or not? (Only slice if it is necessary), and
● How dry should the fruit be before it can be kept safely? Generally speaking, do not dry fruit until it gets hard, although mulberries dried until they are brittle make amusing sweets for children.

Continually watch the stove when you are drying, especially to check ventilation.

## Chewy sweet-making – fruit leather

This is a promising field waiting to be developed. Fruit such as paw-paw or mulberries, or a mixture of both is mashed, flavoured if desired with orange or lemon and sugar to taste. The mixture is then spread on the (very slightly greased) glass tray about 8 to 10mm thick and dried like fruit. The surface dries, while underneath the mixture is still moist. The glass can then be inverted with the mixture still stuck to it, and drying completed in that way. When dry, but not hard, the sweet can be cut into squares, or into long strips and rolled. It keeps well in screw-top jars (see accessories).

**CAUTION:** Solar cookers, like electric and gas cookers as well as open fires can be dangerous. People need educating in the use of solar cookers so no harm comes through them. People who make solar cookers and particularly those who buy them, besides being shown how to care for them and use them, must be made aware of three dangers to be guarded against, which are:

● Poisoning – from eating food which has been made warm for a long time without being cooked, or which has been cooked but left to cool slowly with the lid on in the stove. This danger applies particularly to meat, and weak children have been known to die as a result of eating warmed but uncooked meat. Meat the

cooker fails to cook should be well-cooked on the fire the same day or be thrown away

● Explosions – this danger has already been mentioned. Explosions of containers should be possible, but have not been reported. What can happen is that a jar is inadvertently screwed down and heated then unscrewed, or the cork of a boiling bottle is against the top glass of the stove and is moved. In such cases (which should never happen) the contents spurt out dangerously, and

● Fire – in theory this is a danger. The sun shining through clear glass bottles may burn little holes in the back of the stove. The bottoms and sides of some of our ten-year old stoves seem to be quite charred, but no actual fire has been heard of.

It is essential that education about the dangers, as well as the use of solarware should be included in any programme on the subject. The author has written this chapter as an expert in APT. He is not an expert on solar energy and nutrition. There is obviously a need for positive research by practical experts in these fields.

# PART THREE
# Decorating and Finishing

# Chapter Eleven: Decorating and finishing APT articles

This chapter, like Chapter One, deals with general technology, but there is a difference. It describes a number of ways, some well-known and some new, of decorating APT articles. These ways have been tried and proved suitable. You may use some of them. On the other hand, you should try out new ways and do your own thing. This final chapter also gives advice on finishing APT articles, including varnishing.

## A. Decoration

In the preceding chapters instructions have been given for the first two stages of making an APT article, that is, building and strengthening/tidying. Little has been said about decorating. The reason for this is that there is no single way to decorate an article. Anybody performing APT needs to learn as much as possible about decorative materials and processes so they can select what is most appropriate for an individual article from their knowledge base. It is hoped that this chapter will give APT technicians a start in building up that base.

Because the range of decorative processes is so wide there will be exceptions, but the following points have very wide application.

**1. Decoration is very important.** Chapter one stressed this point. By giving an article an attractive appearance you enhance its value. If you are obliged to make an article within the limits of the materials you have at the time this may give it the added value of originality. People take special care of things they value, so you add also to its durability.

**2. New and appropriate decoration is needed.** Decoration should not merely be attractive. Through decoration the maker should express himself or herself. The decoration should say something to those who see it. APT is a new creative technology. It must not limit itself to the common forms of decoration such as those used on commercially made articles. New and appropriate forms must be used. APT was originally Zimbabwean and Zimbabwean culture, both traditional and modern, was evident in its decoration. The range of APT decoration will, as APT continues to grow and spread, be enriched by other cultures, their concepts, designs and techniques.

**3. Decoration takes time and time is sometimes money.** On the one hand, you must always be on the look-out for ways and devices to do routine jobs which will save time without detracting from the quality of your work. Suggestions will be given later in this chapter (see Decorating paper, (d)). On the other hand, never save time by not decorating an article as beautifully as you can. Remember that above all your decoration establishes the reputation of your work.

**4. Decoration needs much thought** about practical and aesthetic aspects before you can start, such as:

(a) What quantities of materials will be required? The carcass of a six-board round table has 12 sides to decorate. A legged table has six short legs, six short rails and six very short rails. The board table needs four times more decorative material than the legged one.

(b) How valuable is the material, that is, how difficult is it to get? The answer to this question has to be linked with the previous one, for example, if coloured decorating paper is valuable it should not be used on the base of a board table.

(c) How much time does it take to apply certain types of decoration? Preparing and applying mosaic papers takes a very long time. You might need a whole day to decorate an armchair in this way. It could be painted and decorated with earth paints in two hours. If earth painting will make the article beautiful, use it.

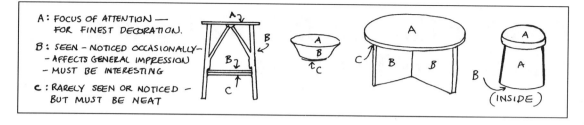

Figure 11.1 *Areas of decoration*

**Note**: it is because of these three considerations that large utility furniture is most often decorated by painting with coloured earths.

(d) How will the finished article be used? Is it a stool for a play centre where it will get heavy use every day? Or is it a stool to be used as a table in an elegant lounge? Or is it a solar oven that will stay outside all day? Different uses require different decoration.

(e) Who is going to use (or look at) the article most? Is it a chair for a little child who is still at the stage when he or she likes to pull off pictures? Or is it a table for older children to work or play on? Older children prize their table more if it has nice pictures on it. Or is it a coffee table for the lounge of a certain person? In which case the colour must match the decor of the room and a picture, if used, would have to be very carefully chosen.

(f) What use will the different parts of the article get? A table top may be looked at even more than it is used, so beautiful decoration is a must. A desk top is, above all, a writing surface, so decoration must not make it uneven. Play school chairs are sat on by little pants that cost Mum money – it would be a shame to decorate the seat with coarse earth paint that would wear them out.

(g) What is the exact part of the article you are thinking about? In most articles we distinguish between three areas for decoration (see Figure 11.1), which are:

(i) Parts not normally seen (the underneath area of a table top). Such areas do need to be neatly finished, but they do not need to be attractively decorated

(ii) Parts that are seen and may be closely examined on first sight of the article. Being seen they will contribute to the impression that the article gives, but they are not the main focus of attention, for example, the outside and bottom of a bowl, the carcass of a stool or table. These parts need to have some interest and should harmonize with the colour and design of the focus of attention, but not be so elaborately decorated that they compete with it for attention (see three kinds of decoration later in this chapter), and

(iii) The part looked at most, that is the focus of attention, for example the top of a stool or table, the inside of a bowl, or the top surface of a tray. These are the areas that will bear the most important decoration. This is where after much thought, and with careful skill and artistry, you create something of special beauty and give the article its character.

All the above considerations and more must be borne in mind, and in some cases be thought hard about before beginning to decorate the article. They should in no way frustrate you. The choice of decoration is very wide. The considerations centre largely on use and should enable you to create articles in line with the principles of traditional art, in which beauty and use are integrated in one creation.

## B. APT materials and techniques

### 1. Decorating paper

Most APT decoration consists of applying colour. This is in the form of either paper or earth paint. Coloured paper can be divided into the following four types (a, b, c and d below).

(a) Paper that is more or less ready when found. This is not usually brightly coloured, for example, cement bag paper, old envelopes (especially those which are a bit yellow or orange) and pieces of wrapping paper.

(b) The layer of coloured paper that decorates some boxes. This is often brightly coloured and patterned paper of good quality, but you have to peel it off! You can learn, largely by experience, until from most coloured boxes you can peel off the paper in one sheet. The following tips may help to peel off paper (they work, but why they work is not always clear):

(i) The glues holding them on seem to vary. Some allow you to peel off the paper dry. Some need to be softened first by immersing the card in water for some time. The time to get the paper off easily is when the card and glue are still wet but the paper surface is almost dry. Some cards hold the paper too securely. Such coloured card is best used as it is, for example, in one piece as the top card layer of a chair seat

(ii) The grain of the top paper and that of the card (which are usually different) affect things. The paper can often be peeled off best in a diagonal direction (neither with or across the grain). Also, when you have failed to peel it from three corners you sometimes succeed at the fourth. Making the card surface hollow as you pull helps

(iii) Rolling the card, colour-side up, with and across the grain sometimes loosens the paper

(iv) First separate the paper at a corner with a fingernail. Then try different ways until you succeed. If the paper is coming off easily the sheet can be placed flat and the paper rolled off on a roller.

(c) Coloured paper (either as whole pictures or as torn-out pieces of colour) from magazines, calendars and books. As well as looking for colour look for pieces that make interesting textures in a mosaic or built-up picture. Pay attention to thickness and finish of this paper. Some paper is too thin to use. Some is so thick it will make ridges unless you layer the whole sheet, calendar pictures are sometimes like this. Some paper is waterproof and therefore pasteproof. Some newsprint magazine colour rubs off very easily. Some calendar pictures stick immediately to any pasted surface they touch and need careful handling otherwise their coloured surface will come off.

(d) Sheets of colour painted by you (earth-coloured paper).

Note: it saves a lot of time to keep stocks (banks) of coloured paper from which you can get the type and colour you want. Devise a system for keeping these papers in several different containers according to type. Have sections in each container according to paper colour. Pictures need another container. A large APT-made box file with cards to separate papers and keep them flat is very suitable.

## 2. Earth paints

(a) You may already know successful ways of making natural dyes, but vegetable dyes, because they are not opaque are not very useful in APT. Every country has a wide range of coloured rock and earth. Developing countries, such as Zimbabwe, are especially fortunate because coloured earth and rocks are dug up and spread around every time a new road is made or a deep hole dug, which happens all the time.

The following instructions will enable you to make excellent paints from earth (ochre) by the simplest of methods:

(i) Collect small bags of different soils and rocks. The soil must not be sandy. The rock should be soft, for example, the colour rubs off or a fingernail can scratch into it

(ii) Find a wide-mouthed container, stretch a piece of nylon stocking over it and tie it to make a sieve. Crush and grind the soil. Rub the rock against a hard rough surface. Shake the sieve with the soil on it so that the fine powder goes through

(iii) Store the powder paints in a set of transparent bottles and number them, and

(iv) To mix the paint, put about a dessert-spoonful of paint in a shallow container. Add some water and a little paste. Stir the mixture thoroughly until it is about the consistency of cream.

(b) To use the earth paints, first have a container of water and some paste handy. These have to be added to the paint from time to time. Use the water to wash mud off your brush, because it must be kept clean. Using hands to apply paint is the quickest way. Then, foam rubber or a brush is needed to spread the paint evenly. Work the paint two or three times

Figure 11.2 *Coloured earth paints*

across the surface in different directions finishing with light even strokes.

Speed is essential. Working drying paint can erode the paper surface. Drying paint can be revived by passing a piece of pasty foam rubber over it. Texturing must be done at the right moment while the paint is still moist. The following different effects can be obtained.

(i) Tones and intensity of colour can be varied by several methods:

● Wetting the surface before you paint it

● Making the paint thicker or thinner by applying a second coat when the first is dry, sprinkling some extra powder over the surface as you are painting and working it

● Mixing colours, especially adding soot to darken a brown, and

● Using the same paint on different kinds of paper, for example, when making earth-coloured papers, use white duplicating paper, cement bag (strong paper), envelopes of different colours, and so on. All give different colours from the same coloured paint.

(ii) Texturing is done by scratching a freshly painted surface in various ways. It is another way to achieve an interesting decorative effect. Texturing can be done with almost anything with an edge or narrow surface to it, such as fingers, the back of a finger nail, fork, comb, hard plastic pieces with teeth cut in them to produce the texture you want. These tools are called grainers. Almost any earth paint can be painted on top of another if the first one is dry, but not varnished. Do not apply the paint too thick or it will crack and may come off.

Do not waste leftover paint. If it gets dry it can be softened again with paste and water and is just as good as before. Small leftovers can be quickly used to paint a few more sheets of coloured paper.

Earth paints are the only type of paint that APT uses. As said before they can be applied in the usual ways. However, earth paints are opaque and on a brown surface they should not be applied very thinly. Their main uses are various forms of pattern work which are described

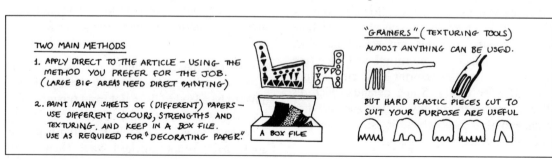

Figure 11.3 *Decorating with earth paints*

146

later in this chapter. For some of these brushes are needed.

## 3. Brushes and brush-making

Figure 11.4 shows how APT brushes are made. Of course, the brushes can be used also in non-APT painting.

The brush part is either animal hair, sisal from the plant, or unravelled string, or foam rubber. Figure 11.4 shows how the hair and sisal is doubled at the middle to prevent pieces from falling out and the foam rubber (usually a strip) is doubled at the painting end to give it firmness.

Figure 11.4 also shows how the brush part has a band of nylon stocking string looped around it and, with the aid of a wire hook, the string is pulled up into the end of the tube as desired. For example for the marker only a very little foam rubber is left projecting, but a lot is tightly pulled up into the tube to hold some of the paint – the brush will nevertheless still need to be dipped from time to time. The stencil brush needs short straight stiff bristles.

The string is then wound and tied around the brush tube. This enables you from time to time to remove the brush part to wash it thoroughly or to add hair to it or to remove some from it and to pull it back in again.

Most APT artists use old pen barrels of various sizes for tubes but hollow sticks, real straws or canes, plastic drinking straws, and even tubes of rolled paper can be used.

## 4. Decoration of different areas

Refer to Decoration, A.4(g) earlier in this chapter.

(a) Overall plain decoration – mainly used for the parts of an article not normally seen. It is sometimes used as a background to cover other areas with some other decorations applied to it. Most often ready-found coloured paper or earth colour is used for area A (see Figure 11.1).

(b) Overall patterned decoration – commonly used for areas that are seen but are not the focus of attention. It is also used as a base on to which detailed decoration is applied. Pat-

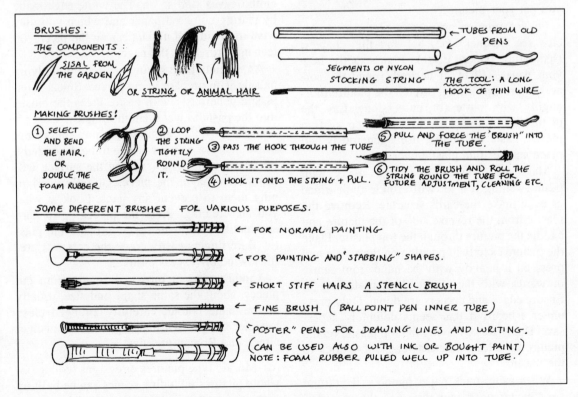

Figure 11.4 *Earth-painting accessories — brushes*

terned paper from boxes, wrapping paper and textured painted paper is used. Sometimes the patterned paper is carefully applied so the pattern looks intact on the article. Sometimes it is torn into mosaic-sized pieces so a new irregular pattern is made when they are layered on the article. Coloured paper mosaic can be included in this category.

(c) Detailed or fine decoration – mainly done to be the focus of attention on the parts which are most often looked at. It can be done in innumerable ways.

## 5. Fine or detailed decoration

(a) Whole pictures – select only those which will give permanent pleasure. Picture shapes should normally harmonize with the decorated area, that is not a square picture on a round tray. A thin frame round a picture gives the picture depth. Surfaces on which pictures are applied should be perfectly smooth and flat. They can be applied on cylinders and cones, for example lamp pillar, round stool carcass. Be sure there is no grainy earth paint where you put your picture.

For information on pasting pictures to articles see Chapter One: 8e, and this chapter: Decorating paper, B.1(c). Plan exactly how your paper will fit. If desired, round the corners to prevent lifting. Stretch the picture thoroughly with paste (or immersion). Lay the picture face-up on a well-pasted sheet of thin plastic. Paste the picture itself generously and place another thin plastic over it.

Make the article surface just sticky with paste (wetting it a lot will crinkle the surface or even make the cards separate. Remove the plastic from the reverse side of the picture and handle the picture through the top plastic. Place the picture exactly in position on the article and press on it heavily with the hand from centre outwards, with the plastic sheet protecting it. Ensure edges and corners are down. Only press under a board if this seems definitely necessary. Doing so, or leaving the top plastic on the picture for a long time may cause it to stick to the plastic.

When using thick paper pictures, if you are very experienced you may use the race-the-stretch method. Press the picture so that every part of it is under pressure, for example with a piece of thick flat cloth or foam rubber between the plastic and the pressing board.

(b) Cut-outs – these may be small pictures carefully cut out around their outlines. They may be shapes of animals, people, and so on and also geometrical and other shapes cut out from coloured paper. Leaves may be printed on paper and cut out. Pictures may be arranged or scattered to make a pattern. Shapes can be arranged to make patterns including traditional African patterns.

(c) Mosaics – these are torn out pieces of paper, usually coloured, and layered on a surface to make an overall cover. Mosaics could cover a whole surface, or a small area or border. Good mosaic requires thought. Select colours that go together and that harmonize with the rest of the decoration, even with the room where the article will be used. Do not only select colours, look for interesting textures, that is lines and shapes and patterns like you see in pictures of grass, hair, woven cloth, leaves, and so on. The white edge made by tearing coloured paper and which you may wish to avoid will not appear on the piece you tear upwards from the page.

An efficient time-saving method for applying mosaic is to prepare many pieces. Smear a flat plastic generously with paste. Press the pieces into the paste to wet them thoroughly. Cover if necessary with a thin plastic to prevent drying. Make the area on your article to be decorated a bit sticky with paste (soaking the surface will unstick it). Layer the pieces, slightly overlapping them to prevent any gaps. Look at what you are creating! Press the pieces down hard and mould them over edges through thin plastic. Bare fingers easily erode the colour. Carefully wipe off excess paste.

Another type of mosaic is made from cut pieces, about the same shape and size, usually of the same colour, carefully arranged close together but not overlapping, like the ancient Greek and Roman mosaics.

(d) Mosaic type pictures or designs (collage) – whole pictures including scenes can be built up with cut-out pieces of coloured and textured paper. This is a combination of (b) and (c)

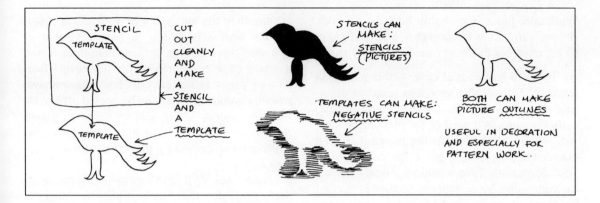

Figure 11.5 *Stencils and templates*

above and the technique is the same. Like many other decorative processes it can be done even by small children, but carried out by a creative artist with skill and patience the result can be very impressive.

(e) Painting whole pictures or designs using earth colour – techniques for applying earth colour have already been mentioned. After experimenting on sheets of card you will know what methods you prefer and the kinds of effect you can produce. The danger you have to watch for is making the surface so wet that it comes unstuck and bulges up. Of course, it can be repaired but your picture will have been spoiled and you may have to layer over it.

(f) Stencils and templates used as negative stencils – this is a safe form of painting as the paint has to be a bit thick, like cream and does not penetrate the card surface.

To stencil successfully:

● Cut stencils from strong thin card, thin hard plastic or old X-ray film. The edges must be sharp and clean. When you cut a stencil you also cut out a template which can be used to make negative stencils or outlines for cut-outs
● Small stencils are much easier to use than big ones. Cut all the shapes wide and long enough, because when stencilled they will be reduced a little
● Use a short stiff brush (fibre or foam rubber)
● Apply the paint (which must not be at all runny) with stabbing strokes that go slightly inwards but make a sharp outline. Hold the stencil tight down. Lift off neatly, and

● Clean and dry the stencil, especially underneath, after each stencilling.

(g) Potato prints – by experimentation you will find several articles or substances that can be substitutes for bought potatoes. The object of this process is to enable you to create patterns quickly and easily.

Use fairly thick paint. Experiment on card to get the best possible results. The print may need a little touching up with a brush. The surface to be painted must be smooth and flat. If it is not, and you only need a few prints to make your pattern, they can be printed on paper, cut out and stuck on. This takes time but the method is recommended for leaf prints as it is difficult to be sure your print will be successful and leaves cannot be touched-up very well.

(h) Patterns made with pressed flowers and leaves — these have been done successfully but are probably best used on surfaces that will not have much wear. You must learn the method by trial and error. Discover which leaves and flowers are suitable. They must be thin, have no thick centres or high hard veins. Dry and press a large quantity, each one carefully arranged flat between newsprint and pressed in a weighted book for a week to ten days. Reject any that are brittle or lose all colour.

Apply flowers only to flat even surfaces, although small flowers have been successfully applied to the inside of a large round bowl.

Paste the pressed flowers using mosaic technique of thoroughly pasting and pressing.

Wallpaper paste is probably best for this job. Before varnishing cover again with wallpaper paste, ensuring that every piece is firmly stuck.

(i) Tobacco leaf overall cover – this makes an impressive cover that serves as focus of attention on the main surface. The process is basically the same as described for pressed flowers, with modifications to suit the material. If you master the process and prove the durability of your decoration there would be a ready market for your work. More experimentation is needed but some advice is offered based on experience already gained.

Leaves should be dried but kept in a plastic bag until used to prevent them from drying out. Use leaves which are as perfect as possible. Parts can be cut and patched and the leaf overlapped as you use it, but overlapped areas look darker.

Plan your arrangement. See the leaf is covered all over on both sides with thin paste. It is waterproof but, pasted thoroughly, it becomes supple, it can even be stretched a little and layered over edges and surplus cut away with scissors. Because of the stretch you have to modify your planned arrangement as you work. Layer and press by mosaic methods using a thin plastic sheet. As you press, gently work out any surplus paste under or on the leaves otherwise it will turn black on drying.

Dry under padded pressure on all possible surfaces for the first drying stage, then repair as necessary and complete the drying as you think best. Protect with two or three coats of varnish.

## 6. Techniques for puppets and dolls

The facial features, that is the eyes and mouth, make a doll life-like and give it its own character. The three options for colour are: earth paint; paper that is coloured right through, such as wrapping paper, envelope paper, even pink duplicating paper; and paper with a strong surface of colour that can be peeled off boxes or posters. Magazine paper is not suitable for overall colouring.

Some useful tips for decorating a doll's facial features follow:

● Skin – technically, earth paints are the best way to colour a doll with dark skin. But find or mix a colour that really looks right and which is smooth to the touch. If you want to use paper for the skin it is easiest to use paper that is coloured right through because then there is not a white edge to contend with. However, that sort of paper is not easy to find. Sometimes, suitably coloured paper can be peeled off boxes or even posters. Using surface-coloured paper is slow work as the skin must not show any white streaks caused by the white edges of the paper

● Hair – jet black earth colour is difficult to find. Possibly, the black found in car-park loose surfacing is best, or the black carbon from inside torch batteries (although this may contain poison), or carbon paper. Carefully plan and mark the hair line before starting painting

● Eyes, nose and mouth (proportions) – these are the doll's main facial features. Check, and if necessary, correct the sizes and positions of the features already moulded. The hollows for the eyes and the eyeballs should be half-way between the top of the head and the chin. The nose should be small and flat.

Colouring the eyes and the mouth is extremely delicate work and cannot be done with earth paint. The recommended method is to do it with suitably coloured paper, including magazine coloured paper. Tear, and sometimes cut, the paper into small, carefully calculated pieces. Apply them with utmost care. The following advice applies to the foundations on which the decoration is laid, as well as to the actual decoration

● Eyes – Figure 11.6 shows a way of doing eyes which looks simple. In reality you work by trial and error. You may reject four or five pairs of eye shapes before you are satisfied.

Eyebrows (not illustrated) are made by experimentation. Place them with great care. While you are decorating look at babies' faces and pictures of them and study their eyes. This exercise will help you see what is wrong with your doll's face.

When you made your doll's or puppet's face you laid the foundations for the eyes by shaping slight hollows, with a raised part near the centre where the eyeball will be. First, place your first pair of eye-whites. If one or both are not satisfactory try others until you have got two eye-whites the right shape, the right angle

Figure 11.6 *How to colour eyes*

and correctly spaced. Tear into them to make them lie flat. Then, do the same with the eye-balls, working with both eyes at the same time. Note that the eyeball should not be smaller than the height of the eye, that is it should touch the top and bottom edges of the eyes. Much trial and error is needed to succeed.

Eyelashes are extremely narrow pieces of paper, the top one slightly bigger than the bottom one. The highlights are very important, although they are very minute pieces of white paper, because they make the eye come alive, and

● The mouth – this is a much more intricate operation than the eyes. Check the mouth has a good foundation on which to lay the decorating paper. The mouth should be properly positioned in relation to the two eyes (as well as to the nose and chin). There should be three levels distinguishable in the mouth: the slightly deeper-inside and tongue part which will be darker than the rest (the tongue will not be noticed); a small curve under the top lip for the gum (where one or two carefully cut fragments of white paper may be placed later); and the outside lip level which you may want to build up a little. The whole mouth, and the corners in particular, should curve slightly upward.

Before proceeding to colour the mouth make any necessary changes to the rest of the face. At this stage alterations dry quite quickly. You will discover that the mouth and face, and the cheeks and chin in particular, are all part of one system and parts may need modifying.

When you are satisfied that you have done all you can, proceed to decorating the mouth. Coloured magazines should provide you with all the colours you need but selecting the right ones is a delicate operation. Magazine colour cracks and comes off paper easily. Work it as

little as possible. The skill now is that of an artist and only you can do it in your way.

You may find that the following tips are useful:

(i) One or two specially cut plastic tools are essential for modifying shapes and pressing papers into position inside the mouth

(ii) Find the right colour. This is not the real colour when compared to the baby's face, but it is the colour that looks right on your doll. Note that the lips on a dark-skinned face are not red at all

(iii) Start with the inside and work outwards finishing with the lips. Be careful in all this operation not to make the mouth or any part of it, including the teeth and lips, too big. Teeth usually improve a face but they must be minute (especially in height) and very carefully positioned on the gums.

In spite of all your efforts you will not produce a perfect baby in this way. But when you have done all you can and hand over your creation you will be surprised at the loving reception it receives from children. That is what matters in the end and makes it all worthwhile.

## C. Finishing

Finishing is an operation in which money is spent. It is a technical process and it is hoped that some technical readers will improve upon it. Finishing involves varnishing. Always read the labels on varnish tins. Make enquiries on ways the varnish could be dangerous before using it on an article.

This section briefly describes the methods that have been used in APT to make articles more permanent by protecting surfaces from spills, to make articles harder, and at the same time brighter in appearance (varnish enhances colour), and to reduce the effects continually damp weather may have upon them (which in most regions is negligible). Varnished surfaces can be wiped over with damp cloths to clean them.

## Applying varnish

Brushes are not usually used for varnishing. They cannot reach some of the places very well. Brushing is slower than using a cloth. It is more difficult to control the amount of varnish if it is applied with a brush than if a piece of cloth or foam rubber is used. Brushes tend to put a lot of varnish in one place to start with and with a paper surface it may soak right through and spoil its colour. Bought brushes are expensive. Even if home-made brushes are used they still have to be cleaned in turpentine.

When varnishing:

● First consider the surface to be varnished. If it has light-coloured news or magazine pictures or patterns it is wise to smear a coat of cellulose wallpaper paste or PVA clear glaze over it to insulate the colour from the varnish, otherwise varnish will penetrate the surface and perhaps bring dark print from underneath to the surface. If you wish, any surface can be sized in this way before varnishing. This process enhances colour, but on polished card surfaces it may prevent the varnish from holding tightly and air bubbles could appear where it is scratched or knocked

● Apply varnish with a pad of cotton cloth. Hands can be protected for a while by using one or two plastic bags as gloves. Some people use a plastic pad or just a plastic bag-glove or a piece of foam rubber to apply a quick coat to an article. However, these materials disintegrate quite quickly which could spoil the surface.

The varnish should be rapidly spread to cover the whole surface thinly and stroked evenly before it gets sticky. Do not return to improve it once you have left it as you will spoil it.

● Give a second, even a third coat of varnish, to any article or area, for example, a chair seat that will have heavy wear. Apply this when the first coat is quite dry, and touch it very lightly with some very fine sandpaper before revarnishing

● As a general rule start with the inside and difficult parts of an article (the underneath of a table or stool). Then proceed to the parts that are not noticed very much. Varnish the tops and the finer decoration last.

(a) Polyurethane varnish is soluble in mineral turpentine. This can be used to thin down thick varnish. It is also the best thing for getting varnish off the hands and off many surfaces, if varnish has accidentally fallen on them. It will not completely remove varnish from clothes.

(b) Varnish is hardened (it sets) through constant contact with the air. Heat and sun by themselves do not dry it. If there is enough air in a tin it will harden (and spoil) the varnish. Close the tin immediately after use. Press the lid right in and shake the varnish upside down to seal any leaks round the lid. When your varnish is three-quarters finished transfer it to a smaller tin or screw-top jar where there will be less room for air.

(c) There are some PVC clear glazes that can be used instead of varnish. They are water-based. If you do not leave glaze splashes for a long time, they can be removed by washing with water (not turpentine). Hands can be washed clean in the same way.

(d) Glazes can be made from the gum of some trees but owing to lack of information on positive results no advice is offered here.

## Doing your own thing!

This chapter has tried to give sufficient information and examples for you to decorate APT articles by techniques that have proved successful. If you stop there the chapter has failed in its main purpose. The aim is to give you a basic knowledge of APT decorative, technology to use and develop to produce new ranges of beautiful and durable APT creations.

# Glossary

Some common words are used in APT with a special or limited meaning. Most are explained in the text where first used. The following list with references may save you time. R indicates the rehabilitation section at the end of some chapters (*In the context of rehabilitation*).

**Angle pieces:** pieces of card with a fold down the middle mainly used for strengthening the angles where two boards join. Often made from off-cuts (Chapter One:19b and Figure 3.3).

**Armature:** a fairly hard core, for example, tightly tied paper or clay, around which an article is constructed – usually by moulding.

**Base:** the part of an article that stands on a table or floor – or the whole of the carcass.

**Bar:** fairly narrow board made extra thick in order to be strong.

**Basic kit:** the tools and materials needed for most jobs and prepared beforehand (Chapter One:10)

**Bearing:** the tube into which an axle fits and in which it is held as it turns.

**Belt:** a band of stretchy material, such as nylon stocking or inner tubing; or a wide strip of strong paper pasted, rolled, then squeezed or pressed flat. Belts are used to pull and hold parts together. Strong paper belts are wound around and pressed in position and layered over.

**Block:** a thick piece of board, usually fairly small and of a particular shape. Blocks may be fitted or fixed to other boards.

**Board:** cards laminated to make a hard board. For different kinds of boards see Chapter One:18.

**Bone:** strong smaller tube forced into the end of a wider tube to strengthen its end or project so another tube can be joined over it (Chapter One:17b and Figure 1.7).

**Bota:** Shona name for thin porridge (Zimbabwe). Used as a paste (Chapter One:9b).

**Card (or thin card):** card from shoe or cereal boxes or shirt boxes.

**Carcass:** the main body of an article (of furniture) which supports a top.

**Carton or corrugated card:** thick card of which heavy boxes are made.

**Chassis:** the strong middle board of a vehicle to which the wheel assemblies are fitted.

**Chisel:** a tool, for example, a 15cm nail, with a sharp blade at one end for cutting holes in boards. The nail point would be flattened and sharpened.

**Classic style:** legged furniture made from thin card (Chapter Six). Light and elegant compared with utility-style furniture.

**Clay:** any kind of clay, normally just dug from the ground.

**Collar:** for strengthening the join of a tube to a board. A piece of card with flaps cut into one end, wrapped on to the tube. The flaps secure it to the board (Chapter Four: chair).

**Decorating:** see Chapter One: 22 and Chapter Eleven.

**Earth colours or earth paints:** paint made fron grinding and sifting soil or soft rock and mixing the powder with paste and water (Chapter Eleven).

**Elastic:** any narrow length of stretchy material, pantyhose top, inner tubing string with a piece of inner tubing tied to it. Used for binding around an article or parts of it to hold them together.

**Fatten:** to make an article or parts of it bigger or thicker by binding and layering.

**Finishing:** mainly by varnishing (Chapter Eleven)

**Fitting:** a feature that can be fitted to a piece of apparatus but is removable (Chapter Four: R).

**Fixture:** a feature attached immovably to a piece of apparatus, that is a permanent fitting (Chapter Four: R).

**Four rules of APT:** strong, useful, attractive, no money spent (see Chapter One: 4).

**Grain:** direction in which the fibres run in any piece of paper or card (Chapter One: 8a).

**Insulated (insulation):** to keep two surfaces apart (usually by a thin plastic sheet placed between them) so one does not wet the other or stick to it. For solarware insulation refers

153

to the means used for preventing heat from escaping from the box.

**Join (noun):** a joint, but in APT parts do not normally fit into each other to make a joint – they are most often pressed and bound, or strapped together, joined.

**Kaylite:** see polystyrene.

**Knife:** must be strong and very sharp. A trimming knife with renewable blades is an expensive but very useful tool.

**Layer:** a general term for placing and pressing any piece or strip of pasted paper to the article you are creating (Chapter One:15).

**Laminating:** layering cards together to make a board (Chapter One:18).

**Loop:** a single segment of nylon stocking string, tied through two parts to hold them together.

**Mash (papier mâché):** ground paper mixed with thick paste (Chapter One:14).

**Measure:** any gauge, for example, made of card or paper, for marking or testing a measurement. APT does not usually use rulers or measure in centimetres on the job.

**Mosaic:** design, pattern or picture made by skilfully layering small pieces of coloured paper (Chapter Eleven).

**Mould (noun):** object over which paper card or mash is pressed and shaped.

**Mould (verb):** to work and form paper, mash or card with the hands into the shape you want.

**Nail (wooden):** a sharpened piece of wood used like a nail to hold components together in the early stages of construction (Chapter Four: box structures).

**Needle:** usually a home-made tool (partly straightened staple or paper clip) for threading string through holes.

**Nylon and nylon string:** nylon in the manual refers to stockings or pantyhose. Narrow segments are cut across the legs and pants to make string. The string is strong, thin elastic and strongly recommended for APT construction.

**Off-cuts:** see Angle pieces and Chapter One:19b and Figure 3.3.

**P and P** or **the two Ps:** stand for paste and pressure, the two essentials for things to stick well. Hence the APT slogan is: **Two P's Spell Stick**.

**Packing:** hard material such as thin card pieces pasted and forced into a cavity to build it up solid.

**Paste:** paste made from flour of one kind or another (Chapter One: 9). The only adhesive used in APT.

**Padding:** material, often lightly pasted paper, moulded and layered on to a surface to build it up, or pressed into a space to fill it.

**Piercer:** a tool (usually home-made) for making holes through boards.

**Peg:** a cylinder of bamboo twig, plastic or rolled card used for fitting or holding two parts together (Figure 5.2a and Chapter Four: R, movable accessories).

**Polystyrene (Kaylite):** white, extremely light, substance used in packing goods in cartons. It is used in APT to make armatures, or broken into crumbs to make solar insulating material. Polystyrene is also used to make tubes and pipes.

**Rail:** card tube, usually horizontal, that joins and supports other tubes or boards.

**Roller:** straight round rod (stick or polythene piping) on which card is rolled to make tubes.

**Rub:** usually refers to rubbing the edges of a bowl or board; wet or dry with a stone or in the case of boards on a concrete surface, to wear them smooth.

*Sadza:* Shona name for a maize-meal pudding eaten by many African people in Zimbabwe.

**Shoe:** section of hard plastic tubing fitted on to a (tubular) leg.

**Sift (verb) and sieve (noun):** nylon is stretched over a wide-mouthed container, and ground soil is passed through it (sifted) to make a fine paint powder.

**Smoothing stone:** very rough hard stone used as a rasp to rub edges smooth.

**Stabilizer:** a modification to an article to control tipping. (Chapter Seven: R).

**Steaming:** holding an article or board in hot steam to soften it so that its shape can be corrected.

**Steering bar/board:** a strong bar to which a wheel assembly is attached and which is part of the steering system (Chapter Seven: R and Figure 7.15).

**Strapping:** strong, quite short, paper strips, often double thickness, used to pull and hold parts of an article together, or bind flaps to another surface.

**Stretch/shrink factor:** see Chapter One: 8e.

**Strengthening:** the second stage in constructing an article – strapping over all joins and layering the article all over with strong paper (Chapter One:20).

**String:** almost always means nylon string (see nylon).

**Strong paper:** In Zimbabwe this usually means cement bag paper. In some countries potatoes are wrapped in the same kind of strong khaki paper.

**Strut:** supporting tube set at an angle.

**Support:** general term for any tube, board or bracket designed to hold another part firm and to prevent it from sagging. A strut is one form of support.

**Surgery:** treatment given when a board or a laminated article has separated inside. Cuts that cross each other are made through the surface so that paste can be inserted and worked in between the separating layers and the board repaired and strongly pressed.

**Tube:** paper or card, pasted and tightly rolled on a roller (above) and pulled off, then dried (Chapter One:17).

**Top:** either the top side of a board, or the board itself which forms the top of a stool, table, and so on.

**Utility style:** range of furniture made from the corrugated card of old cartons (Chapter Four). Utility items are heavier and usually larger than classic-style articles.

**Varnishing:** see Chapter Eleven.

**Waterproofing:** see Chapter One:17c, tubes.

**Weights:** anything heavy to press on a join or weigh down a pressing board, that is, plastic bags of sand, bricks in plastic bags, stones, heavy batteries, and so on.

**Wheel assembly:** the three components, that is, bearing and axle with wheels, when all have been fitted together (Chapter Seven).

# Index

This index enables you to locate articles described in this manual according to chapter. **Note:** (i) R refers to rehabilitation section at the end of some chapters (*In the context of rehabilitation*); (ii) decoration materials and processes are not listed here (they are located in Chapter Eleven); (iii) figures refer to chapter numbers.